ELITE IMAGES OF DUTCH POLITICS

Elite Images of Dutch Politics

Accommodation and Conflict

Samuel J. Eldersveld
Jan Kooiman
Theo van der Tak

The University of Michigan Press • Ann Arbor
Martinus Nijhoff • The Hague

for Europe: Uitgeverij Martinus Nijhoff bv
Lange Voorhout 9
's Gravenhage, The Netherlands
ISBN (Neth.) 90–247–9085–9

Library of Congress Cataloging in Publication Data

Eldersveld, Samuel James.
   Elite images of Dutch politics.

   Includes bibliographical references and index.
   1. Government executives—Netherlands—Attitudes.
2. Legislators—Netherlands—Attitudes. I. Kooiman, J.,
joint author. II. Tak, Theo van der, joint author.
III. Title.
JN5851.E44   1981   306'.2'09492   80–29559
ISBN 0–472–10009–2

Paperback ISBN: 978-0-472-75126-6

Preface

Elite research is perhaps more sensitive than any other type of political science research. It requires sophisticated interviewing and insightful analysis. The cooperation and advice of many people are necessary if the goals of objective and scientific inquiry are to be realized. In working toward these goals in the project presented here we are deeply indebted to many people: First, to the respondents themselves, the civil servants and members of Parliament who gave us liberally of their time. Next, to the very able women who so efficiently handled the sensitive interview situations in which we tape-recorded our sessions with the leaders: the Ms. S. Van Esterik, M. J. Jonkers, W. J. Soullié, G. Van Tijn, and A. Wolterbeek. These same women were also responsible for the complicated task of coding the interviews from the typescripts. We are particularly grateful to Mrs. Van Esterik/Boon-Zaaijer, who was the project supervisor in its early stages. Her attention to the organizational details of the planning and the arrangements for interviewing and coding was extraordinary.

Funds for the project were provided by the Ford Foundation as well as the National Science Foundation and the European Cultural Foundation. A variety of resources were put at our disposal by the political science department of the University of Leiden and the Interfaculteit Bedrijfskunde at Delft. The Netherlands Institute for Advanced Study (NIAS) provided secretarial support as well as a delightful locale in which most of the manuscript was written. Computer assistance as well as typing assistance were provided by the University of Michigan and the Interfaculteit at Delft. Robert Friedrich and Jack Katosh were primarily responsible for the computer work at Michigan, while Theo van der Tak was responsible for the computer programming at Delft.

Many of our colleagues in political science advised and assisted us in this research. The University of Michigan group which originated the comparative elite project of which this is a part did the invaluable preparatory work of designing the study, developing the questionnaire, preparing the cross-national codebook, and undertaking many of the early analyses with the data from other countries. Thomas Anton, Joel Aberbach, Ronald Inglehart, Robert Putnam, and Bert Rockman were colleagues whose contribution to this project was invaluable. Other associates at Leiden also provided assistance from time to time. Discussions with Professors Arie Van Braam, Hans Daudt, and Arend Lijphart were of value for particular sections of the study. Above all, we are indebted to Hans Daalder, who took an early interest in the study, helped in getting it accepted by Dutch leaders, and pioneered in this area with his own research on Parliament.

Finally, we wish to thank all the secretaries at NIAS, Leiden, Michigan, and Delft for their patient typing and retyping of the many versions of this manuscript. Their work put the final touches on a research enterprise that was truly a cooperative effort.

Contents

Figures

Tables

CHAPTER 1

Elite Integration in the Political System: Theoretical Perspectives

Political systems produce elites: individuals recruited, selected, and presumably trained to make decisions for a society. Among these elites, ranging in status from cabinet ministers to local officials, there are two sets of actors of preeminent national importance—the higher civil servants and the members of Parliament. They have been called, respectively, the "core of modern government"[1] and "strategically central to the system."[2] Their attitudes and behavior as leaders and their relationships to each other determine in large part, though certainly not completely, the ways in which the system solves its problems, the substantive direction of public policy, and the degree of public support for government. The study of such elites also tells us much about the norms, practices, and values—in short, the political culture—of that society.

In the past hundred years in modern societies, particularly in Europe and North America, politicians and bureaucrats have assumed a commanding influence and importance in the functioning of these societies. It was in the latter part of the nineteenth century that political parties as we now know them really began to develop into organizations with special constituencies, led by leaders who made a career out of politics, who developed programs and ideologies, and who mobilized votes in free elections in order to achieve power, particularly in Parliamentary assemblies. And it was during this same period that modern governments developed bureaucracies which expanded drastically their size and complexity and their influence over the governmental process. As societies faced increasingly different problems in social and economic development during and after the industrial revolution, the structures and institutions of the political system also developed. The electorate expanded in size, the political leadership selection process became more institutionalized, the electoral system was reformed presumably to make it more deliberative and democratic, representative institutions were strengthened, and policymaking processes were altered to make them both more efficient and more responsive to public needs. In this period from about 1870 on, two sets of national political system elites emerged as being of great importance—the civil servants who managed the national bureaucracy and the party leaders who together controlled the national legislative process. The preeminence of these two elites and the importance of their relationships have been widely recognized. Max Weber saw these two elites as determining the character of the modern polity—hopefully and ideally in cooperative patterns of behavior, but actually and eventually in conflict. To study these elites is, then, crucial for any serious inquiry into the modern political system.

In the spring of 1973 we tape-recorded a set of interviews with samples of Dutch higher civil servants and members of the lower house of the Dutch Parliament, 120 leaders in all. We asked them about their social origins, their career patterns, their views about the nature of and solutions to political problems, their perceptions of the Dutch power structure and each other's roles in that structure, their interactions and linkages with each other and other elites, their perceptions and beliefs about the political process and the system in the Netherlands, and their values. We were interested in their images of the political world since we assumed that what and how people think and what and how they believe about the world in which they live influences greatly the way they as leaders will act, behave, and decide.

Our study in the Netherlands was part of an international project in which, from 1970 to 1973, the same sets of elites were interviewed in five other European countries (Britain, Germany, Italy, France, and Sweden) and in the United States. These studies focused on the same objectives and will permit us to compare Dutch elites with those of other systems, an analysis of major theoretical relevance. For, while systems do indeed produce elites, the characteristics of these elites may, indeed, transcend individual systems.

Our Dutch study is, then, a detailed analysis of the backgrounds and ideas of 120 M.P.'s and civil servants who had come from a variety of social, family, and geographical backgrounds to The Hague, where in 1973 they were playing important roles in the Dutch government. We attempted through interviews and analysis to discern their basic orientations and beliefs about politics, power, and policy. And in the process of such an undertaking we hoped to learn more about how the Dutch political system works, as well as the nature of political leadership in modern societies generally, in conjunction with the work of our colleagues in other countries.

Theoretical Approaches to Elite Integration

There have been many studies of political elites, the product of many different substantive interests. One major theoretical concern that dominates our study of Dutch elites is elite integration and conflict. The character of the relationships between and among elites in modern societies is, we would argue, central to the achievement of certain system goals—whether stability, policy change, effective elite-mass relationships, governmental efficiency, legitimacy, or political development. Further, the patterns of elite relationships are substantively diverse. The integration of elites is manifested in a variety of ways, including mutual acceptance of roles, congruence in perceptions of the political environment, similar ideological preferences, frequency of communication, and nonconflictual value priorities. Systems differ in the nature and extent of elite integration or conflict. Systems also differ in the extent to which elite integration is necessary and elite conflict is tolerable. Indeed, one can argue that in most systems certain types of elite conflict are not only tolerable but necessary, while other types of elite conflict are dysfunctional to system performance. We are concerned here with identifying the dimensions on which there is elite conflict or integration and what factors explain these patterns, and then evaluating these findings in terms of the functional needs of the system.

In the vast literature on political elites, there are three major approaches in dealing with this question of elite integration or conflict. First, there are those writers who have emphasized the cohesion of elites, arguing that there is *a* political elite and it constitutes a "class." Thus, Mosca writes, "In all regularly constituted societies . . . we find a ruling class . . . and they are a minority."[3] And Michels similarly talks of the ultimate consequences of the oligarchical developments in a system producing a new class of leaders.[4] C. Wright Mills speaks of the "class consciousness" among the American "power elite."[5] The essence of the position of such writers is that the elite is indeed very integrated. It consists of a group of like-minded individuals, probably closely interactive, sharing a desire for power, in no fundamental disagreement in their perceptions and preferences about their political world, and committed to the same ideologies, goals, and values. In Meisel's words, using the "three c's," they manifest group "consciousness, coherence, conspiracy."[6] As applied to our study of higher civil servants and

M.P.'s, this theory would predict a high frequency of interaction and certainly considerable elite congruence in attitudes and solidarity in action perspectives, despite differences in role and position.

A second group of scholars have emphasized elite conflict, combat, and hostility. Weber is in one sense an exponent of this position, particularly when he writes of the natural opposition between the bureaucrat and politician in modern democracies.

> Democracy inevitably comes into conflict with the bureaucratic tendencies which, by its fight against notable rule, democracy produced. . . . Under normal conditions, the power position of a fully developed bureaucracy is always overtowering. The "political master" finds himself in the position of the dilettante who stands opposite the "expert". . . .[7]

Other scholars have emphasized other basic elite conflicts within systems, such as ideological differences, which make it difficult for elites to work together (Sartori, Almond). Differences in skill training and in orientation may produce fundamentally opposed views of the policy process (Saint Simon, Burnham, Bell, Galbraith), as may generational conflicts and differences in clientele relationships of elites to social sectors or groups. These writers differ in their emphasis on the extent of polarization or the seriousness of it for the polity. But the essence of their position is that, rather than elite cohesion, one should expect and will find elites which are not homogeneous, indeed elites that differ among themselves in critical ways and who may oppose each other with varying degrees of hostility. Students of developing societies, such as Riggs, point to the patterns of tension and conflict between elite sectors. Riggs himself sees as the fundamental problem in such societies the deterioration in bureaucratic autonomy and efficiency in the face of a power-expansionist set of party leaders.[8] For scholars in this second group, *the* elite does not exist as a singular collectivity, but rather the political and administrative leaders of a system are very diverse and incongruent in perspective, despite being socialized in the same system and having common backgrounds. This is due to their different power statuses in the system, their role or position socialization, their partisan or ideology orientations, their communication linkages, or the institutional contexts in which they work.

A third group of scholars emphasize, in contrast to the theorists of elite class or elite conflict, the phenomenon of elite convergence in perspectives, of mutual respect and rapport and a capacity to work together. This convergence occurs, it is argued, despite certain differences in views about the political world, possibly with limited communicative linkage, and with a socialization to different roles. The point of this theoretical position is that elites learn to work within a system or naturally develop patterns of mutual tolerance and cooperative behavior. For some this is a product of similar social and political backgrounds—scholars of the British system have emphasized this position. For others, the emphasis is on functional overlap of the institutions in which elites work. Thus Huntington argues that the American system evidences less functional specialization and thus more overlap (for example, in the functions of the bureaucracy and of Congress) than has been historically true in Europe.[9] Still other writers have emphasized the purposive cooperative behavior of elites as a result of their recognition of this as a system requisite. The "accommodationism" theory of Lijphart, as applied to the Netherlands, is an example of this. There are, finally, those who would argue that, insofar as the relationships of bureaucrats and politicians are concerned, modern politics inevitably leads to elite convergence. The functions of the civil servant and politician, because of the complexity of the policy process, have become intermixed, and they therefore, as elite actors, need each other more than ever. The bureaucrat has to mobilize political support, and the politician has to mobilize expertise. The need, therefore, for pragmatic cooperation is enhanced, and the probability develops that they will exhibit more convergent perspectives. This set of theories is distinctive, then, in its emphasis on the fundamental institutional integration of elites even though they are not a unified and self-conscious class.

In these theoretical models of political elite relationships, a variety of dimensions and variables stand out: homogeneity in social background, density of communicative linkage, value or ideological consensus, congruence in political perspectives, class consciousness (solidarity), as well as others. In figure 1 we suggest how these different ways of thinking about elite integration can be conceptualized. It is possible certainly to think of elite integration simply in terms of social backgrounds or sociometry. But if one is preoccupied with the substantive meaning of elite integration, then the objective is to determine whether the elites actually reveal agreement in their views about politics, issues, the political system, and the values of the society. It is this latter objective that is our major concern here; while contributory forces are examined in detail, our aim is to use them to elucidate the extent of elite integration.

Using two of these dimensions together—communicative linkages and congruence in perspectives—produces the theoretical types represented in figure 2. Where elites are highly interactive they can be either coalescent (demonstrating high agreement in their perspectives) or combative (polarized or in considerable disagreement). Where the elites do not communicate with each other with a high degree of frequency, they could reveal, despite this isolation, very similar orientations, due to other factors such as socialization. Or they could oppose each other sharply in their views of politics—the immobilist pattern of elite relationships. One can also conceive of special subtypes—such as the "power elite" class consciousness conception of the elites of C. Wright Mills—characterized by high frequency of interaction, high social homogeneity, and high congruence in power perspectives, which approximates the Michels conspiratorial conception of oligarchy.

In our comparative research and in this study of the Netherlands we are interested in using empirical analysis to see which model of the structure of political elites accords with reality. In studying the Dutch senior civil servant and the politician, we are concerned with the distance between them in their contacts, in their images of politics, in their acceptance of each other, and in their values. Linked to this concern is an interest in the balance in these relationships: what are the differences in emphasis in the contact patterns of these two elite sets of actors in their relationships to the cabinet ministers, to party leaders, to interest groups, to citizens, and to each other? Are civil servants and legislative politicians, in their own eyes, equal or unequal actors in the system? Do they feel they should have different and unequal influence roles? If we compare their views on politics, is there serious disjunction between these two sets of actors in their perceptions of reality (how the political process does function) and in their normative preferences (how, in their opinion, the political process should function)?

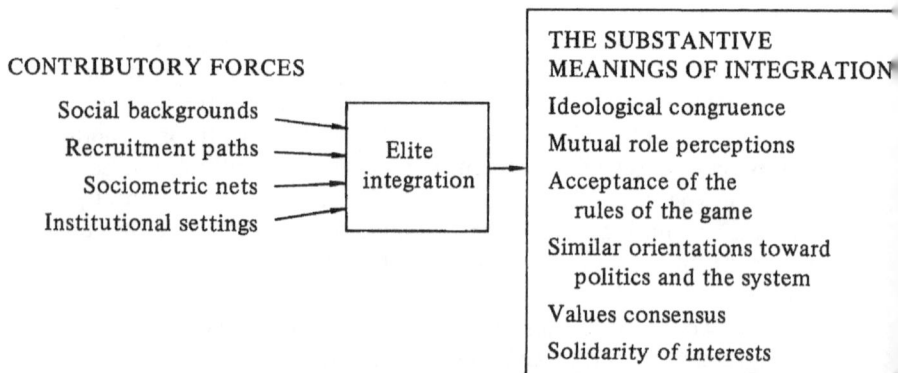

CONTRIBUTORY FORCES

Social backgrounds
Recruitment paths
Sociometric nets
Institutional settings

Elite
integration

THE SUBSTANTIVE
MEANINGS OF INTEGRATION

Ideological congruence
Mutual role perceptions
Acceptance of the
    rules of the game
Similar orientations toward
    politics and the system
Values consensus
Solidarity of interests

Fig. 1.   A conceptual diagram of elite integration

The classical view, of course, is that the bureaucrat and politician live in two different worlds or cultures. The bureaucracy, after Weber, is presumably a special subculture emphasizing, among other characteristics, organizational efficiency, technical competence and expertise, hierarchical authority patterns, impersonal human relationships, careerism, and eventually hostility to the politician because of conflicts over power status and over what are considered proper and acceptable criteria for the making of policy. The power orientations of the legislative politician, it is argued, are intolerable to the classical bureaucrat. The bureaucrats' images of politics theoretically collide fundamentally with those of the elected parliamentarian who seeks votes, mobilizes political support, calculates electoral strategies, and is patronage-conscious. In such a two-cultures view of the political elite system, one can expect either an immobilist type of confrontation between equals, or some development leading to imbalance in the status of these two elite sectors—the dominance of the M.P. or the dominance of the bureaucrat.

In recent literature there is much support for this two-culture approach, particularly in the assessment of trends in developing societies. However, there are serious problems with this view of the way bureaucrats and politicians function. One is that it assumes that each elite sector is socialized separately, or that socialization, if similar, is irrelevant. It also ignores the extent to which these elites need each other, their mutual dependence, their functional overlap. It is certainly possible to start from an opposite set of assumptions and arrive at expectations about elite relationships quite contrary to those of Weber. In analyzing the distance between elite sectors and the bal-

ELITE CONTACT PATTERNS

	Mutual	*Unbalanced*	*Minimal*
High congruence	Coalescent		Convergent
Some dissonance		Potentially exploitative and conflictual	
Hostile conflict	Combative		Immobilist

(Left vertical label: ELITE PERSPECTIVES)

Fig. 2. A typology of elite integrational patterns

ance in their relationships we can test the validity of both theoretical approaches.

Major Propositions Derived from Elite Theories

If one analyzes critically the assumptions, assertions, and the logic of these elite theories, with particular attention to the question of elite integration as posed here, one can extract from such theories rather specific operational expectations (to be used, for example, in our study of higher civil servants and M.P.'s). The trouble is that one finds considerable conflict in these expectations depending on which body of theory one is utilizing.[10]

Illustrations of contrasting theories in the literature readily come to mind. For example, for some scholars *social backgrounds* of elites are a major clue to elite integration, because homogeneity of backgrounds presumably leads to congruence in elite attitudes. As Quandt puts it, "The integration of a political system may be viewed in terms of the degree to which members of the political elite share common socialization experiences."[11] Others argue that this cannot be demonstrated, and that later socialization experiences are more important, Putnam and Bonilla both being skeptical of the linkage of attitudes to social backgrounds.[12]

Again, there are those who feel *sociometric networks* and elite contacts are a major clue to elite integration (as Michels and C. Wright Mills argued). But the density of elite contacts at the top of the system is not always found, and such contacts may be very selective. Above all, they may be irrelevant to the emergence of congruence of elite attitudes.

Other scholars emphasize the importance of *institutional role or "position"* (Suleiman) and the influence of experiences while "working in a given field or institutional setting" (Barton).[13] On the other hand, the alternative proposition is advanced that leaders arrive at their positions because they already held certain perspectives. As Putnam cryptically puts it, "Role constraints may demand certain beliefs and behavior. . . . Where you get to sit depends on where you stand."[14]

Finally, there is a considerable body of theory which postulates that elites are after all the product of a *particular culture and society,* and they have to be understood in those terms primarily. For example, there are some scholars (Armstrong and Suleiman are good references here) who see bureaucrats as achieving a special status in their systems historically and acquiring a sort of legitimacy, tradition, and expectations concerning their behavior.[15] The system has certain norms, "rules of the game," political practices which impose limits on how elites think and behave. These norms and rules, the "political formula" in Mosca's language, are accepted, transmitted, indoctrinated. Systems differ in the institutional contexts within which elites must function (the power of legislative assemblies, bureaucracies, cabinets) and thus, so the argument goes, elite performance will also vary by system. In opposition, it is often argued that there are cross-systemic uniformities—bureaucrats will always be bureaucrats, differing from politicians in role conception, views of partisan politics, preferences about the policymaking process, and so forth. Functional specialization and differences in socialization experiences, as well as quite disparate power bases, will lead to within-system differences and cross-national equivalencies. Thus, again, we have two contrasting sets of expectations. Clearly, there is considerable theoretical argument as to the consequences of social background, sociometric nets, institutional roles or positions, and system differences for elite attitudes and performance. There is, thus, much theory to test, if one is interested in the study of elite integration and conflict.

Our overriding concern in the study of Dutch elites is the nature of elite integration. By this we first mean the extent of consensus or dissensus among M.P.'s and top civil servants in their mutual role perceptions; their views about the power and role of other actors in the system; their conceptions of the political process (including the functioning of parties, interest groups, Parliament, and the bureaucracy in that process); their attitudes toward political conflict; their political ideologies; and their values. Second, our objective is the analysis of the linkage of elite integration as thus conceptualized to the contributory forces of social background, sociometric networks, recruitment patterns, and institutional position (see fig. 1, p. 6). Only through such a two-phased analysis could we establish what the nature of Dutch elite integration is *and* what factors help to explain it.

The Netherlands Political System as Our Laboratory: The Historical Perspective

The Netherlands is a country that is extremely useful to study in terms of these theoretical perspectives, because of its historically fragmented culture and the heavy system requisites for cooperative, if not consensual and integrated, elite behavior. Its historical development must be kept in mind, however. In 1848 the beginnings of parliamentary democracy came to Holland with the constitutional revision of that date, and in 1868 cabinet responsibility to Parliament was definitely established.

Thereafter, organized political parties began to appear first as loosely organized cadres of leaders and then, particularly from the 1880s on, as more articulated structures with clienteles. By 1918 universal manhood suffrage was adopted, as well as proportional representation, leading to a fully democratic order. During this entire period, from 1848 to 1918, the particular form of the Dutch parliamentary democracy took shape, with its special multiparty system at the local, provincial, and national levels; its constitutional monarchy; its own type of representative institutions; its distinctive cabinet government concept; and its bureaucracy, which grew into an effective and efficient, although technically politically neutral, branch of government. The industrial revolution came late to the Netherlands (about 1870), but the process of industrial change was rapid. The society was faced with a variety of crises from 1870 on, and it became increasingly difficult to contain the conflict among the key religious and class groups in the country. A distinctive pattern of democratic government gradually emerged, with its own special rules of the game, specifying particularly the roles and behavior of the political elites. This pattern of democratic government has been aptly called "consociational democracy," and one shorthand term for characterizing the style and behavior of elites (and the public) in such a democracy is to refer to it as "the politics of accommodation."[16] The elements in this model provide a backdrop for us in terms of which the attitudes and behavior of Dutch top civil servants and politicians can be understood.

The Dutch system has certain key features, similar in certain respects to other systems but also cumulatively having a special character. These features must be seen in the historical context of both *pluralism* and *accommodationism.* First, the Dutch political system has always been a highly pluralized society from its earliest days, with extreme territorial dispersion of authority until 1795, after which it became a much more centralized state but with continuing geographical diversity. In the nineteenth and twentieth centuries its pluralism has become more a function of religion and class than of locality or region. But the need for developing rules and procedures for a culture for negotiating among competing interests, has always been paramount. Second, the slow process by which the Dutch state was centralized and developed into its present unitary state with an effective, legitimate central governmental structure saw the emergence of particular political practices and institutions, with their roles and functions having a special, definitional character, to accord with the Dutch elite's views as to how to achieve a central governmental authority that could make acceptable decisions while recognizing and respecting the conflicting demands of intensely involved, rival groups.

The Dutch concept of cabinet government and the cabinet's relation to the Parliament is a very particular contribution in this sense.
The cabinet is a collegiality made up usually of a widely disparate set
of party leaders who negotiate at length before coming to an agreement on a working program. Yet it is, once formed, a body collectively
responsible to Parliament, while at the same time standing apart from
Parliament and often in confrontation with Parliament. The ministers
(sixteen in recent years) cannot be members of Parliament. They have
a separate status. But they must defend themselves before Parliament.
On the other hand, they are ministers of the crown.

    Along with a strong system of cabinet government, the role of
Parliament has been relatively subordinate to the cabinet once it is
formed, although its relationship is somewhat rationalized as one of
the "cooperation of powers." Parliament has certain rights, powers,
and resources in its relationship to the cabinet, such as the right to
interpellation, to inquiry, to information, to make legislative motions,
to take initiatives, and to vote the cabinet down. But generally the
initiative comes from the government (i.e., the cabinet). There is general recognition that the government dominates the political agenda,
has the responsibility for presenting the major policy proposals, de-
cides on what information is to be disseminated, and usually prevails
on legislation in its disagreements with Parliament. Parliament does
perform important functions of scrutiny of proposed laws, debating
their content and thereby securing publicity for the different positions,
querying ministers over administrative matters, and occasionally forc-
ing the cabinet to reverse or withdraw proposed legislation. The role of
the M.P. as the representative of political interest groups and sectors
has become more important, as has his role in maintaining contact
with, and developing support from, the public. The Parliament, in a
larger systemic sense, has a triple functional status—as articulator of
political or sectional group needs and demands, as cooperator with the
cabinet in adopting legislation, and as interrogator and confronter of
the government in an adversary sense. In the final analysis, the tradition of independent cabinet government in the Netherlands means that
Parliament's major influence occurs during the formation of the cabinet. Then the basic political bargains are struck, the broad political
lines drawn.[17]

    What has historically been the role of the higher civil servant in
the Dutch system? Although not all scholars agree, and there is some
concern that the bureaucracy has recently become a "fourth power,"
its historical role was subordinate, nonpolitical, and advisory in the
policy process. Daalder observes that in the early history of the United

Provinces there was no central bureaucracy, and later it "remained of modest size until the early twentieth century." In Dutch nineteenth-century history, he says, "one also looks in vain for a salient role of . . . the bureaucracy. . . ."[18] Other scholars have noted also the "strict hierarchical structure" of the bureaucracy, the loyalty of civil servants to the ministry in which they serve, the capacity of the civil servant to work effectively with any minister regardless of his political persuasion, the relative independence of the bureaucracy from Parliament in the performance of administrative tasks, and the development of close social and personal ties among civil servants.[19] On this latter point, Van Braam has an apt description of the situation in the 1950s.

> Higher civil servants are more than their colleagues of lower rank socially oriented in their own group. They marry more in their own milieux, live concentrated in certain neighborhoods, choose their friends largely from their colleagues, participate more than lower-rank officials in (social) organizations and clubs of civil servants.[20]

This picture of a rather exclusive, politically neutral, nonactivist bureaucracy is not shared today by all scholars. And in actuality one gets the impression from what little research has been done that the role of the top bureaucrat is more complex, less simplistically administrative, and thus more controversial. While formally the rules of behavior for the top civil servant remain the same (loyalty to the minister, no political bias, no political activism, etc.), observance of civil servants in reality has led to statements about their policy role, and concern about their power as having become too great and not subject to proper controls. Van Braam in 1970 spoke of "the fourth power syndrome," the fear of some people that the bureaucratic apparatus had become both separate and independent. Others argue that the bureaucracy is not a bloc, that it reflects internal differences and seeks a great deal of participation from the base of the system.[21] It is pointed out also that the policy role of civil servants varies greatly by sectors of policy, some ministries being very restricted while others are given more latitude. The role of advisory boards, a well-known Dutch tradition, is also pointed to as imposing restraints on civil servants, because on such boards they must sit with pressure group representatives and specialists from the outside and develop a consensus in policy recommendations in a socially diverse context. Nonetheless, the view emerges more and more that the Dutch higher civil servant is not merely a reticent technician who takes a back seat in the policy process. Rather, one senses more policy activism. As a former cabinet minister put it recently, "A clear tendency exists toward a real say in policy matters instead of merely advising, for the closest assistants of the Minister, as well as for the persons responsible for the execution of policies; that is to say, a change from an 'advisor' to a 'manager' role."[22]

Though still unsubstantiated empirically, the implications of these observations for the relationship between M.P. and higher civil servant are obvious. Historically, as Daalder has noted, the Dutch politician had a "more comfortable relationship" with the administration than was the case in many lands where a strong formal separation existed between the two.[23] Since the application of the concept of "proportionality" to recruitment into the bureaucracy, he argues at another point as follows:

> In a segmented society like the Netherlands, carefully balanced political appointments would even seem to have smoothed the relations among the parties and between politicians and governments. They have given parties the certainty that their views were taken into consideration at the beginning of policy formation and in the details of policy execution; they have provided officials with a new avenue by which to obtain political support for administrative concerns; they have thus acted as brokers between officials and politicians and between various parties, softening political conflict in the process.[24]

This characterization of civil servant-politician relationships as historically one of mutual rapport, assistance, and balance is convincing, although one should note that the empirical support for it is not clearly available. It is a view which today some scholars would contend still is correct. One student of the subject recently emphasizes the maintenance of a "professional reserve" in the relationship of politicians and higher civil servants today so that since both sets of actors are engaged in the policy process, they "understand each other's position, (and) are conscious of and accept each other's role in the system." Further, he argues that while the higher civil servant reacts to political initiatives, he observes the differences in opinion in Parliament and, above all, does not become "subordinate to political control."[25] There are others, however, such as Daalder, who suggest that the relationship may have changed. He wrote in 1974:

> The entrance of a new type politician, and the increasing replacement of the former pluralistic accommodation with a conscious polarization, can lead to increasing conflicts between politicians and higher civil servants and to a new kind of politicization of administration.[26]

Such theoretical questions and issues concerning the basic character of the relationship between the Dutch civil servant and M.P., in the context of the changing conditions of Dutch society and politics, particularly interest us here.

The Consociational Model and Its Contemporary Relevance

The well-known theory of consociational democracy has been formulated and utilized to explain how such a set of political institutions as described here for the Netherlands can be made to work effectively to achieve democracy and stability while also producing a government responsive to sharp cleavages and conflicting interest group demands. We need not here explain in detail this theory, since it has been well described by many scholars.[27] The salient points for our purposes can be briefly summarized. The Netherlands has traditionally been seen as having the following basic characteristics: a sharply and deeply segmented society, cleaved particularly in terms of historic religious conflicts; comprehensive and penetrative integration for each major subcultural bloc of the population; a highly pluralized party system reflecting these segmentation patterns; very limited cross-cutting contacts to relieve the subcultural separation; considerable ideological disagreement by blocs and only a narrow national consensus; and political passivity by the public and deference to subcultural leaders.

In a fragmented society such as the Netherlands, then, there are well-organized sociopolitical subcultures which have their own ideologies and among which there is minimal social or political contact. In such a society certain basic elements of a politics of accommodation are necessary if effective government is to be achieved. The Netherlands is a dramatic example of the survival of a nation state as a stable democracy despite extreme social pluralism. Lijphart emphasizes particularly the need in such a system for "overarching cooperation at the elite level." This includes many particular requisites. Among these, as he and Daalder as well as other theorists of conflict in segmented societies have argued, are: agreement among the elites on the fundamentals of the system; belief in the legitimacy of the system; pragmatic political bargaining styles; a deemphasis on ideological politics at the apex; procedures for depoliticization at the subelite level; insulation of elites from direct political protests; and the acceptance by elites of particular rules of the game (such as proportionality, concurrent decisions, secrecy, grand coalitions, and specific cultural practices in the formation of cabinets). The theory of consociational democracy emphasizes the role of elites in managing

the conflicts of a highly compartmentalized and ideologically pluralized system, and accomplishing a consensus on policy in the face of
such conflicts. As Lijphart puts it, "The politics of accommodation
places heavy burdens on the political leaders. Successful policymaking
and settlement of divisive issues require a clear recognition of the
perennial disintegrative tendencies in the system and the capability to
take either preventive or remedial action."[28] Daalder reiterates this
position: "Consociational democracy therefore tends to show a curious
mixture of ideological intransigence on the one hand and pragmatic
political bargaining on the other. . . . relations among subcultures are
settled by a process of careful and businesslike adjustments."[29] This
emphasis on the presence of (perhaps need for) both conflict and
integration is important to keep in mind in comprehending the Dutch
system.

There has been considerable agreement that this model of consociationalism was valid for the Netherlands up to 1967, but that since
that date basic changes in Dutch society *and* in political elite behavior
have occurred. In chapter 2 we will review some of the empirical
evidence of change. There is allegedly in the last decade less rigidity in
the pillarization of the society and more interaction between the *zuilen*
(social sectors). At the mass level there has been more political action
and less indifference as shown by the appearance of action groups, for
example. The party system has been changing, including both the
emergence of new small parties and the merger of the three confessional parties into a federation with one parliamentary *fractie* (group).
At the sociopolitical level these changes are highlighted by the unifica-
tion of the two national trade unions (socialist and Roman Catholic)
into one body.

It is argued that there is less overarching cooperation and certain
infractions of the rules of the game at the elite level. All this, it is
claimed, has led to more political instability recently. Daalder argues
that one sees in Dutch leaders "fundamental changes in philosophy"
and "less readiness to seek political cooperation," leading to possibly
increased friction between elites, particularly between politicians and
civil servants.[30] Daalder contrasts the pre- and post-1967 conditions of
Dutch politics dramatically by contrasting the "moderate politics" of
the earlier period with the "unmasking of ideology" by 1974, the tolerance of the pre-1967 period with conflict in the later period, "top
deliberation" with more attempts at decentralizing decision making at
the base, "proportionality" with polarization, secrecy with publicity,
and "depoliticization" with politicization.[31] Although an oversimplification, such a set of contrasts identifies the key components of both

the classical consociational model and the character of a system in which a revision is presumably taking place.

In a provocative book on the "crisis" in Netherlands politics (1976), van den Berg and Molleman discuss at length the changes leading to the emergence of a newly stabilizing system: the reform of governmental institutions (as the election system), the reordering of the party system, the reintegration of social relations (*ontzuiling*) and democratization. They argue that the Netherlands is still in the middle of a transitional crisis, a period of considerable political change and renewal linked to social and economic changes and, it is hoped, leading to a greater political stability.[32] The role of elites in this process of revision, and in the causes of instability, however, are continually emphasized. Thus, Lijphart says that one "explanation for the instability of Dutch post-accommodation politics is the nervous, ambivalent and, as a result, ineffective reaction of the political leaders to such unfamiliar phenomena as the breakdown of bloc cohesion, declining deference, demands for democratization, and political polarization."[33]

The Higher Civil Servant and the M.P.: Old and New Theoretical Models

This set of theories or interpretations about the Dutch political system provides the setting for our research on Dutch M.P.'s and bureaucrats. Our study was conducted in 1973. We seek to test the extent to which the older model of consociationalism, insofar as it is applicable to the elites we studied, has been replaced by a model of politics which is more conflictual, polarized, and politicized.

In specifying our expectations concerning the attitudes and behavior of members of Parliament and higher civil servants, it is useful to keep in mind the distinction between those requisites which should be valid over time and those which may indeed vary as consociationalism gives way to a more transitional politics. With different patterns of party competition, ideological polarization, decentralization, and democratization, one might well expect different patterns of elite behavior. Thus one could expect both sets of elites—higher civil servants and M.P.'s—to reveal high congruence irrespective of time period, on commitment to the Dutch political system per se, as well as high support for the basic features of the socioeconomic order. But beyond commitment to such fundamentals, one might well expect that the elites of the mid-1970s would vary in certain significant respects from the image held of these elites in the pre-1967 consociational period. Further, while change might not be found in the attitudes and orientations of all elites, one might well expect to find pockets of elite opinion and orientations which were at odds with that image of the earlier elites.

We can represent in summary form some of the contrasting expectations, using the same device which Daalder used in identifying the pre- and post-1967 components of Dutch politics[34] (table 1). As indicated, hypotheses are derived concerning the expected role of the higher civil servant, of the M.P., of the relationships between the elites, and their joint orientations towards politics. Theoretically, one should expect the Dutch civil servant in a consociational system (pre-1967) to be depoliticized. He would not be seen as central to the resolution of political conflict, or, indeed, as involved in partisan controversies at all. His policy role is advisory and mainly technical. Higher civil servants under consociationalism would support system goals, work loyally within a ministry despite the partisan leanings of the minister, and observe the rules of political neutrality and secrecy. Their contacts with M.P.'s would be minimal. Indeed, outside of the bureaucracy their contacts would not be extensive, except with clientele interest groups and as members of advisory boards. Yet, they would accept the role of politicians in the policy process, although perhaps themselves utilizing more technical criteria for the analysis of policy matters. If there was any friction between civil servants and M.P.'s, it would be very latent. After 1967, as consociationalism declines, theoretically the higher civil servant would be functioning in the context of a transitional or evolving set of political-cultural norms. And thus he might be expected to be more politicized, as figure 2 indicates; he is more engaged with conflict and tolerant of it, more partisan and even ideological, less preoccupied with political neutrality and more interested in an activist policy role. This might also lead to more friction within the bureaucracy and with certain types of M.P.'s.

The M.P. before and after consociationalism theoretically could differ considerably in political perspectives. If Daalder and Lijphart are correct, the M.P. sees his role somewhat differently; he is more likely to challenge the government, more a champion of citizen causes, more interested in developing and articulating ideological positions. His style becomes less pragmatic, less tolerant, and more combative. His pattern of contacts becomes more dense and cosmopolitan. Although he accepts and is loyal to the fundamentals of the Dutch system, he views the political process as more properly conflictual and seeks to participate more aggressively in it.

Thus the moderate, businesslike, nonideological politics of the past have been replaced by a more strident, controversial, and ideo-

TABLE 1. Expectations of Elite Behavior during Accommodation and After

Consociational Model (pre-1967)	Postconsociational Transitional Model (1967 and later)
Expectations for both elites	
Low salience of ideology	Conflict at least partly seen as functional
Disapproval of conflict	Evidence of intolerance of ideas of politi-
Tolerance of ideas of others, particularly of partisan opposites	cal opponents (M.P.'s particularly)
Pro-compromise attitude; against extremism	Inclination to be more skeptical of compromise; willing to take more extreme positions
Elitism; not strongly in favor of citizen involvement	Democratic and populist views; favor citizen participation more
Emphasis on secrecy of governmental actions; anonymity favored	Desire more publicity of governmental actions
Ideological emphasis and awareness	
Expectations for higher civil servants	
Political neutrality emphasized	Less emphasis on neutrality
Technical; advisory, passive policy involvement	Active, managerial, political, as well as technical policy involvement
Partisan preference latent and unimportant	Partisan preference may be linked to political perceptions and attitudes
Ministerial loyalty irrespective of party	Concern about change of ministers
Restricted patterns of contact with actors in the system	Greater contacts outside the bureaucracy
Expectations for M.P.'s	
Subordinate to cabinet; limited assertion of parliamentary initiatives	Assertion of parliamentary initiatives and rights; willing to confront the government
Important relationships with social-political groups within own pillar; contacts with public not emphasized; pragmatic political styles	Open relationships with interest groups, but much more emphasis on citizen contacts
	Ideological political styles
Expectations for M.P.-civil servant relationships	
Minimal contacts between the two elites	Critical of each other's roles, and more
Mutual tolerance and acceptance of each other's roles; policy role of civil servants minimized	disagreement in perceptions of roles of other actors (particularly of ministers)
High congruence in perspectives about the political process, especially political conflict and its resolution; opposition to the role of citizens in the process; the importance of the role of political parties in the process	Development of disagreement among elites on perspectives—M.P.'s view conflict less traumatically, favor more citizen involvement, and see parties as important actors in the political process
Ideological and partisan differences *between* the two elites are not important—*within* Parliament they are significant	Ideological and partisan differences both *within* the bureaucracy and the Parliament are emergent and may influence
Contacts increased, especially for younger elite members	intraelite consensus, as well as cross-elite relationships

logical politics of the present. And elites reflect these basic changes in political culture. These expectations about civil servants and politicians, outlined above, set the stage for our inquiry. They suggest some reconceptualization of roles by these elites, a new emphasis in elite contacts, different political styles, and significant reorientation of beliefs about the political process. They suggest, above all, greater elite conflict and, perhaps, friction. In the politics of the transitional period elite integration may be harder to achieve than ever before.

Looking at Dutch elite data, one might keep in mind the classification of democratic regimes used by Arend Lijphart (see fig. 3). The questions constantly before us are: What does our data tell us about the continuance of the accommodation model? To what extent does the Dutch system seem to be moving toward another model—depoliticized, centrifugal, or centripetal democracy? Or is a new model of the Dutch system appearing, one which emphasizes the existence and need for elite accommodation as much as before, but which reflects certain characteristics of other systems also, such as polarization, politicization, populism, and decentralization? Is, in other words, a much more complex system emerging reflecting different values, goals, and political practices? That in a sense is the key query which dominates our analysis.

POLITICAL CULTURE

		Homogeneous	Fragmented
ELITE BEHAVIOR	Coalescent	Depoliticized democracy	Consociational democracy (accommodation model)
	Competitive	Centripetal democracy (pluralistic model)	Centrifugal democracy

Fig. 3. A typology of democratic regimes (after Lijphart)

Our Study Procedure

If one is to check reality against elite theory, one should talk to those in leadership positions. With this firm conviction a comparative study was designed of which the Dutch research is one part. We sought to test theories about political elites in general and the Dutch elites in particular. In the Netherlands we conducted interviews in 1973 with forty-four members of Parliament and seventy-six higher civil servants. This was part of the international study of elites begun in 1970 at the University of Michigan, employing in each country the same basic design and field procedure. As indicated earlier, the countries included were five other European parliamentary democracies plus the United States. The Dutch study must be seen, thus, as part of a cross-national project. It was felt that the propositions about elite theory should be tested in countries with a variety of cultural and institutional contexts, though with generally similar political and economic systems. The special features of Dutch politics—subcultural pluralism, fragmented multiparty system, strong cabinet government, and a tradition of an independent, politically neutral bureaucracy plus the feeling that this system was undergoing modification—encouraged us to test elite theory in the Netherlands. It would, we thought, provide both significant system similarity and striking contrast to other countries in our project.

The sample eventually consisted of three segments, selected to meet the criteria of cross-national comparability. Approximately one-third of the members of the lower house of Parliament were selected randomly, excluding only first-year M.P.'s.[35] Since two studies of the Dutch parliament had been completed in the few years prior to our study, including many questions similar to our own, we felt that such a sample was adequate. We also selected a sample of higher civil servants from the two levels of the service below the *secretaris-generaal* (i.e., *directeur-generaal* and *directeur*) in ministries primarily concerned with domestic affairs. (Thus, the Ministries of Foreign Affairs and Defense were excluded, for reasons linked to the international project.) We sought to include the career civil servants at the top ministerial policymaking level, individuals who had the responsibility for program administration in a division, section, or bureau. These individuals were randomly selected, seventy-six being finally interviewed, constituting close to one-third of the universe as thus defined. Finally, we sought a group of "high flyers" (a British term), a group of younger civil servants at the lower levels of the bureaucracy who, because of age, position, and mobility patterns, were identified for us (by senior civil servants) as likely to move to the top of the ministries in the

succeeding ten years. We finally selected seventeen of these for limited
comparison with the senior civil servants.

One can visualize where in the bureaucracy we did our interviewing from the listing of the levels of the civil service in three countries
found in figure 4.

Our interviews with these leaders in the first half of 1973 were
largely open-ended, structured but informal, and tape-recorded. We
did employ some closed questions providing precise responses on certain topics, utilizing scales and agree-disagree items. But in the main
these were conversational interviews, following a set of basic questions used in all our studies. The advantages of such a technique with
such leaders are obvious, providing a flexibility in interaction of inter-
viewer and respondent and an opportunity to explore the nuances of
meaning and the underlying structure of a leader's ideas. The disadvantages were severe, however, in achieving standardization in the
coding of responses and in the costs of time and money in transcrib-
ing the tape-recorded interviews into typescripts from which coding
could finally be done. We employed highly educated interviewers
who had previously interviewed Dutch M.P.'s. They also did the
coding, which was standardized as carefully as possible, supervised,
and checked by the project coordinator as well as selectively by the
principal investigators.[36]

The Dutch project encountered particular problems because of its
timing. After the parliamentary election of November 29, 1972, over
five months elapsed before the Den Uyl cabinet was confirmed on May
11, 1973. Since we could not wait for our interviewing, we went ahead
with the project during this cabinet formation period. The responses of

	Netherlands	*Germany*	*Britian*
	Minister	Minister	Minister
	Staatssecretaris	State secretary	Permanent
	Secretaris-generaal		undersecretary
	Directeur-generaal	Ministerial direktor	Deputy
Our *interviews*	Directeur	Ministerial dirigent	Undersecretary
	High flyer	High flyer	High flyer

Fig. 4.   The civil servant sample

political and administrative leaders are often time-bound, and the un-
certainties of the Dutch political situation may have contributed somewhat to the attitudes expressed. On the other hand, the type of questions we utilized, dealing with basic orientations towards politics, could
well be asked and answered, thoughtfully and reflectively, during such
a period without seriously being affected by the long deliberations in
cabinet formation. Indeed, there are those who would argue that for
many civil servants at least (and possibly also for some M.P.'s) the
relaxed atmosphere preceding a new cabinet, when new legislative
proposals are held in abeyance, might be rather conducive to such an
investigation as ours. One should add that the cooperation of our
respondents was excellent; access was not difficult once the proper
arrangements and explanations had been made, recording of interviews was not refused, and the patience and willingness of these
leaders to explain their positions and beliefs in depth was impressive.

This was the empirical basis, then, for studying elite political culture in the Netherlands. It was a study of the leader at the *individual
level,* but we were interested in arriving at interpretations at the macro
or *system level* that would eventually help us to generalize at the *cross-
system level.* Our immediate focus was the images of political elites;
our ultimate interest was the functioning of the system.

Over a decade ago Lasswell said the study of elites was "indispens-
able to all serious inquiry into political processes."[37] For him such
study was critical for retracing history, understanding present power
relationships, and predicting future events. Above all, for Lasswell
elite study was important for clarifying the goals and values of society.
While much writing on elite integration has appeared and, as Robert
Putnam says, "the main theoretical dimensions of elite integration
are . . . reasonably clear," solid empirical evidence on the incidence,
interrelationships, and implications of elite integration patterns is, as
he also says, "very rare."[38] This book, it is hoped, can contribute to
that intellectual task.

NOTES

1. See Carl Friedrich, *Man and His Government* (New York: McGraw-Hill,
   1963), p. 464.
2. Avery Leiserson, *Parties and Politics* (New York: Alfred A. Knopf, 1958),
   p. 35.
3. Gaetano Mosca, *The Ruling Class* (New York: McGraw-Hill, 1939), p. 50.

4. Robert Michels, *Political Parties: A Sociological Study of the Oligarchical Tendencies of Modern Democracy* (Glencoe, Ill.: The Free Press, 1915).
5. C. Wright Mills, *The Power Elite* (New York: Oxford University Press, 1956), p. 283.
6. James Meisel, *The Myth of the Ruling Class: Gaetano Mosca and the Elite* (Ann Arbor: University of Michigan Press, 1958), p. 4.
7. H. H. Gerth and C. Wright Mills (eds.), *From Max Weber: Essays in Sociology* (London: Kegan Paul, 1948), pp. 226, 232–34.
8. Fred W. Riggs, *Administration in Developing Countries* (Boston: Houghton Mifflin, 1964), p. 237.
9. Samuel P. Huntington, *Political Order in Changing Societies* (New Haven: Yale University Press, 1968), p. 109.
10. We have leaned heavily here on Robert Putnam's most comprehensive and useful summary of the literature on elites, *The Comparative Study of Political Elites* (Englewood Cliffs, N.J.: Prentice-Hall, 1976).
11. W. Quandt, *The Comparative Study of Political Elites* (Beverly Hills, Calif.: Sage Professional Papers in Comparative Politics, 1970), p. 198.
12. Putnam, *Political Elites*, p. 93; Frank Bonilla, *The Failure of Elites* (Cambridge, Mass.: MIT Press, 1970), p. 149.
13. Ezra Suleiman, *Politics, Power, and Bureaucracy in France: The Administrative Elite* (Princeton, N.J.: Princeton University Press, 1974); Allen H. Barton, "Determinants of Leadership Attitudes in a Socialist Society," in *Opinion Making Elites in Yugoslavia*, ed. Allen H. Barton et al. (New York: Praeger, 1973), p. 242.
14. Putnam, *Political Elites*, p. 97.
15. John Armstrong, *The European Administrative Elite* (Princeton, N.J.: Princeton University Press, 1973); Suleiman, *Politics, Power, and Bureaucracy.*
16. Arend Lijphart, *The Politics of Accommodation: Pluralism and Democracy in the Netherlands* (Berkeley: University of California Press, 1968, 1975).
17. See, for analyses of the Dutch Parliament, Jan Kooiman, *Over de Kamer gesproken* (The Hague: Staatsuitgeverij, 1976), and, in an English summary, his paper, "Aspects of Role and Function of Parliament in the Dutch Political System—As Seen by the Members Themselves" (Paper prepared for the International Political Science Association Conference, Montreal, August 1973).
18. Hans Daalder, "On Building Consociational Nations: The Cases of the Netherlands and Switzerland," *International Social Science Journal* 23, no. 3 (1971): 358–60.
19. A summary of much of this "knowledge" is found in Jan Kooiman, "The Higher Civil Servant in Holland: Role, Status, and Influence" (Paper prepared for European Consortium for Political Research Workshop, Mannheim, Germany, April 1973).
20. A. Van Braam, "Sociale herkomst en mobiliteit van ambtenaren," in *So-*

ciale stijging en daling in Nederland, ed. F. van Heek and E. V. W. Vercruysse (Leiden: Stenfert Kroese, 1959), vol. 1, pp. 195–239.

21. K. Millenaar, "Parlement en beleidsambtenaar," in *Parlement en politieke besluitvorming in Nederland,* ed. H. Daalder (Alphen aan den Rijn: Samson Uitgeverij, 1975), p. 55.

22. See Kooiman, *Over de Kamer gesproken,* for elaboration of these positions and for the quotation used here.

23. Hans Daalder, *Politisering en lijdelijkheid in de Nederlandse politiek* (Assen: van Gorcum, 1974), p. 69.

24. Hans Daalder, "Parties, Elections, and Political Developments in Western Europe," in *Political Parties and Political Development,* ed. Joseph La Palombara and Myron Weiner (Princeton, N.J.: Princeton University Press, 1966), pp. 60–61.

25. Millenaar, "Parlement en beleidsambtenaar," p. 54.

26. Daalder, *Politisering,* p. 69.

27. Of course, Arend Lijphart's book, *The Politics of Accommodation,* states this classic theory extremely well. See also Eric A. Nordlinger, *Conflict Regulation in Divided Societies* (Cambridge, Mass.: Harvard University Center for International Affairs, 1972), and the excellent review article by Hans Daalder, "The Consociational Democracy Theme," *World Politics* 26, no. 4 (July 1974): 604–21. Much of the summary of consociationalism used here rests on these sources. Writers have also questioned Lijphart's model as applied to the Netherlands. See particularly M. Fennema, "Professor Lijphart en de Nederlandse politiek," *Acta Politica* 11 (January 1976), pp. 54–77.

28. Lijphart, *Politics of Accommodation,* pp. 122–38.

29. Daalder, "Consociational Democracy Theme," p. 607.

30. See Daalder, *Politisering,* pp. 52–53, 62, and 69 for these observations, as well as Lijphart, *Politics of Accommodation,* 2d ed., chap. 10 ("The Breakdown of the Politics of Accommodation").

31. Daalder, *Politisering,* p. 38.

32. J. Th. J. van den Berg and H. A. A. Molleman, *Crisis in de Nederlandse politiek* (Alphen aan den Rijn: Samson Uitgeverij, 1974), pp. 214–19, 226.

33. Lijphart, *Politics of Accommodation,* 2d ed., chap. 10.

34. Daalder, *Politisering,* p. 38.

35. The exclusion was based on the premise that they had limited experience in Parliament, and, particularly, had not yet developed a relationship with the bureaucracy, the focus of our study.

36. Costs prevented double coding of all interviews, but a 20 percent sample of the interviews were coded twice. The results of this confirmed our feeling of high confidence in the basic reliability of the coding operation.

37. Harold D. Lasswell and Daniel Lerner (eds.), *World Revolutionary Elites* (Cambridge, Mass.: MIT Press, 1966), p. 4.

38. Putnam, *Political Elites,* p. 123.

CHAPTER 2

Recent Trends in
Society and Politics:
Empirical Realities

Before presenting our analysis of Dutch elites, it is necessary to describe and evaluate the major developments in Dutch society and politics at the mass level since the 1960s. The attitudes and orientations of the political elites can well be seen as related to changes which have been occurring in public attitudes and behavior. The political system as well as the social system of the Netherlands has been undergoing a transformation, a periodic phenomenon for all modern democracies. What has been happening to the governmental elites at the apex of the system, particularly in their views about the political process and their conceptions of the roles of elites and the public in that process, must be seen against this backdrop of social and political change at the citizen level. The essential nature of integration or conflict at the elite level must be interpreted in the light of new public social and political orientations.

Basic Subcultural Cleavage Patterns

As a prelude to understanding the segmented nature of the society, one must look first at religious affiliation trends (table 2). The Catholic proportion of the population has held steady since 1920 at more than one-third. Both major Protestant denominations constitute together slightly more than 30 percent on the basis of 1970 data, and this is significantly down from 50 percent in 1920. While this has been happening, there has been a sharp rise in the percentage of those who profess no religion—to 28 percent.

If one combines religion with regularity of church attendance and then includes information about social class, linking these to party preference data, one finds Dutch society divided basically into four blocs or "pillars": the regular and faithful Catholics, the regular and faithful Calvinists, and a secular bloc which is split along class lines into socialists (primarily working and lower class) and liberals (primarily the middle and upper class). A national survey in 1964 revealed the approximate distributions shown in figure 5.[1] Population and voter aggregates very similar in size make up these four blocs in the population. No bloc comes close to having a majority. In actuality the Calvinist bloc includes the members of two distinct denominations, the Reformed (or Gereformeerd) and the Dutch Reformed (Nederlands Hervormd). Although the latter group is quite a bit larger (28.3 percent of the Dutch population in 1960, compared to 9.3 percent for the Reformed), regularity of attendance is much greater in the Reformed group, so that they each constitute about 50 percent of the Calvinist bloc. The secular bloc consists of the nonreligious, the irregular Catholics, many of the Dutch Reformed who are not regular churchgoers, and members of minor dissenting churches. This melange of secularists then separate out into two blocs—socialists and liberals—with differences in class status and perspectives providing the basis for cohesion within each bloc. This division of the society, it is argued, goes back generally to the sixteenth century, resulting from the Dutch war of independence with Spain, the subsequent conflict between Catholics and Protestants, as well as the Reformation and Renaissance movements which accentuated these conflicts and split the Protestants. The industrial revolution, of course, added the class division of the society which helps explain the split in the secular bloc.[2]

The linkage of these blocs to the parties is clearly demonstrated in table 3. For the Catholic and Calvinist blocs there has been strong support for overwhelming adherence to the Catholic Peoples party (KVP) and Calvinist Anti-Revolutionary (ARP) and Christian Historical Union (CHU) political parties, at the 80 percent level or better.

TABLE 2. Religious Distributions in the Dutch Population (in percentages)

	1920	1930	1947	1960	1970
Roman Catholic	35.6	36.4	38.5	40.4	36.9
Dutch Reformed (Hervormd)	41.2	34.4	31.1	28.3	22.6
Reformed (Gereformeerd)	9.5	9.4	9.7	9.3	8.8
Other	5.9	5.4	3.7	3.6	3.9
No religion	7.8	14.4	17.0	18.4	27.8

Source: Netherlands Central Bureau of Statistics, *Statistical Yearbook of The Netherlands* (The Hague: Staatsuitgeverij, 1971), p. 75; the 1970 percentages come from the national survey of that year.

The secular bloc consists of over 50 percent who support the Party of Labor (PVDA), other smaller parties on the Left such as Democrats '66 (D'66) in 1970, the conservative Peoples Party for Freedom and Democracy (the "Liberals," or VVD), or the latter's conservative allies such as the Democratic-Socialists '70 (DS'70).

What is particularly remarkable about this party adherence data for blocs up to 1970 is the negligible cross-bloc party support between the religious blocs. Simply put, there was *no support* for the Protestant parties by the members of the Catholic bloc, and similarly *none* of the Calvinist bloc regulars supported the Catholic party. The 15 percent to 20 percent of these blocs who defected did so to the smaller parties, and particularly to the secular sector: 8 percent of the Catholics affiliated with the Labor party and another 8 percent with the Liberal party or small parties; 8 percent of the Calvinists also preferred Labor, 3 percent preferred the Liberals, and the remaining 8 percent opted for small parties (some of whom were also Protestant). Thus, deviations in political behavior by the two major religious blocs were to the Left and to the Right (ideologically) but not to each other!

The evidence of the pervasiveness of this segmentation in many other aspects of the Dutch society has been presented with a wealth of data by Lijphart. For example, in 1964 trade union data revealed that 94 percent of the Catholic union members, 92 percent of the socialist

1964 Population Survey   *1967 Party Vote*

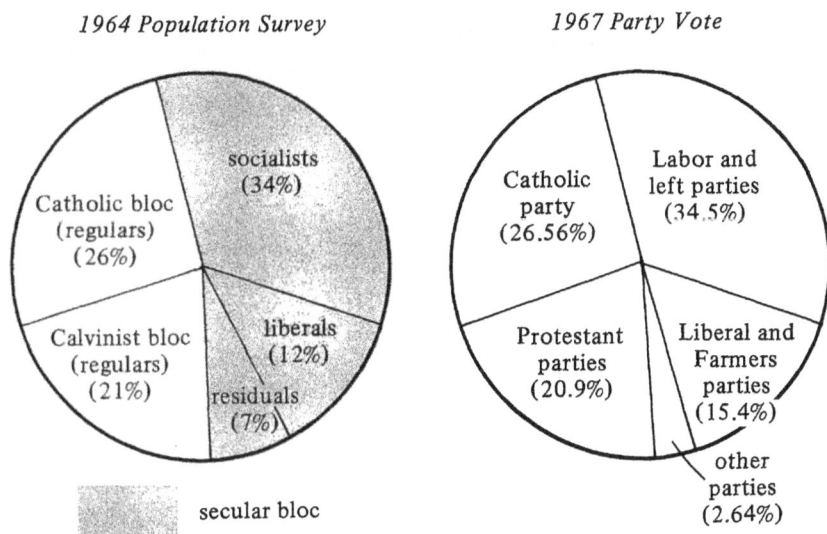

Fig. 5. The pillars in the Dutch population in the 1960s

union, and 77 percent of the Protestant union came from the Catholic, secular, and Calvinist blocs, respectively. Another example is membership in radio-television associations: 89 percent of the Catholic, 75 percent of the Calvinist, 96 percent of the socialist, and 78 to 86 percent of the liberal associations came from liberal or socialist bloc followers.[3] Even the friendship patterns of Dutch citizens reflected subcultural distinctiveness. In 1964, when asked to reveal the bloc identifications of their five best friends, 85 percent of the regular Catholics, 78 percent of the Reformed, and 85 percent of the Dutch Reformed said their friends came from their own religious circles; 90 percent of those with no religion said their friends were not religious, were socialist, or liberal.[4] Clearly the vertical pillarization of the society has been rigorous and comprehensive in the past. Even during the war the underground press reflected this pattern of regimentation, and the one newspaper that cut across these blocs did not last long after the war![5]

Changes in the Pattern of Social Cleavages in Recent Years

In the last decade the Dutch system at the mass level has been changing considerably. This is manifest in a variety of ways. It has been

TABLE 3. Party Preferences of the Blocs up to 1970 (in percentages)

	Catholic Party	Major Protestant Parties		Labor Party	Right-wing Liberal Party	Other Parties
		ARP	CHU			
Catholics						
1964	87	1	0	8	2	1
1970	85	0	0	3	4	4
Calvinists						
Reformed						
1964	0	72	9	6	1	12
1970	0	78	0	1	1	18
Dutch Reformed						
1964	0	15	65	10	4	6
1970	0	11	61	16	7	4
Secular Blocs						
(Liberals and Socialists)						
1964	5	2	6	59	18	9
1970	2	3	2	53	17	11

Sources: For 1964, the survey used by Arend Lijphart in *The Politics of Accommodation: Pluralism and Democracy in the Netherlands* (Berkeley: University of California Press, 1968, 1975; for 1970, a Dutch national election study conducted under the auspices of the Sociologisch Instituut of the Katholieke Hogeschool, Tilburg, described in Philip C. Stouthard, "De verkiezingen van maart 1970," *Acta Politica* 6 (January 1971), pp. 18–28.

leading to what Lijphart calls "the breakdown of the politics of accommodation." The 1967 election appears to have been the turning point. From that date one observed changes in party loyalty and in the basic subcultural segmentation patterns.

The breakdown in the rigid lines of religious encapsulation has become particularly apparent in the political preferences and voting behavior of the public. As table 4 indicates, deconfessionalization occurred in the late 1960s and 1970s. The drop in Catholic support for the Catholic party was precipitous and continuous, 45 percentage points from 1963 to 1972. For Protestants the defections were not quite as great, but a decline did take place. This was a bit more noticeable among active Catholics than among Protestants, and actually more serious than among irregular churchgoers. In 1956, for example, 95 percent of active Catholics and 50 percent of other Catholics supported the Catholic party (KVP); by 1967 these figures had declined to 77 and 37 percent, and by 1972 to 53 and 25 percent. In contrast, 90 percent of active Protestants and 62 percent of other Protestants supported the ARP in 1956; those figures fell only to 88 and 58 percent by 1967 and to 61 and 36 percent by 1972.[6]

While the decline has occurred for both regulars and irregular churchgoers, the regular attendants of the Reformed church were more loyal to their party during this period. There has generally been an attitudinal movement away from the idea of religiously based parties. A question put to a cross section of voters from 1971 on as to whether parties should be confessional associated with a particular

TABLE 4. Deconfessionalization in Party Preference Patterns (in percentages)

Election Year	Catholics Supporting Catholic Party (KVP)	Dutch Reformed Supporting Their Protestant Party (CHU)	Reformed Supporting Their Protestant Party (ARP)
1963	83	—[a]	—[a]
1967	67	24	82
1971	51	22	61
1972	38	18	56
1977[b]	51	28	66

Source: Thomas Rochon, "Local Elites and the Structure of Political Conflict: Parties, Unions, and Interest Groups in the Netherlands" (Ph.D. diss., University of Michigan, 1980). Based on J. van den Berg and H. Molleman, *Crisis in de Nederlandse politiek* (Alphen aan den Rijn: Samson Uitgeverij, 1974), p. 65.
    a. Data not available.
    b. In 1977, the KVP, CHU, and ARP combined into one religious party, the CDA. Data from G. Irwin, J. Verhoef, and C. Wiebrans, *De Nederlandse Kiezer '77* (Voorschoten: VAM, 1977), p. 151.

religion or not brought an increase of support for nonreligious parties from 38 percent in 1971 to 52 percent in 1977.[7]

This is all part of a developing secularization of the society and a loosening of bloc ties. The voters have also gradually opted for labor unions which are more disassociated from religion.[8] Further, a new labor union, the Federation of Dutch Unions (FNV), has come into existence which combines the socialists and Catholics in one union, a move which evoked no opposition from the Catholic bishops. Additional evidence of the decline of the exclusivity of society's pillars is the rise of neutral newspapers and a surge in the membership of radio and television associations not committed to a particular bloc. Lijphart concludes that "the social cleavages between the blocs have lost their sharpness as well as much of their political salience."[9] The formation of the Christian Democratic Appeal (CDA), merging Protestants and Catholics in one party, is a major development in this direction. This began in 1970 and 1974 at the local and provincial elections and culminated with the new party replacing the three old parties in the 1977 national election.

The Pluralized Nature of the Dutch Party System and Changes Since 1967

The multiparty system has existed in the Netherlands for a long time, since the turn of the century at least, and long before proportional representation was adopted as a system of representation in 1918. There were eight established parties at the time of the great crises in Dutch politics over suffrage and religious education in the period from 1910 to 1917, the resolution of which led to the foundation of the present consociational democracy. It is important to note the timing of the development of the party system, for it refutes the argument that in terms of system origins election systems *cause* party systems. In the Netherlands it was originally the other way around. Nevertheless, proportional representation has been linked to more pluralization. Until World War I there were three liberal parties, a Catholic party, two Protestant parties, a socialist party, and a Communist party. In 1918, seventeen parties won seats in the lower house of the Parliament, although the five largest parties secured 87 percent of the vote and the seats. Since then, on the average, ten parties were represented in the 100- to 150-member national legislature between 1918 and 1963, but the "Big Five" (the Catholic party, Anti-Revolutionary party, Christian Historical Union, Labor party, and Liberal party) normally controlled 88 percent of the vote.[10] But many of the small parties persisted, representing very small but loyal clienteles, examples of which are shown in table 5. In recent years the number of parties appearing on the scene and winning seats increased to fourteen in 1971 and 1972, but declined in 1977 to eleven. This has been one of the most fragmented party systems in modern democracies, perhaps rivaled only by the Israeli party system.

There is no question that modifications in the Dutch party system have been taking place in recent years, manifesting two contrasting (but also complementary) tendencies—more pluralization and more consolidation (table 6). First, there has been the striking decline of the strength of the KVP—from a high of 32 percent to a low of 17.7 percent in 1972. All religious parties secured over 50 percent of the vote in the past (53.7 percent in 1946, 52.3 percent in 1963), but by 1972 this declined to 36 percent. There was a moderate decline in the Christian Historical Union (CHU) after 1956. Much greater was the decline in Catholic support of the KVP, from 84 percent in 1956 to 38 percent in 1972 (for regular Catholics attending church the drop was from 95 percent to 53 percent).[11]

The decline in support for the religious parties was accompanied by another development—the increased support for the smaller parties. The hold that the "Big Five" had on the electorate weakened, dropping from a mean of 88 percent of the voters earlier to 72 to 73 percent in the seventies. This meant a moderate restructuring of the electorate and the party system. D'66, a new party of the moderate Left advocating reform of the existing party system, appeared in the 1967 election and captured 4.5 percent of the vote. The Radical party (PPR), consisting of Christian radicals who were initially unhappy with and deserted the old KVP in 1968, won 4.8 percent in 1972 (1.8 percent in 1971). It drew heavily from the young voters aged eighteen to

**TABLE 5. Percentage of Vote Won by Smaller Parties
in National Elections**

	1959	1963	1972
Farmers party	0.7	2.1	1.9
Communist party	2.4	2.8	4.5
Reformed Political League			
(right-wing Protestants)	0.7	0.8	1.8
Political Reformed party			
(also right-wing Protestants)	2.2	2.3	2.2
Pacifist Socialist party	1.8	3.0	1.5

Source: Central Bureau voor de Statistiek, Statistiek der Verkeizengen (The Hague: Staatsuitgeverij, 1972).

twenty years, who had just received the vote. The DS'70, a more right-wing party, many of whose early supporters came from the Labor party, received 5.3 percent in 1971 and 4.1 percent in 1972. These, together with even smaller parties, the Roman Catholic Party of the Netherlands (RKPN), and Netherlands Middle Class Party (NMP), were all groups who broke away from the old party structure, exploiting the Dutch system and people's tolerance for dissidence and new movements, and modified the functioning of the traditional system. Above all, the system became more pluralized.

Through all of this, the Dutch Labor party maintained and later even increased its major status in the system. Its earlier version, the Social Democratic Workers Party (SDAP), founded in 1894, gradu-

TABLE 6. Realignment in the Dutch Party System

	Distribution of the Vote in Eight National Elections (in percentages)							
	1946	1952	1956	1963	1967	1971	1972	1977
Development of the New Left								
Communists (CPN)	10.6	6.2	4.8	2.8	3.6	3.9	4.5	1.7
Pacifist Socialists (PSP)				3.0	2.9	1.4	1.5	0.9
Radical party (PPR)						1.8	4.8	1.7
Democrats '66 (D'66)					4.5	6.8	4.2	5.4
Total	10.6	6.2	4.8	5.8	11.0	13.9	15.0	9.7
Decline in Major Confessional Parties								
Catholics (KVP)	30.8	28.7	31.7	31.9	26.5	21.9	17.7	(CDA
Protestants (ARP)	12.9	11.3	9.9	8.7	9.9	8.6	8.8	coali-
Protestants (CHU)	7.9	8.9	8.4	8.6	8.1	6.3	4.8	tion)
Total	51.6	48.9	50.0	49.2	44.5	36.8	31.3	31.9
Resurgence of the Old Liberals and the Right								
Liberals (VVD)	6.4	8.8	8.8	10.3	10.7	10.4	14.4	18.0
Political Reformed party (SGP)	2.1	2.4	2.3	2.3	2.0	2.3	2.2	2.1
Reformed Political League (GPV)	0.0	0.7	0.6	0.8	0.9	1.6	1.8	1.0
Farmers party (BP)				2.1	4.7	1.1	1.9	0.8
Democratic Socialists (DS'70)						5.3	4.1	0.7
Catholic National party (KNP) (Roman Catholic party [RKPN])		2.7					0.9	0.4
Midden Stands party (NMP)						1.5	0.4	
Total	8.5	14.6	11.7	15.5	18.3	22.2	25.7	23.0
Stability of the Socialists								
Socialists	28.3	29.0	32.7	28.0	23.5	24.7	27.4	33.8

Source: Ministry of Economic Affairs, Central Bureau for Statistics.

ally increased its strength to over 20 percent of the votes before World War II, but stayed out of the cabinet. After the war it was reorganized as the PVDA, an interconfessional party, receiving support from supporters of the former SDAP as well as Protestants and Catholics. It based its appeal on "personal socialism," a moderate approach to the class struggle, recognition of the private sector, and called on all groups opposed to the continuance of capitalism in its present form to unite to secure a "just order for labor." The PVDA served 28 percent of the vote in the first postwar election of 1946 (compared to 10.6 percent for the Communists) and maintained its strength at this level despite a drastic (for the Netherlands!) drop of 4.5 percent in 1967. By 1977 it had increased its strength actually to over 33 percent. Although the party has not achieved its goal of increasing its electoral strength quickly, it has not continued to decline, as some people had predicted. Desertions to the new Left (Communists and pacifists, for example) or to the new Right and Center parties, and the internal demands for reform by what was called the "New Left," were weathered by the party that actually at first tolerated the left-wing radicals and later saw them take over a majority of positions in the organization's executive committee. Thus, the Labor party adapted to the changes in Dutch society not by becoming more bourgeois or moving to the center but by maintaining itself as the genuine socialist alternative for the electorate.[12]

One interesting and possibly significant consequence of change in the party system (or a trend associated with these developments) is that a relatively small proportion of the Dutch public has a strong sense of party identification. Recent studies done over a three-year span have revealed that in 1970, 1971, and 1972 18 percent, 17 percent, and 22 percent (respectively) of the Dutch population claimed a strong adherence to one political party; 27 percent, 24 percent, and 22 percent stated they had a weak adherence to one party; and 55 percent, 59 percent, and 56 percent said they preferred no party over another. Thomassen argues that in the Netherlands "party identification is less stable than voting behavior" and the "weak psychological attachment to political parties" is linked to the Dutch public's association with the subcultures which has weakened in recent years.[13]

What is cause and what is effect in the changes in the party system, however, is hard to say. The low level of loyalty may have contributed to the rise of new parties and the fragmentation of the system. However, there is some evidence that prior to the 1960s a larger proportion of the electorate (as many as 80 percent) had a party preference.[14] This suggests that fragmentation of the party system and decline of party adherence may have gone hand in hand. There is evidence also that this decline in party identification was particularly noticeable, as in some other countries like the United States, among young citizens.[15]

While the party system has been changing and its pluralized character essentially maintained, there has also been some reconsolidation of the system. In the early seventies the three major religious parties began to discuss the possibilities of fusion at the national level (in some localities combined slates had already been presented in elections). After much negotiation (which many had considered impossible) a new party, the Christian Democratic Appeal (CDA), appeared. It presented a list of candidates in the 1977 election which replaced and combined the lists of the KVP, ARP, and CHU parties. And it did reasonably well, securing slightly more of the vote than these parties had received in the 1972 election. One study suggested that the CDA brought some Catholics and Protestants back to this party. Thus 38 percent of the Catholics supported the Catholic Peoples party in 1972, but 51 percent of the Catholics supported the CDA in 1977.[16]

Further evidence of reconsolidation of the party system occurred in the 1977 election in the decline in public support of the small parties. All but the D'66 suffered losses, and in certain cases the loss was severe enough to exclude them from the Parliament. The smaller left-wing parties had 22 seats in Parliament in 1972; in 1977 they dropped to 14 (the Communists lost 5 seats, the Pacifists [PSP] lost 1, the Radicals [PPR] lost 4, and D'66 gained 2). The smaller center-to-right-wing parties suffered as well, dropping from 15 seats in 1972 to 6 in 1977 (DS'70 lost 5, the Political Reformed party [SGP] lost none, the Reformed Political League [GPV] lost 2, the Farmers party lost 2, and the Catholic party [RKVN] lost its only seat). Thus the overall loss in the seats that splinter parties held was 17 (from 37 to 20), or 46 percent. Whether this again is a temporary phenomenon, or part of a restructuring of the system remains to be seen. There is still considerable fragmentation in the meantime—eleven parties have seats in a Parliament of 150!

Changes in the Dutch Public's Role in the Polity

Traditionally the Dutch people have had a true sense of nationalism which goes back to the struggle for independence and which began to develop first, probably, towards the end of the sixteenth century. This antedated the rise of the blocs or pillars. Calvinism was dominant in the early republic because of its role in the struggle against Spain. But the Catholics also were patriotic and committed to the nation-state, even though they had to fight for recognition in the new Dutch nation. As Lijphart points out, the Catholics never seriously considered leaving and becoming part of Belgium, partly because the doctrine of the Catholic church did not permit it and partly because of their affection for their country. Nevertheless, the tensions in the nineteenth century between Catholics, Calvinists, and seculars were severe, threatening often to break "the narrow national consensus."[17]

If the Dutch public was patriotic, it was also passive. The nature of the political culture led both elites and the masses in the traditional Dutch system to deemphasize political participation by the public. Historically people deferred to their leaders and emphasized respect as an important characteristic of good citizens. To Hans Daalder it was a "mixture of both deference and indifference" that distinguished Dutchmen.[18] An early study documented Dutch passivity compared to other countries. When asked what the ordinary citizen could do if confronted with an unjust or harmful law, 54 percent of the Dutchmen queried said they could "do nothing," while only 7 percent responded that they could use "direct personal contact" to solve the problem. Compare this to the United States, where 25 percent said they could do nothing but 57 percent would try to use direct personal contact, and Great Britain, where 38 percent responded "could do nothing" and 44 percent answered "direct personal contact."[19] Clearly the Dutch were, in the past at least, less inclined to be activists in politics. Daalder refers to the observation of Lord Napier, the British ambassador to The Hague, writing in 1860: "The Dutch are little disposed to take a busy and sustained part in politics. They rather enjoy their liberties than exercise their rights." Daalder felt in 1964 that that condition still prevailed.[20]

A major development at the mass level was the reorientation of the attitudes of Dutch citizens towards their political institutions. Voting turnout has always been high, 95 percent before the 1970s and 87.5 percent in 1977. But in the past this did not signify an assertiveness by the public of any role in the system, other than an electoral one (in the Schumpeter tradition). More recently one finds evidence of a desire for more influence. Thus in 1971, 85 percent of the national sample said they had little or no influence in politics, and 69 percent said they wanted much more influence.[21] A series of questions on political efficacy, trust, and cynicism used in the seventies (unfortunately not in the earlier studies) reveal from 40 percent to 50 percent of the public as critical of their roles in politics and lacking "political self-confidence"; specifically, 56 percent to 58 percent from 1971 to 1973 (46 percent in 1977) agreed with the statement that "people like me don't have any

influence on governmental policy."[22] A statement concerning the secrecy of the governmental policy process (a basic rule of Dutch elite
politics in the past) was objected to by 40 percent in 1972.[23] And a
certain cynicism has crept in to evaluations of ministers, state secretaries, and M.P.'s—39 percent of the public were inclined to think that
their (elite) contacts rather than their qualifications got them into
office.[24]

What is particularly surprising to Dutch scholars is the large proportion of Dutch citizens who support radical reforms in the system.
Close to 50 percent want a reduction in the number of parties to five or
less (as well as 52 percent, in 1977, wanting parties not tied to particular religions). Even more striking is the 60 percent who want to elect
the prime minister (the Minister-President), the burgermeester (now
appointed by the national government), and who wish to have popular
referenda. Table 7 indicates the strength of sentiment for these reforms since 1967. The trend is certainly in the direction of giving the
public more control. One particular reform approved by a majority of
the public recently concerns a basic principle of Dutch coalition politics—whether the parties should cooperate and work together (to
compromise differences) before or after the election. The principle and
practice in the past has been to wait until *after* the election. In recent
surveys the Dutch public by a large majority (64 percent in 1977)
prefers such cooperation *before* the election.[25]

So attitudes are changing. A case can be made that a new politicization of the public has occurred. Action groups have appeared on the
scene as a major new political force in Dutch politics. Nonparliamentary
actions and demonstrations are supported more than ever by the Dutch
public (33 percent favoring such political action in 1971).[26] The appearance of new parties on the Left and the Right have given people more

TABLE 7. Public Support for Reforms of the Dutch System

Proposal	Percentage in Favor			
	1967	1971	1972	1977
Elect the prime minister	50	51	60	57
Elect burgermeesters (mayors)	53	60	61	61
Permit popular referenda	61	49	61	57
Elect Parliament on a district basis		60	51	41
Reduce number of parties by				
having a vote threshold		64	66	59

Sources: De Nederlandse Kiezer '71 (Meppel: Boom, 1972); *De Nederlandse Kiezer '72*
(Alphen aan den Rijn: Samson Uitgeverij, 1973); G. Irwin, J. Verhoef, and C. Wiebrans, *De Nederlandse Kiezer '77* (Voorschoten: VAM, 1977).

opportunities to dissent from the established party system. Together with what some see as a more polarized politics ideologically this means that there has developed an attitudinal and organizational base for a new type of involvement by the public in the political process.

The argument that change has been taking place at the mass level in the Netherlands finds support also in national surveys concerning the values and goals of ordinary citizens. The research of Inglehart in western Europe indicates that the Dutch public has, from 1970 on, become more "post-materialist" in its value orientations than most other Europeans. When asked about their goals for their society in a 1970 study, the Dutch were more likely to emphasize "belongingness" and "self-actualization" goals (such as "more say in the job," a "less impersonal society") than in other countries and to emphasize economic objectives much less. For example, only 26 percent of the Dutch sample said "fighting rising prices" should be one of the top two goals of their society, compared to 44 percent of the German sample and 50 percent of the British sample. Only 14 percent of the Dutch said economic growth should be a top national priority, while 24 percent of the Germans and 29 percent of the British said it should; 16 percent of the Dutch chose the goal of a stable economy, compared to 39 percent of the Germans and 25 percent of the British. These data on value commitments (and value conflicts) suggest a significant reorientation, and the trends continued on in the seventies according to Inglehart's analysis, holding steady in studies of 1973 and 1976. But there were two aspects of this value change process in the society which are important to note: (1) the younger cohorts revealed the most striking decline in materialism, particularly those in the middle and upper middle classes; and (2) support for new parties on the Left seemed to be linked to new postbourgeois value orientations. All the data in support of these observations cannot be presented here. But it is important to note that in the 1972 survey the youngest cohort (19 to 28 years old) is classified as 27 percent "materialist" in its values while the oldest cohort (69 years old and over) is 51 percent materialist. Those in the student milieu were 50 percent postbourgeois, the highest of all European countries. As for the party relevance of this value change, Inglehart demonstrates that the largest proportion of the postmaterialists supported the socialists and the new Left parties (such as D'66). Indeed, in 1970 almost 70 percent of those with such postmaterialist values preferred the Left parties while 54 percent of those considered acquisitive in their value orientations were supporting parties of the Center and the Right. This, indeed, strongly suggests a major developing conflict in Dutch society.[27]

Other data from Dutch national surveys during this period also suggest that the public perceived important conflicts to exist in the society. Some of the more significant conflict perceptions are illustrated in table 8.

One must add to this conflict picture the evidence from the Dutch studies that large proportions of the Dutch public think there are serious problems and that the government should take more action on them (on housing needs, inflation, educational system reform, etc.). Further, there is evidence of the increasing willingness of Dutch citizens to defend the need for protest actions against the government, something rarely heard of in earlier days. Indeed, 31 percent of the public in 1971 and 38 percent in 1973 approved such actions, including support for protests by over 50 percent of the more progressive or leftist sector of the population.[28]

These findings from national and European surveys from 1970 on provide a cumulative body of evidence that (1) segmentation is breaking down to some extent, (2) new public attitudes toward politics have appeared, and (3) values are changing in the Dutch polity, particularly in the young, middle-class, educated, and left-wing sectors of the society. All of this seems to be leading to a new polarization in values and ideology and a politicization of the electorate. As the pillars of the segmented society begin to crumble and transreligious bloc behavior mounts, the public's role in the consociational system, a role which in the past emphasized passivity, is being redefined. It is this development that the political elites of the seventies and eighties must cope with.[29]

The Relevance of Changes in Dutch Society for Political Elites

We have noted certain changes in mass society and politics in the Netherlands in the period since 1967. Social segmentation is less rigid,

TABLE 8. Percentage of Public Perceiving "Great" or "Very Great" Conflicts in Society

Conflict	1971	1973	1977
Between young and old	63	57	45
Between employers and employees	57	67	53
Between persons with high and low incomes	73	82	70
Between the religious and the nonreligious	31	40	26

Sources: De Nederlandse Kiezer '73 (Alphen aan den Rijn: Samson Uitgeverij, 1973), pp. 126–27; G. Irwin, J. Verhoef, and C. Wiebrans, De Nederlandse Kiezer '77 (Voorschoten: VAM, 1977).

transreligious contact has been occurring more frequently, deconfessionalization and secularization of politics have characterized social and political relations, and the public has been asserting a much more positive political action role as well as revealing an interest in radical politics and system reform. What consequences may these trends have for the politics of accommodation, and particularly for the orientations and behavior of political elites?

The empirical evidence presented here as to trends at the mass level essentially underscore the theoretical expectations elaborated in chapter 1. Scholars such as Lijphart have contended that what the Dutch needed, and what they got, to make their political system function effectively, despite extreme social and political pluralism was "prudent leadership."[30] As the theory goes, the system did survive because of the wisdom, unity of purpose, and cooperative behavior of the political elites at the top of the system. But with the changes in the society that we see as having taken place in the past decade and more, the type of prudent leadership needed by the Dutch now may be of a somewhat different nature. At least one would be inclined to look for new elites or elites with somewhat new orientations to politics. One might well expect, for example, that the newer, younger types of leaders in Parliament, and possibly also in the bureaucracy, would manifest in their attitudes some of the views of the action elements in the Dutch public. Indeed, if the middle-aged elites are also attentive to the new developments at the mass level, one might well see them also revealing more populist orientations. Their views about the roles of citizen participation in the political process would be especially interesting. Then too, as Daalder suggests, one would expect more ideologically divisive, if not polarized, elites with bureaucrats also less neutral and more partisan than previously was apparently the case. Further, if the rigid bloc structure of the society is breaking down, one might well expect to find trans-bloc elite contact and support patterns. And above all, as the basic rules of the game in the system are being questioned, we should probably find political elites (such as M.P.'s and top civil servants) redefining their own roles, and also the roles of others, in the system. This may very well mean less willingness to subscribe to summit diplomacy, more insistence on involvement in the policy process, less secrecy in decision making, a greater role for parties and partisanship, and more emphasis on the mobilization of public support in order to strengthen elite roles in the system. These are all very hypothetical, but they are theoretical expectations to which our data can speak. Finally, these new trends at the mass level suggest there may be a transformation in the special patterns of elite integration in the system. On the one hand, there could develop greater conflict between and among elites in their views of politics, in ideologies, and in values. On the other hand, a new approach to and conception of elite integrative perspectives and behavior may be emerging—a new elite accommodationism. In the last analysis this is the real test for the Dutch system as it passes through this transitional period: can the political elites maintain their basic unity of purpose and capacity for working together despite their conflicts? We hope that our data on elite attitudes and perspectives can throw some light as to how in the seventies Dutch elites appear to be adapting to the new realities of their system.

NOTES

1. Derived from data presented by Arend Lijphart, *The Politics of Accommodation: Pluralism and Democracy in the Netherlands* (Berkeley: University of California Press, 1968, 1975), p. 31. "Regular" refers to attendance at church at least once a week; "residuals" support religious parties. These are approximations only. The data are from a table using both religious preference and party preference, but smaller-party preferences were not specified, and had to be estimated. Those responding "don't know" to party preference were excluded here. The connections made here with the party vote in 1967 assume for these purposes that we can combine the Communists and PSP with the Labor party (the socialists), and the Farmers party with the liberals. This is not, of course, strictly defensible, but it does help to validate partially the bloc divisions.
2. See ibid., pp. 16–23, for the description of and rationale for these divisions into blocs.
3. Ibid., pp. 37, 49.
4. Ibid., p. 55.
5. Ibid., p. 47.
6. Ibid., p. 205.
7. G. Irwin, J. Verhoef, and C. Wiebrens, *De Nederlandse Kiezer '77* (Voorschoten: VAM, 1977), p. 151.
8. Ibid., p. 154.
9. Lijphart, *Politics of Accommodation*, p. 197.
10. Hans Daalder, "De Kleine Politieke Partijen," *Acta Politica* 1 (1965–66): 177–78.
11. Steven B. Wolinetz, "The New Left and the Transformation of the Dutch Socialist Party" (Paper delivered at the 1975 Annual Meeting of the American Political Science Association, San Francisco, September 1975), p. 4; Irwin, Verhoef, and Wiebrens, *De Nederlandse Kiezer '77*, p. 34; Arend Lijphart, data supplied to Wolinetz.

12. A good discussion of the transition to the new Labor party is found in Wolinetz, "The New Left and the Dutch Socialist Party."

13. Jacques Thomassen, "Party Identification as a Cross-Cultural Concept: Its Meaning in the Netherlands," *Acta Politica* 10 (January 1975): 40, 53–55.

14. See Lijphart, *Politics of Accommodation*, pp. 26–36. The "don't know" category was 18 percent in the 1964 study.

15. Steven B. Wolinetz, "Electoral Change and Attempts to Build Catch-All Parties in The Netherlands" (Paper delivered at Canadian Political Science Association, Montreal, August 1973), table 5.

16. Irwin, Verhoef, and Wiebrens, *De Nederlandse Kiezer '77*, p. 151.

17. See Lijphart, *Politics of Accommodation*, pp. 80–82.

18. Hans Daalder, "The Netherlands: Opposition in a Segmented Society," in *Political Oppositions in Western Democracies*, ed. Robert A. Dahl (New Haven: Yale University Press, 1966), p. 197.

19. Lijphart, *Politics of Accommodation*, p. 151.

20. Hans Daalder, *Politisering en lijdelijkheid in de Nederlandse politiek* (Assen: van Gorcum, 1974), p. 9.

21. *De Nederlandse Kiezer '71* (Meppel: Boom, 1972), p. 72.

22. *De Nederlandse Kiezer '72* (Alphen aan den Rijn: Samson Uitgeverij, 1973), p. 89; *De Nederlandse Kiezer '77*, p. 33.

23. *De Nederlandse Kiezer '72*, p. 70.

24. *De Nederlandse Kiezer '77*, p. 43.

25. *De Nederlandse Kiezer '77*, p. 83.

26. *De Nederlandse Kiezer '71*, p. 96.

27. Ronald Inglehart, *The Silent Revolution: Changing Values and Political Styles Among Western Publics* (Princeton, N.J.: Princeton University Press, 1977), particularly pp. 36–37, 49, and 104–5. See also Inglehart, "The Silent Revolution in Europe: Intergenerational Change in Post-Industrial Societies," *The American Political Science Review* 65, no. 4 (1971): 1003, 1007, and 1011, which includes a breakdown by age and class.

28. See *De Nederlandse Kiezer '71*, p. 95, and *De Nederlandse Kiezer '73* (Alphen aan den Rijn: Samson Uitgeverij, 1973), p. 97, for evidence on these points.

29. For an excellent analysis of these trends at the local level of the Dutch society, see Thomas R. Rochon, "Local Elites and the Structure of Political Conflict: Parties, Unions and Interest Groups in the Netherlands" (Ph.D. diss., University of Michigan, 1980).

30. Lijphart, *Politics of Accommodation*, p. 188.

CHAPTER 3

Paths to the Top:
Social Origins and Career Routes

Who gets to the top, to the "political elite," and how they get there, is a fascinating inquiry in any system. In ideal theoretical terms those who get there reflect the social forces and satisfy the credentials of the selectors, whoever these may be. The question of the social representativeness of the elites in relation to the masses, while a matter of considerable intellectual curiosity, is therefore not the crucial issue. Rather, the most salient concern is whether and how the preelite social backgrounds and career development patterns of leaders determine their access to elite status and their behavior once they have arrived in their elite positions. This basic query breaks down into several specific questions. Are political elites linked so intimately to certain social (class) or status groups which influenced their preadult development that a social bias persists in their subsequent leadership performance? Does family socialization to politics have a lasting influence on their interest in political and governmental activity and their attitudes and styles once in political positions? Are social backgrounds so homogeneous that a consensual elite emerges; or are backgrounds diverse, and do they thus lead to conflict in elite views about the political system? In essence, the major query is whether an individual's past—the type of family, the social environment, the educational and occupational history—is important for understanding elite attitudes and behavior. For some it may be dominant and controlling as these leaders fulfill their roles. For others the past may be of marginal relevance as they seek to be responsive to contemporary forces, current pressures, new interests, new demands, and new opportunities. This is the key question we seek to probe here as we look at the background data and career paths for Dutch political and administrative elites.

The Representativeness of Elites

Studies of political leadership regularly document the fact that administrative and political elites disproportionately come from the upper levels of the social status hierarchy. Those with political authority, status, and power have high social status also—the "agglutination" concept of Harold Lasswell.[1] These studies also find that as one moves up the ladder of political power one finds increasingly that the elites are socially unrepresentative of the masses—"the law of increasing disproportion."[2] We find both of these phenomena in the Netherlands, but M.P.'s and bureaucrats differ in certain respects. Table 9 indicates the extent to which that is true. M.P.'s seem to have more diverse social backgrounds—55 percent had completed a university education (compared to 84 percent of senior bureaucrats), and 9 percent had had only a primary school education. For M.P.'s there is also a greater spread among the age groups, 14 percent in fact coming from the youngest age cohort, those under 35. Further, their geographical origins are slightly more diverse, and there are at least *some* women (usually 10 percent) in the Dutch Parliament. The higher civil servant group, however, is male, much older (none under 34), and better educated (only 5 percent did not attend a university). Religiously the two groups look very similar, with about two-fifths unaffiliated and one-fifth Catholic. Weekly church attendance, considered by some to be the critical evidence for the persistence of the religious pillar, is rather low—only a fifth of higher civil servants, and one-third of M.P.'s.

In comparison to the general population, these elites are extremely unrepresentative in educational status, since only 1 percent of all citizens completed school through the university level. They are also less religious (two-fifths with "no religion" compared to one-fifth of the population), less female, less rural, and, for the civil servant, much older than the adult population. These data suggest above all that while religion is no barrier to entrance into the elite, a key elite credential is a university education. This is strikingly so for the administration.

These findings appear to be also true for the same elites in the United States and other European countries. Putnam's 1970–71 comparative study of Britain, Germany, Italy, and the United States revealed that a large majority of high civil servants had university degrees, ranging from 83 percent in Britain to 100 percent in Italy; for legislators, the figures ranged from 59 percent in Germany to 88 per-

TABLE 9.   Social Status of Dutch Elites (sample percentages)

	M.P.'s	Higher Civil Servants	General Population
Education			
Completed university	55	84	1
Attended university	25	9	2
Middle level	11	5	54
Elementary-primary level	9	0	43
Religion			
Catholic	23	21	40
Protestant			
Hervormd	21	21	23
Gereformeerde	7	6	7
Other Protestants	2	10	—[a]
Other religion	7	8	8
No religion	40	36	23
Church attendance			
Weekly	35	23	31
At least once a month	14	21	10
Occasionally	9	15	13
Never	2	4	13
No religion	40	36	30
Age			
under 25 years	0	0	43
25–34	14	0	15
35–44	34	11	12
45–54	39	38	11
55–64	14	49	9
65+	0	3	10
Place of birth			
Amsterdam, Rotterdam, The Hague	16	24	27
Other large cities (100,000 and over)	17	12	
Medium-sized cities (50,000–100,000)	17	13	25
Small urban places and commuter suburbs	22	26	
Small towns and villages	29	22	42
Sex			
Male	86	100	50
Female	14	0	50

Sources: De Nederlandse Kiezer '72 and *De Nederlandse Kiezer '73* (Alphen aan den Rijn: Samson Uitgeverij, 1973); Central Bureau of Statistics, *Statistisch zakboek* (The Hague: Staatsuitgeverij, 1974).

a. No data available.

cent in the United States. In contrast, only 2 percent (Britain) to 11 percent (United States) of the adult population of those countries had completed a university education.[3] Unquestionably, in Western democracies educational status is closely linked to political elite status.

One other type of underrepresentation should be mentioned—that of Catholics in *both* Dutch elite groups. In the bureaucracy, particularly, only 21 percent of this sample of higher civil servants were found to be Catholic.[4] Catholic underrepresentation in the elites might be partially explained by the fact that most Catholics in the Netherlands live in the two southern provinces, while the majority of higher civil servants come from provinces in the north and nearer to The Hague. Actually, our data reveal that 64 percent come from Utrecht, North Holland, or South Holland, while only 17 percent come from the two southern Catholic provinces plus Zeeland. Members of Parliament are less concentrated by province—only 43 percent come from the provinces of Utrecht, North Holland, and South Holland.

In summary, then, this is a high status set of Dutch males, well educated, diverse in age, religion, and geographical origin. The politicians, however, are more diverse in these respects than the bureaucrats.

The political representativeness of the higher bureaucracy is rather impressive. We asked the civil servants which party they preferred, as well as which party they voted for in the 1972 national election. Nine parties were mentioned in their preferences and votes, with the distribution as shown in table 10. The representation is somewhat unbalanced in that the Left and the Protestants are underrepresented. The Labor party and the Anti-Revolutionaries are particularly disadvantaged. Right-wing partisanship is decidedly overrepresented. The Catholic party is only slightly underrepresented. The VVD and DS'70 are the primary beneficiaries of this unbalanced system. Nevertheless, there is great partisan diversity in the civil service, including supporters of the newer small parties. Whether there is partisan intensity of feeling is a matter to be discussed later.

Family Social Class Origins of Elites

Despite the political representativeness of Dutch elites, the image of relative social exclusiveness must be kept in mind. It is reinforced if we look at the family backgrounds of these leaders. Their social class origins are clearly indicated by their father's occupations (table 11). One notices, first, that these leaders are offspring of upper-middle- and upper-class fathers—from 50 to 60 percent come from families in the upper-prestige occupational levels.[5] One can see that those with fathers in professional, managerial, and business occupations clearly predominate, while only 5 to 11 percent have fathers who were manual laborers—a striking difference from the rest of the population.

Second, one notices again that M.P.'s are somewhat different from civil servants in social class origins. Thus, twice as many came from working-class families, fewer from the professions and higher governmental levels, and 41 percent from the lower three ranks in the occupational prestige scale for fathers. In one sense, this means that children of lower-class families had three times as good a chance to be elected to Parliament as to enter the civil service and arrive at the top. What this also means is that the occupational mobility of M.P.'s has been much greater than that for the higher civil servants, for 85 percent of the latter come originally from fairly high prestige families.

We can trace the occupational mobility of M.P.'s with three types of data: father's occupation, respondent's first occupation, and respondent's occupation just before entering Parliament. The data are presented in table 12. The striking change in occupational career paths is obvious. They carried on their father's interest in government (eventually, of course, all becoming M.P.'s), but they moved away from busi-

TABLE 10. Party Affiliations of Bureaucrats and the Public (in percentages)

Party	Voters' Preference, 1972	Civil Servants' Party Affiliation[a] (N = 76)
KVP	17.7	15.8
ARP	8.8	1.3
CHU	4.8	5.3
Left-wing		
PSP	1.5	1.3
PPR	4.8	5.3
PvdA	27.3	17.1
D'66	4.2	2.6
Right-wing		
DS'70	4.1	10.5
VVD	14.5	28.9
No preference		11.8
Total		99.9

a. Determined by stated preference or, if no preference given, by 1972 vote.

ness positions and from working-class status. They moved into educational and professional careers (27 percent in education and 32 percent in the professions) before going into Parliament. In social class mobility terms, they revealed a phenomenal intergenerational mobility. Only 27 percent of their fathers were in the highest prestige level, but by the time the M.P.'s in our sample took their first positions, 41 percent were at the highest level, and this increased to 69 percent just before they entered Parliament.[6]

It is interesting to compare the social origins of Dutch elites with those of other Western systems. The high class status of Dutch bureaucrats is similar to their counterparts in other countries (table 13). The backgrounds of M.P.'s differ by country, however. Dutch bureaucrats are as likely to come from high-status families as in other Western

TABLE 11. Social Class Origins of Elites by Father's Occupation (in percentages)

	Higher Civil Servants	M.P.'s
Father's occupation		
High governmental positions		
(Minister, M.P., etc.)	11	7
National civil servants	21	11
Local civil servants	1	2
Teachers (all levels)	11	5
Professions (other than teaching)	4	7
Total	48	32
Trade, industry, shipping,		
banking, insurance	16	27
Middle-class shopkeepers	15	14
Farming and fishing	8	11
Total	39	52
Manual laborers	5	11
Special and other (military, police, religious		
organizations, social agencies, etc.)	8	4
Prestige level of father's occupation		
I (highest)	37	27
II	23	18
III	26	14
IV	11	32
V	4	9
VI (lowest)	0	0

societies. But Dutch M.P.'s had fathers who were less likely to have the highest prestige positions, in comparison to M.P.'s in other systems. Thus, 58 percent of British M.P.'s came from high occupational status families, while only 27 percent of Dutch M.P.'s did. Further, 22 percent of British M.P.'s (18 percent of American, 36 percent of Italian, and 30 percent of West German M.P.'s) were children of fathers with manual occupations, while 11 percent of the Dutch M.P.'s came from such backgrounds. The Dutch M.P.'s, therefore, seem to be less likely to come from extremely high prestige families, but also from less extremely lower-class families.

The fathers of Dutch elites were also well educated. For the high civil servants, 32 percent had fathers who attended a university, and this was true also for 24 percent of the M.P.'s. At the other extreme, one-third of the M.P.'s had fathers with only a primary school experience, which was the case for 17 percent of the bureaucrats. Thus, educational level of family as indicated by father's education was an important factor for these elites. The elites themselves in the majority of cases were relatively well educated; 55 percent of M.P.'s and 84 percent of top civil servants completed university educations. If one keeps in mind that this was the case for probably only 1 to 2 percent of the adult population, one sees both the importance of educational training as a credential for elite status, and the considerable overrepresentation of university graduates among the elites.

TABLE 12. Intergenerational Occupational Mobility of M.P.'s (in percentages)

	Occupation of Father	Respondent's First Occupation	Respondent's Occupation before Entering Parliament
Type of occupation			
Government	20	17	25
Educators and professions	12	45	59
Trade, industry	52	24	7
Manual laborers	11	7	0
Other	4	7	9
Occupational prestige level			
I (highest)	27 } 45	41 } 68	69 } 90
II	18	27	21
III	14	12	5
IV	32	12	5
V	9	7	0
VI (lowest)	0	0	0

The Family Political Environment

The first steps towards political elite status for many individuals occur during youth as a result of exposure to politics and government in the family. This is clearly the case for Dutch elites. As previously noted, the fathers of one-third of the higher civil servants held some type of governmental or civil service position. This was true of 20 percent of the M.P.'s in our sample. Further, other relatives of these elites held governmental positions, so that the total exposure of these leaders in their youth in family circles to socialization influences about governmental work as a career was true for over 50 percent; table 14 summarizes these data. There was a fairly even balance between exposure in the family to the civil service and to legislative-political influences.

Intergenerationally, there is considerable interchange in career decisions. Thus, it is interesting that the sons (and daughters) of civil servants go into legislative careers (11 percent of our M.P.'s fit this category), while the sons of legislative politicians go into the civil service (11 percent of our high civil servants had such backgrounds). These percentages increase to almost 20 percent when other relatives are included. This suggests considerable diversity in the influences that elites bring to their positions, influences not exclusively from the national level.

Many of these leaders came from homes where parents were deeply involved with partisan politics. Thus, 61 percent of the M.P.'s had fathers who were members of political parties, and 43 percent had mothers with such membership. One-third of the M.P.'s had fathers who were active in an official position in a party, true of 22 percent of their mothers.[7] Politics was discussed in their homes "much" or "very much" for 56 percent of the M.P.'s in our study and 44 percent of the

TABLE 13. Comparative Data on Family Occupational
Backgrounds (in percentages whose
fathers had high managerial or
professional occupations)

Country	Legislative Elites	Administrative Elites
Britain	58	35
Italy	28	42
West Germany	35	42
United States	44	47
Netherlands	27	37

Source: Putnam (1976), pp. 23–25 (for all but Dutch data).

higher civil servants. It is interesting to note that less political discussion did occur in the homes of the higher civil servants. Indeed, 43 percent of our bureaucrat respondents (compared with only 24 percent of the M.P.'s) reported no discussion of politics at all in the home while they were growing up.

One can conclude from these findings that 50 to 60 percent of these elites were exposed to some extent, and for some to a great extent, to adults who worked in government, were active in politics, and discussed government and politics in the home. The probable relevance of this for the selection of a career, if not for their socialization to political attitudes, is high.

Dutch elites were brought up in a multiplicity of partisan families. Their fathers and mothers supported parties that covered much of the spectrum of their pluralized system (see table 15). The nineteenth-century "liberal partisan tradition" was particularly prominent for the civil servants, 21 percent of whom had fathers supporting that tradition. But the Catholic and Protestant parties were as well represented among their families, 20 percent and 27 percent respectively having fathers adhering to such parties. It is in the limited representation of the socialist tradition that civil servants' families revealed a decided bias. M.P.'s were much more likely to come from the socialist family tradition (SDAP, PvdA)—32 percent in contrast to only 13 percent of the civil servants. However, there was no evidence of extensive "colonization" of the civil service by particular partisan families. Yet the differences in partisan environments in which these elites were reared, on both the paternal and maternal sides, is evident—fewer socialists, more Protestants, and more conservative partisan families among the civil servants.

To what extent were these leaders still committed to the same partisan and religious preferences of their fathers and mothers? Was

TABLE 14. Family Governmental Careers of Elites (in percentages)

Types of Positions Held by Relatives	Higher Civil Servants	M.P.'s
Administrative or legislative position or both	55	64
Civil service	34	32
National	27	18
Local, provincial	7	14
Legislative	36	50
Parliament	17	21
Municipal, provincial	19	30

Note: The data on types of positions cumulate to more than the overall percentage (given at the top) because of duplication in positions held.

there continuity at this elite level in the political pillars of the system? In the transmission of partisan preference from father to elite offspring, there is much discontinuity, as table 16 reveals. For all senior bureaucrats father to son transmission is 52 percent; for M.P.'s, 58 percent. Particularly noticeable is the decline in confessional party support in the bureaucracy, only 36 percent retaining a preference for father's confessional politics. Among M.P.'s the discontinuity was somewhat less sharp—55 percent supporting the father's confessional party. Those with socialist parentage retained much more support among both M.P.'s and senior civil servants. There is then both intergenerational continuity in party preferences, and "depillarization" at the elite level.[8]

The transmission of religious preference between family and offspring was considerable (table 17). For the bureaucrats, 78 percent continued in the religion of their youth, as did 65 percent of the M.P.'s. Those from Catholic backgrounds were particularly likely to

TABLE 15. Family Partisan Environment of Elites (in percentages)

	Higher Civil Servants		M.P.'s	
	Father's Party	Mother's Party	Father's Party	Mother's Party
Socialist				
PvdA/-SDAP	13	10	32	33
Free Democrats (VD)	10	17	5	2
Catholic (KVP, RKS, KNP)	20	21	25	26
Protestant				
ARP	10	8	11	12
CHU	17	18	5	2
Liberal (VVD, LSP, VB)	21	20	14	19
Other or don't know	10	5	9	6

TABLE 16. Father–Son Party Preference Transmissions (in percentages)

Leader's 1973 Party Preference	Father's Party Preference					
	Higher Civil Servants			M.P.'s		
	Left (N = 16)	Confessional (N = 33)	Right (N = 15)	Left (N = 16)	Confessional (N = 18)	Right (N = 6)
Left	56	21	13	63	39	50
Confessional	6	36	7	6	55	0
Right	26	27	80	31	6	50
No preference	12	16	0			

retain their family's religious tradition (over 80 percent), but those with Protestant backgrounds, particularly the M.P.'s, left the family religion in larger proportions. It is interesting, however, that over 20 percent of these leaders from non-Protestant backgrounds currently profess a Protestant denominational association. One must remember, however, that only 25 to 35 percent attend church weekly, suggesting that religious practice is very irregular among elites, as it is also at the public level.

In sum, these elites usually came from highly politicized families. In their own adult lives, however, while pursuing political careers or being recruited into public service, many of them broke with the partisan and religious traditions of their families.

Career Paths and Recruitment: Civil Servants

Keeping in mind the high social status and special political environment of the families of Dutch political elites and the possible impact of this on them while they were growing up, one must still ask what were the conditions and reasons that led them to government careers. Only a small minority of those from such families did arrive in the civil service. And, on the other hand, one must ask what led those few into the civil service who were not from high-status families.

It is first important to note that 93 percent of the higher civil servants had some higher education beyond secondary schools, and, above all, that 84 percent of them completed their university education. The others went to some technical higher school of a semiuniversity nature (9 percent), while only a few went to the gymnasium (an advanced high school) or similar school and then stopped (6 percent). Second, curriculum concentrations were varied. While law is the most prominent curriculum in their educational training (39 percent), eco-

TABLE 17. Comparison of Religious Conviction in 1973 with Religious Upbringing (in percentages)

| Leader's 1973 Religious Conviction | Religious Upbringing | | | | | |
| | Higher Civil Servants | | | M.P.'s | | |
	Catholic (N = 15)	Protestant (N = 37)	None (N = 21)	Catholic (N = 12)	Protestant (N = 12)	None (N = 19)
Catholic	93	3	0	83	0	0
Protestant	0	73	24	8	58	42
None	7	24	76	8	42	58

nomics is next in frequency (23 percent) followed by the more technocratic skills such as natural science (16 percent) and agriculture (4 percent). Social sciences generally, or "letters" and humanities, contrary to the British tradition, are not apparently frequent areas of university expertise that prepared these men for entry into the civil service.

As for the location of university study, Dutch higher civil servants came from a variety of institutions. There is no tendency for a concentration as at Oxford and Cambridge in England. Rather, we found the following distributions: Leiden (16 percent), Amsterdam (16 percent), Utrecht (22 percent), Rotterdam (20 percent), Delft (14 percent), Nijmegen (2 percent), Free University of Amsterdam (2 percent), other (8 percent). This dispersion in university education was found generally true for M.P.'s also.

Although the majority of higher civil servants entered government work shortly after completing their university education, a sizable minority waited and thus held some prior nongovernmental position. For those civil servants for whom we have complete data (fifty-one cases), we find that 14 percent entered the civil service between the ages of seventeen and twenty-three, 41 percent were between twenty-four and twenty-nine years old, and 45 percent were thirty years old or older. In the first two age groups, about 60 percent never took any other position than a government one, while virtually all of those in the latter category, those who entered after age thirty, had worked in other occupations or professions. In our study there were five cases who entered the civil service after age forty-five, but were at the top of the system when we interviewed them, having been appointed at the top or moving rapidly to the top after entrance. Delayed or "lateral" entrance, thus, was possible.

There seem to be three different career routes to the top of the civil service: (1) those from high status families who went to the university, and then directly into the civil service; (2) those who held some nongovernmental jobs, but yet entered the civil service early, before age thirty; and (3) those who entered relatively late, after holding one or more positions outside of government.[9] One-third of these senior bureaucrats were latecomers to the bureaucracy, had considerable experience prior to the civil service, and revealed fast upward mobility. This suggests three things about the Dutch bureaucracy: (1) the age level is comparatively high; (2) it is a diverse system, with those at the top of the bureaucracy reflecting different ages of entry, different occupational perspectives, different generational periods of recruitment, different socialization patterns; (3) it is a permeable, flexible system, since individuals can enter it at later ages and not necessarily at the bottom of the hierarchy, subsequently moving fairly quickly to the top. While the emphasis is on the selection of persons from universities at a young age, the higher Dutch civil service does not conform to this pattern completely. A sizable proportion (up to 30 percent) have had considerable exposure in business or the professions before going into the civil service.

These findings and interpretations document the observations of other writers. Van Braam has described carefully the formal and informal selection procedures of the Dutch civil service.[10] He noted the absence of any rigid selection approaches or channels. Dutch civil servants are presumably recruited generally from those who complete university work, this being particularly true for those who secure appointments to policy positions. Most departments go through the selection process themselves—from advertising for positions, to interviewing applicants, to making the final decision. But all applications are gathered centrally by the National Psychological Bureau. This agency may also advertise for certain positions and does the psychological testing of candidates who have survived a first selection round performed by the department. So, two agencies are involved in the selection procedure. Van Braam also notes four criteria that are important in the selection: university education, "social involvement and interest," experience (for those appointed at a higher level in the department), and certain traits or abilities (such as intelligence, sociability, stability in personality, or expressiveness). The tendency is, thus, to recruit young persons with certain characteristics, but there is the clear possibility of being recruited into the system at the upper levels of the hierarchy.

We pressed senior civil servants for explanations of why and how they entered the civil service. They gave us a variety of reasons, often related to the pragmatic necessity of finding a job (30 percent) and being offered a position in one's own field of interest and training (25 percent).

Quite a few indicated that it was more or less accidental (20 percent) that they began in the civil service. Few mentioned family pressures or tradition (6 percent). If we evaluate their total set of responses it appears that 11 percent never considered another career or actively sought a civil service career; 46 percent considered other careers but chose the civil service; 39 percent joined the civil service due to circumstances at the time, but have been satisfied and have stayed on; and 2 percent would have preferred another career. For many of these bureaucrats, then, the civil service was not a career they set their eyes on as the *only* vocation for them, even though they had been conditioned early to consider the civil service.

Once these men got into the civil service, they moved in different paths to the top. A very few entered after the age of forty-five and moved very quickly to the top. Others began early with provincial or local government administration (13 percent) before going to The Hague. There was also considerable lateral mobility, or recruitment from inside the service but from other departments. We found that 30 percent came to their present positions after an earlier experience in other departments, which suggests a certain "openness," within the civil service at least, and diversity of experience.[11]

Among the types of attractions and satisfactions that are important to senior bureaucrats, "influence on policymaking" and "helping people" in a general sense are most frequently mentioned. (See table 18 for some comparisons of Dutch senior civil servants with those in Germany and Britain). These were men who were motivated by the variety of intellectual challenges (about 20 percent), opportunities for

TABLE 18.   Job Satisfactions of Senior Bureaucrats: Netherlands, Britain, Germany (in percentages)

	Netherlands (N = 76)	Britain (N = 123)	Germany (N = 133)
Material and social			
Pay and security	3	12	5
Conviviality with colleagues	23	46	12
Intellectual			
Intellectual challenges	23	30	29
Programmatic innovation	12	20	30
Practical problem-solving	20	20	16
Decision making			
Being at the center of things	25	23	10
Influence on decisions	47	23	33
Ideological or substantive policy concerns			
Struggle for cause or group	7	2	4
Interest in specific policy area	16	13	39
Working with or helping others			
Helping other people (in general)	53	13	7
Helping constituents or clients	3	2	3
Contact with public	4	7	6

Source: German and British data are based on identical questions with equivalent samples from Robert Putnam, "Bureaucrats and Politicians, Contending Elites in the Policy Process," *Tulane Studies in Political Science* 15 (1975), p. 188.

Note: Multiple responses were allowed; hence columns add to more than 100 percent. Each proportion is the percentage of respondents who mentioned a particular satisfaction.

service in a general sense (53 percent), and the desire for an involvement with and influence on governmental decision making (47 percent). The Dutch civil servant is much more preoccupied with this "influence" type of satisfaction than in Germany or Britain, as well as a great deal more concerned with service to the public. One is tempted to conclude that although the civil service attracted them initially because it was a job fitted to their qualifications, eventually it has become a job that is intellectually challenging.

What emerges from our data are two basic pathways to the top of the bureaucracy, with a variety of permutations or alternative paths (see fig. 6). Obviously one pathway would place heavy emphasis on high social status, exposure to government and politics in the family with relatives in the public service, and then, after completion of university education, an early entrance to the civil service, and gradual

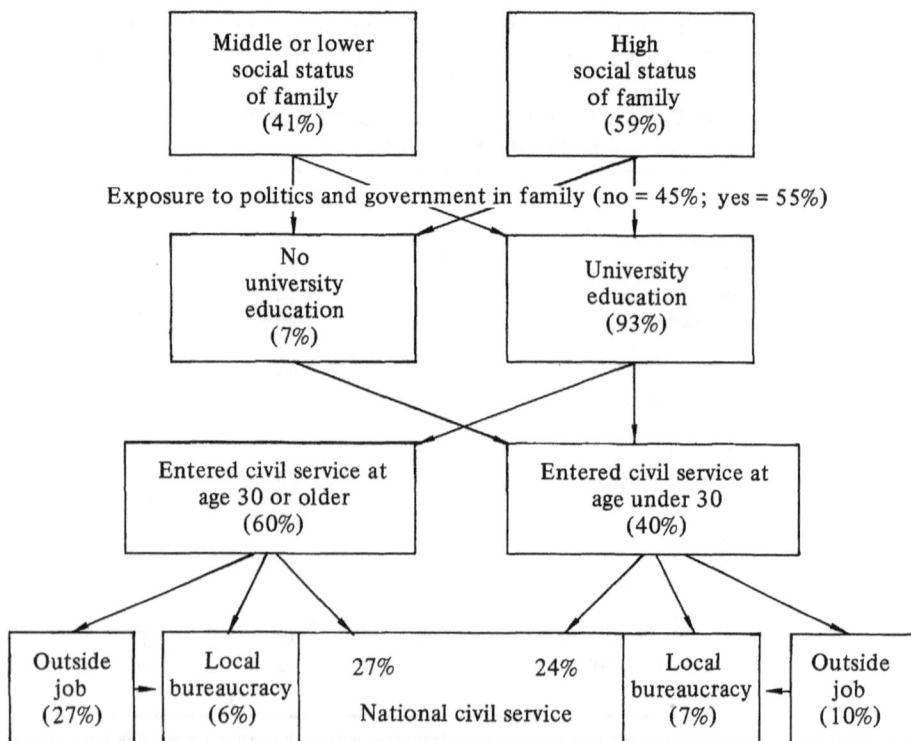

Middle or lower social status of family (41%)	High social status of family (59%)

Exposure to politics and government in family (no = 45%; yes = 55%)

No university education (7%)	University education (93%)

Entered civil service at age 30 or older (60%)	Entered civil service at age under 30 (40%)

Outside job (27%)	Local bureaucracy (6%)	27% National civil service	24%	Local bureaucracy (7%)	Outside job (10%)

Fig. 6. Career paths of higher civil servants. Each percentage is a proportion of the total number of civil servants.

upward mobility to senior status. As many as 30 to 40 percent of our sample seem to fit this path. At the other extreme is another pathway for a few who came from lower social status families, with an incomplete university education or none at all, and who entered the civil service early in life. Possibly 5 percent of our sample fit this model. A third group consists of those who came from a somewhat lower-status family but secured a university education, which led to entrance into the service. As many as 25 percent may fit this pathway. A fourth career channel suggested by our data is one in which a person from a high-status, politicized family does not enter the civil service after completion of the university curriculum but waits, possibly several years, taking a position in business or one of the professions before entering the civil service, probably at the middle management level, and then moving to the top. Up to 30 percent of our respondents seem to fit this conception. The Dutch bureaucracy is, then, one in which those at the top arrive using different routes and do not share, therefore, the same career experiences.

Robert Putnam has suggested four basic models using "social origins" and "education" in relation to "elite status."[12] The key questions posed in this approach are: Can lower-class children achieve elite positions if they secure a higher education? Can those from high social status families achieve elite status without university education? Among the well educated, are upper-class children more likely to enter the elite? If we ask these questions of the Dutch data, it appears that university education is the gateway for almost all those achieving senior elite status in the bureaucracy, and that social status is linked to getting a university education, but not exclusively so. The model, therefore, that seems most applicable is a variation of Putnam's Model II (see fig. 7).

Career Pathways: Members of Parliament

The career routes of M.P.'s are probably even more diverse than for senior bureaucrats. We will not here analyze all aspects of their recruitment, nor in as much detail, since M.P. career development in the Netherlands has been analyzed carefully elsewhere.[13] The major outlines of these careers can be summarized here.

The development of an interest in politics occurred early for the majority of M.P.'s. This is not surprising, since 64 percent had a relative in governmental service (50 percent had a relative in a legislative position), and 56 percent reported that they discussed politics "much" or "very much" in the home while they were growing up. This is similar to the finding in the 1972 parliamentary study that reported on

the extent of political activity in the homes of M.P.'s by their parents—
30 percent reported very much activity, and 22 percent reported moderate involvement.[14] When we probed for the age at which they became interested in politics, therefore, we found 24 percent asserting it
was in early childhood before the age of fourteen, 35 percent between
the ages of fourteen and sixteen, and 35 percent before the age of
twenty-five. Thus 94 percent had a political *interest* during their youth
or early twenties. And 62 percent also told us they were *active* in
politics by the age of twenty-five. This early political involvement was
even more true for those from the middle- and lower-class families
from which 55 percent of our M.P. sample came. Fifty-three percent of
M.P.'s whose fathers had low or middle occupational prestige levels
became active in politics before age twenty-five, while 47 percent of
the same group waited until later. Among M.P.'s whose fathers had a
high occupational prestige level only 35 percent were politically involved before they were twenty-five years old, while the majority (65
percent) became active when they were older. An additional finding
linked to this is that there was much less discussion of politics in these
lower- or middle-class homes—virtually none in 46 percent of these
homes, compared to no discussion of politics in only 21 percent of the
upper-class homes. This appears paradoxical but is understandable. An
M.P.'s family with high social status and with relatives in the government had much discussion of politics while the M.P. was growing up,
leading to an early political interest by children who, nevertheless,
delayed their involvement in political activity. An M.P.'s family with
lower social status and lower frequency of relatives in the government,
had less discussion of politics, but the children got involved in political
activity early, as the result of other stimuli, which led eventually to
Parliament. Recruitment media other than the family, therefore, or a

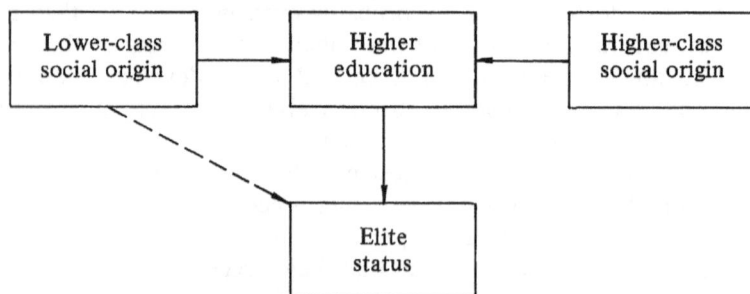

Fig. 7. Alternative paths to bureaucratic elite status

self-generated interest in politics, appear to have compensated for the lower salience of politics in middle- and lower-class homes of future M.P.'s.

The role of particular parties in recruiting elites from lower-class families is particularly striking. Ninety-three percent of the M.P.'s from center-right parties are from the middle and upper middle classes. Two-thirds of the KVP (Catholic) M.P.'s are from lower-middle-class and working-class backgrounds, and one-third are from the middle and upper middle classes. Fifty-five percent of M.P.s belonging to the PvdA and other left-wing parties come from lower-middle- and working-class backgrounds, while 45 percent of the same group are from the middle and upper middle classes. Thus it would seem that the socialist and Catholic parties play an important role in bringing to Parliament those from lower social strata, a finding which appears also in our data for Britain, Germany, and Italy.[15]

The educational paths M.P.'s took while developing this interest in party politics were diverse. Only 24 percent of their fathers had any kind of higher education (17 percent at a university), but 80 percent of the M.P.'s had some advanced education beyond secondary school (55 percent at a university).[16] Although their upward mobility educationally is clear (at the 50 to 60 percent level), they still came to elite status from different educational backgrounds. This is also clear if we look at the university curricula that they represent (table 19). Although the study of

**TABLE 19. University Curricula of M.P.'s, 1973 and 1968
(in percentages)**

	1973 Study (Sample) (N = 44)	1968 Study (Total Membership) (N = 141)
No university degree	43	41
University curriculum:		
Law[a]	23	29
Economics	14	14
Natural science	7	4
Social science	5	5
Agriculture	0	2
Letters and theology	5	4
Medicine and pharmacy	2	1
Military	2	0
Total	101	100

Source: For 1968 data, H. Daalder and S. Hubée-Boonzaijer, "Sociale herkomst en politieke recrutering—I," p. 301.

a. The 1968 study included here under the rubric "law" "Law, Indology, and the Science of the State" ("Rechten, Indologie, Staatswetenschappen").

law is the single most frequently followed curriculum, it is not the route that the greatest number of M.P.'s use. Less than 30 percent are trained in the law. Specialized disciplines like economics, natural science, medicine, and agriculture are the curricula for one-fifth of the M.P's. "Letters" or humanities is a curriculum rarely taken by future M.P.'s. A parliamentary career is open to those with many different types of training, which means M.P.'s have quite different intellectual perspectives—vocational education, law, economics, the exact sciences.

The occupational pathways of M.P.'s are also more varied than those of civil servants. As noted previously, the M.P.'s were strikingly upwardly mobile in occupational history before coming to Parliament—from 45 percent (father) to 68 percent (first occupation) to 90 percent (occupation just before entering Parliament) at the two highest prestige levels. The occupational milieus from which M.P.'s came before entering Parliament varied greatly. Five occupational areas provide the bulk of the M.P.'s: governmental service, including the civil service (about one-fourth); the teaching profession (perhaps one-fifth); other professions (about 12 percent, especially law and journalism); trade and industry (about one-tenth); and those who have held positions in party organizations, labor unions, and other social groups or institutions (from 25 percent to 30 percent). The actual proportions of those in each category have varied slightly in the last thirty years, according to the statistics compiled by the Central Bureau of Statistics, and the calculations of scholars of Parliament.[17] The most noticeable decline has been in the professions, with lawyers dropping from 16 percent in 1946 to less than 10 percent now. The decline in those with business backgrounds is also noticed in certain of the data. Governmental service as a preparation for a Parliamentary post has continued at a fairly high level, though fluctuating between 20 and 25 percent.

One notices certain tendencies in occupational movement in their preparliamentary period. They left positions in trade and industry, and tended to take positions in educational institutions, party organizations, and other social and economic service organizations, including trade unions. One senses a movement occupationally toward the public sector, and groups or institutions close to the public sector.

Aside from their formal occupations, those moving toward a Parliamentary position were often active with the party organizations. We found that 58 percent had held a party position at the local level, 56 percent at the regional level, and 51 percent at the national level. Most of those who were involved with the party began rather low in the hierarchy, as the following data concerning their first political job indicate: 30 percent began in the local party executive, 19 percent with the executive of the youth organization of the party, and 14 percent with the regional party executive. Thus, they often began at the bottom of the party structure and, later, one-half of them moved to the national party executive before entering Parliament. Their exposure to party and legislative politics from the local level to the top was considerable.

The circumstances and conditions that impelled these persons to a political career are difficult to identify with certainty. We asked them how they developed their political interest and why they became active. A great variety of explanations were given us. The role of the family in developing an interest is mentioned by 55 percent of our sample, but approximately the same proportion mentioned school or college influences. The only other specific recruitment medium mentioned was labor unions, mentioned by 10 percent. Yet over 36 percent also mentioned particular crises or issues that triggered an interest. For some the decision was made on their own initiative, for one reason because they felt politics was an exciting life. About one-third referred to this as an important factor.

Why are M.P.'s in politics? What are the satisfactions and attractions of parliamentary life? We discussed this with them and again found a great variety of answers. We can compare those answers here with the replies of M.P.'s of other countries to whom the same basic question was put (table 20). Dutch M.P.'s are very preoccupied with their decision-making role; 70 percent mention this. Next in importance are the causes they espouse (38 percent refer to this) and their

TABLE 20. Job Satisfactions of M.P.'s in Three European Countries (in percentages)

	Netherlands (N = 40)	Britain (N = 83)	Germany (N = 100)
Pay and security	3	0	0
Conviviality of colleagues	10	10	7
Intellectual challenges	35	7	7
Programmatic innovation	15	8	10
Practical problem solving	13	6	11
Influence on decision making	70	42	66
Being at the center of things	18	31	13
Interest in specific policy area	8	1	11
Struggle for a cause or group	38	23	23
Helping other people (general)	35	31	17
Helping constituents or clients	38	48	11
Contact with the public	40	16	16

Source: For Britain and Germany, Putnam, "Bureaucrats and Politicians," p. 188.
Note: Since multiple responses were allowed, the proportions add to more than 100 percent.

contacts with their constituents and the public (40 percent). The material, practical, and specific policy expertise aspects are deemphasized. They are men and women who are interested in power, and political causes, and in helping people; they are intrigued by the intellectual and decisional challenges and opportunities. In this respect they are very similar to M.P.'s in other countries, who may not explicity refer to the intellectual challenges as such, but are also most attracted by the decisional power of the job, not by its material values or its practical problem-solving opportunities.

In an attempt to summarize the data presented here on social and political backgrounds and recruitment of M.P.'s, we can visualize pathway models again, as we did with the higher civil servants (fig. 8). One model traces M.P.'s from families with high or low social status, through a university education, to rather high prestige occupations, and then Parliament. Those with no university education are more likely to hold lower status jobs, subsequently increasing in status be-

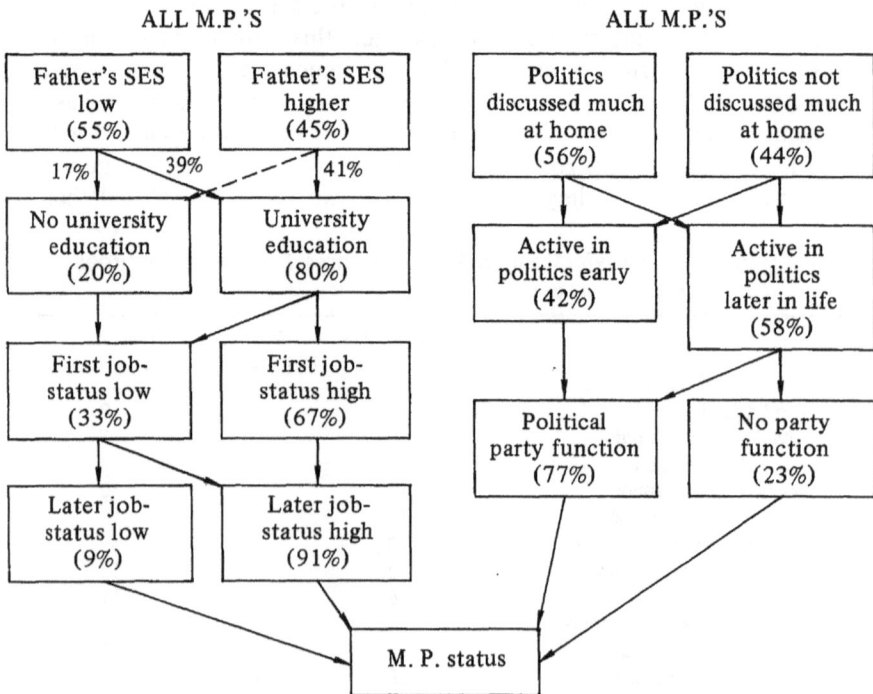

ALL M.P.'S   ALL M.P.'S

| Father's SES low (55%) | Father's SES higher (45%) | Politics discussed much at home (56%) | Politics not discussed much at home (44%) |

17%   39%   41%

| No university education (20%) | University education (80%) | Active in politics early (42%) | Active in politics later in life (58%) |

| First job-status low (33%) | First job-status high (67%) | Political party function (77%) | No party function (23%) |

| Later job-status low (9%) | Later job-status high (91%) |

M. P. status

Fig. 8.   Career pathways of M.P.'s. Each percentage is a proportion of the total number of M.P.'s in the study.

fore entering Parliament. An alternative way of tracing the M.P. career can be visualized from our data, using political socialization and party activism variables. Some M.P.'s come from families that were not highly politicized but, due to a variety of stimulation outside the family, became active in party politics, some late, some early. Other M.P.'s came from very politicized families and also were split into those who entered politics late or early in life. The activity of M.P.'s in parties and other groups (particularly labor unions), was considerable (for almost 80 percent), and often seemed linked to being recruited for a position in Parliament. Only a minority of M.P.'s held no party function.

Clearly there was great variety in the routes taken by M.P.'s and their recruitment backgrounds and experiences were thus very diverse. What seems constant for most of them is great social class and occupational mobility, relatively high educational attainment, deep involvement with political party affairs, and an admission later that opportunities to influence political decision making, as well as to work for causes and serve the people, were extremely attractive. By varied and sometimes circuitous routes, these M.P.'s moved to the power positions that many of them find challenging.

The Relevance of Backgrounds and Careers for Attitudes

Scholars have always asked a basic question in studying elite attitudes and behavior: do the backgrounds of these leaders help us to understand them, or are these backgrounds irrelevant once they achieve elite status? Often, scholars have dismissed these variables as poor predictors of elite attitudes. They are sometimes considered possibly relevant, or, as Putnam has argued, they may be "plausible, but ambiguous and unsubstantiated."[18] We will suggest here under what conditions these backgrounds and career variables may be helpful in understanding political elites.

The discontinuity in life-style and social orientation of political leaders in comparison to their families suggests that for many their social status origins and religious subculture in which they were raised may be irrelevant on many of these attitudinal dimensions. Their own skill-training backgrounds, their political career patterns, their party preferences, and their early occupational experiences (including, for civil servants, their bureaucratic career routes and type of ministry) may be much more important in understanding their beliefs about politics. Above all, one must keep in mind that many of these leaders came to power during the postwar period when Dutch society was undergoing significant transformations. They either were part of those movements or close observers of them, and their beliefs must certainly be reflectors of that transformation. Their age and the generation in which they came to government, therefore, may be important factors in understanding their beliefs.

We can illustrate the differential role of social background with several variables. First we can analyze the role of religion. One might expect that leaders who do have a religious affiliation might perceive certain aspects of politics somewhat differently from those with no religious commitments. Yet when we asked them, for example, how much influence in political decision making the churches should have in the Netherlands today, we find very little evidence that Catholics and Protestants consistently desire much more influence for their churches than other leaders do. Among senior bureaucrats, 14 percent of the Catholics interviewed responded that they felt churches should have much or very much influence on political decision making; 38 percent of the Protestants felt the same way, as did 21 percent of those who claimed no religious affiliation. Among M.P.'s 20 percent of the Catholics, 25 percent of the Protestants, and 6 percent of those with no religion gave the same response. The nonreligious M.P.'s are more negative, but in no elite sector is there much support for a large role for the church. Similarly, we asked these elites to discuss the differences between the political parties, and then we coded the types of differences they emphasized. We found no evidence that those with a religious affiliation were more cognizant of religious differences between the parties.

Another factor presumptively associated with elite beliefs is social class origin; yet previous studies have not been able clearly to establish a linkage. In our study we find some evidence that elite ideology (for example, whether they take a conservative or progressive view about state intervention in the society) may be traceable to class background. Of the M.P.'s we asked whose fathers were in government, 38 percent agreed with the statement that fears about state intervention in society are justified. Of those whose fathers were in trade, industry, or business, 28 percent agreed. Of those whose fathers were in education and the professions, 6 percent agreed. None of the M.P.'s whose fathers were in labor (including fishing and farming) agreed with the statement. These findings are, indeed, very suggestive—those whose fathers worked in government and business were influenced in a more conservative ideological direction than those brought up by professionals or in working-class homes.

Age also appears to be a factor discriminating among these leaders.

Many of the younger elites, those who have entered public service and achieved a senior position in the past decade or less, often have distinctive views about politics. For example, we asked them about the role of ordinary citizens and the voters in the policy process, particularly whether they desired them to have much influence on parliamentary decisions. We found that 90 percent of the youngest cohort of M.P.'s agreed that voters should have a good deal of influence, 64 percent of the middle-aged cohort agreed, and so did 67 percent of the oldest cohort. Among senior bureaucrats agreement of the youngest, middle, and oldest cohorts was 61 percent, 48 percent, and 50 percent, respectively. The positional differences between M.P.'s and civil servants are great; civil servants of all age groups are more skeptical of more democracy. But one notices the increase in support for citizen participation as one moves from the older to the youngest elites. On another measure, the concern among elites about conflict in the political system and the role of parties in exacerbating that conflict, we found a similar relationship for M.P.'s, but not for senior bureaucrats. Forty-two percent of the oldest cohort of M.P.'s felt strongly that parties increase conflict unnecessarily, and 10 percent of the middle-aged cohort agreed, but all of the M.P.'s from the youngest cohort disagreed. Among senior bureaucrats, 42 percent of the oldest cohort, 29 percent of the middle-aged cohort, and 40 percent of the youngest cohort agreed that parties unnecessarily increase conflict. These findings should not be exaggerated. As is obvious already from these data, we do not find a clear relationship between age and elite attitudes on all measures. Indeed, for much of our analysis age is not very relevant. Yet young elites often may have perceptions and beliefs that may be construed as more reflective of newer, more recent (in this latter case, more populist) developments in Dutch society and the political arena.

One other type of variable concerning backgrounds might be utilized here to suggest the type of influence that may be very important: the university training curriculum of the elites. We already noted the different curricula that civil servants took while at their universities, distinguishing those trained in law from those who took natural sciences or social sciences. On some of our attitudinal measures we find a sharp difference by such training backgrounds (see table 21). Although not completely consistent, these findings indicate the possible relevance of this background variable. The "technocratically trained" civil servant is apparently one who emphasizes technical expertise and efficiency, and is uneasy about political conflict and too much citizen participation. We will elaborate further on these relationships later in the analysis.

Summary Observations on Pathways to the Top

We have been concerned in this chapter with the youth, the families, the early upbringing, and beginning careers of Dutch elites. What emerges from the data are certain impressions that should help us understand the type of men and women who occupy top positions in Parliament and the bureaucracy. The backgrounds of these leaders reveal a diversity of social origins and milieus; in that sense this is no monolithic elite. They came from Catholic, Protestant (of many types), and nonreligious families, at least half still committed to the religious (or nonreligious) preferences of their early life. They came mostly from upper- and middle-class backgrounds, although a minority of M.P.'s had fathers with lower-class occupations. Many were frequently exposed in their families to adults who were in government, who belonged to parties, who talked politics, attesting thus in their own careers to considerable "sequential overlap" and intergenerational continuity in career interests and political activity. Yet some came from families in which politics was not manifestly a major interest, and the children in such families seem to have picked up their potential cues and motivations elsewhere. Further, they came from families with very diverse party traditions, with experiences in parties that in some instances have disappeared, replaced more recently by new versions. And, finally, they came to public service as a result of a variety of circumstances and attractions, some rather accidentally, others more

TABLE 21.   Relationship of University Training to Bureaucrats' Political Orientations (in percentages)

	University Curriculum		
	Natural Science	Social Science (primarily economics)	Law
Strongly emphasizes govern-mental efficiency rather than program	47	33	15
Emphasizes technical aspects of civil servant's role	63	28	21
Believes technical consider-ations are more important than political ones in policymaking	40	50	18
Feels conflict in politics is beneficial and good	13	41	59
Favors increased citizen participation in politics	7	44	33

purposefully. Some were looking for a job to fit their talents; others were interested in working for a cause; still others were motivated by other drives (power-oriented or not) that it is virtually impossible to identify precisely. Our data suggest that the service-to-others orientation was important for a large number. Whatever their initial reasons, a significant proportion now find themselves in a career that they admitted to us is attractive because it brings them influence, and means they are near the center of things. This is true of a majority of M.P.'s and almost half of the senior civil servants.

This is indeed a very heterogeneous set of leaders. While not a completely open elite, coming as they do from families with fairly high social status, and certainly not representative of the public in social backgrounds, it is also not an exclusive, closed, singular elite class. It includes many individuals who have broken with their pasts in certain ways, or includes individuals who cannot be characterized as part of the old social networks or influence sets, the older, traditional elite sectors of Dutch society. This indeed is the most interesting question posed by these data: to what extent are these leaders part of a new elite, a modern elite, reflecting the changed conditions of Dutch society and presumably responsive to the new groups, new ideas, new interests, and new values of that society? We know from the data that these leaders include those from lower-class occupational backgrounds, highly mobile in socioeconomic terms, less religious than their fathers, oriented to party politics (the senior bureaucrats also), and often the product of university educations emphasizing scientific disciplines. They were often also experienced in party organizations, labor unions, and social service groups. Their experience in business has been minimal. A small minority came from law. Their recruitment patterns have exposed them to a variety of educational, political, and occupational experiences that should have made them as elite groups aware of the new problems and directions of Dutch society. The question is, have these new elites developed new leadership styles and orientations to politics, departing in subtle (or not so subtle) ways from previous styles or beliefs about politics, or do they fulfill the same historic expectations of Dutch leadership? Are they still thinking and behaving as leaders, theoretically, according to the politics-of-accommodation model of the Dutch system, with its emphasis on leadership consensus, bureaucratic depoliticization, minimal ideological tension, and comfortable relations between leadership sectors? Or is there evidence that a change in leadership orientations, perspectives, and relationships is occurring? We have suggested already that certain elements in their backgrounds and careers, their paths to the top, may have conditioned them in their views about the political system. Whether this means a new politics, or a continuation of traditional politics, or a redefinition of old politics and its transformation and adaptation to a changed polity may be a subject on which these elite data can shed some light. We shall seek to do that by presenting here the patterns of consensus and dissensus, the congruence and the distance in the beliefs of these heterogeneous sets of Dutch administrative and political elites.

NOTES

1. Harold Lasswell and Daniel Lerner (eds.), *World Revolutionary Elites* (Cambridge, Mass.: MIT Press, 1966), p. 9.
2. See Robert Putnam, *The Comparative Study of Political Elites* (Englewood Cliffs, N.J.: Prentice-Hall, 1976), pp. 33–38, for a discussion of this "law."
3. Robert Putnam, "Bureaucrats and Politicians: Contending Elites in the Policy Process," in *Perspectives on Public Policy-Making*, ed. George C. Edwards and William B. Gwyn, Tulane Studies in Political Science, vol. 15 (New Orleans: Tulane University, 1975), p. 86. See also idem, *Political Elites*, p. 27. Jan Kooiman reports similar percentages for Parliaments in *Over de Kamer gesproken* (The Hague: Staatsuitgeverij, 1976), p. 86.
4. In a recent limited study, only 8 percent of those in the public service were found to be Catholic. Mohd. Salleh bin Koyakoti, "De Toegankelijkheid tot de openbare dienst," *Bestuurwetenschappen*, November 1975, pp. 489–502. The data on which Salleh bases his conclusions, however, come from those with the rank of referendaris and above, but only in the Ministries of Interior and Social Affairs.
5. The occupational prestige scale used here is the same as the one developed by F. van Heek and E. V. W. Vercruysse, eds., *Sociale stijging en daling in Nederland*, vol. 1 (Leiden: Stenfert Kroese, 1958), and J. J. M. van Tudler, *Beroepsmobiliteit in Nederland* (Leiden: Stenfert Kroese, 1962). Stratification of occupational prestige is a classification of the occupational population in the Netherlands after the results of a test held in 1953. The occupations by prestige level are as follows:
    Level I. The professions, high civil servants, big-company directors, professors in secondary schools (in 1953, 3 percent of the occupational population)
    Level II. High employees, senior officials, small-company directors, big farmers, middle technicians (8 percent)
    Level III. High middle classes/tradesmen, middle grade civil servants, middle farmers, middle employees (20 percent)
    Level IV. Low middle classes, small shopkeepers, skilled laborers, small farmers (34 percent)

Level V. Trained laborers, subordinate officials (27 percent)
Level VI. Untrained laborers (8 percent)

6. According to data from other scholars, this is a trend which has been apparent since 1930. In that year, 16 percent of M.P.'s held government positions just before entering Parliament; that number had increased to 26 percent by 1973. Similarly, in the same time period the number of those who had held positions in education increased from 15 percent to 19 percent, while those involved in industry or trade fell from 12 percent to 9 percent. See Kooiman, *Over de Kamer gesproken*, p. 88. Data are also presented in Kooiman's analysis of the occupational prestige level of grandfathers of M.P.'s (14–16 percent at the highest prestige level), p. 83. See also the extensive analysis of the social backgrounds of the members of both the first and second chambers of the Dutch Parliament in Hans Daalder and Sonja Hubée-Boonzaaijer, "Sociale herkomst en politieke recrutering van Nederlandse Kamerleden in 1968—I," *Acta Politica* 5 (1969–70): 292–345.

7. These data are similar to those of Kooiman, *Over de Kamer gesproken*, p. 258.

8. For M.P.'s this is less continuity than reported in the findings of the earlier Dutch studies of Parliament—in approximately two-thirds of the cases second chamber M.P.'s followed the partisan preference of their fathers. See Hans Daalder and Sonja Hubée-Boonzaaijer, "Sociale herkomst en politieke recrutering van Nederlandse Kamerleden in 1968—II," *Acta Politica* 5 (1969–70): 379–82. This article discusses in great detail the political backgrounds of members of both houses of the Dutch Parliament.

9. For all senior civil servants in our study, 47 percent had always worked in government service, while 53 percent had not.

10. Arie van Braam, "Sociale herkomst en mobiliteit van ambtenaren," in *Sociale stijging en daling in Nederland*, ed. F. van Heek and E. V. W. Vercruysse (Leiden: Stenfert Kroese, 1959), vol. 1, pp. 195–239; idem, "Enkele aspecten van recrutering van ambtenaren in de Nederlands rijksdienst," *Civis Mundi*, 1974, pp. 203–13.

11. See van Braam, "Sociale herkomst," and Salleh, "De Toegankelijkheid," for discussion of this same phenomenon of lateral mobility in the Dutch system.

12. Putnam, *Political Elites*, p. 30.

13. See particularly Kooiman, *Over de Kamer gesproken*, chapters 13 and 14; also, Daalder and Hubée-Boonzaaijer, "Sociale herkomst en politieke recrutering," for a most thorough presentation, in great detail, of the careers of Dutch M.P.'s based on the 1968 data.

14. Kooiman, *Over de Kamer gesproken*, p. 259.

15. These data come from our comparative project, the analysis being originally presented by Joel D. Aberbach and Robert D. Putnam in their unpublished paper, "Paths to the Top: The Origins and Careers of Political and Administrative Elites," table 4.

16. This is almost identical to the finding in the 1968 study where the prestige of M.P.'s with university education is reported as 58.6 percent. See Daalder and Hubée-Boonzaaijer, "Sociale herkomst en politieke recrutering—I," p. 300. As reported there, this percentage increased from 44 percent in 1930.

17. For the exact numbers of M.P.'s by occupations held before entering Parliament, and an analysis of these data, see Daalder and Hubée-Boonzaaijer, "Sociale herkomst en politieke recrutering—I," pp. 303–12. See also Kooiman, *Over de Kamer gesproken,* pp. 87–90. They reveal these trends:

	1946	1956	1968	1973
Government service	17%	25%	16%	26%
Education	17	19	10	19
Industry and trade	15	11	14	9
Political and social				
organizations	27	28	34	28
Professions	23	17	18	12

18. Robert Putnam, *Political Elites,* p. 44.

CHAPTER 4

Role Perceptions
of Bureaucrats and M.P.'s

Much of the early, classic literature on government made the basic distinction between administrative and political functions and activities. Max Weber, among others, described in some detail the expectations associated with the role of the bureaucrats in contrast to the role of the politician. The image of the politician he conveyed was that of a representative and supporter of particular interests, an advocate for causes, an ideologue, a power-oriented partisan. The image of the bureaucrat, however, was quite different: he was the "expert," neutral executor, concerned about efficiency, subordinate to others in a hierarchical structure, seeking technocratic solutions, and not acting from biased, personal, or partisan orientations.

> According to his proper vocation the genuine official . . . will not engage in politics. . . . he should engage in impartial "administration." The politician's conduct is subject to quite a different, indeed exactly the opposite, principle of responsibility from that of the civil servant. . . . The honor of the civil servant is vested in his ability to execute conscientiously the order of superior authorities. . . . The honor of the political leader . . . however lies precisely in an exclusive *personal* responsibility for what he does.[1]

Of course, Weber also saw the inevitable confrontation between M.P. and civil servant.

> In facing the Parliament the bureaucracy out of a sure power instinct, fights every attempt of the Parliament to gain knowledge. . . . Bureaucracy naturally welcomes a poorly informed and hence a powerless Parliament. . . .[2]

This dichotomy between administrative and political roles and activities, and the assumption that they are distinct, not overlapping, and lodged in separate structures, has come to be increasingly challenged. Scholars have noted that there is no such neat division of responsibilities or styles in the modern nation state. Bureaucrats have to become involved with politics, it is argued, and politicians in Parliaments, for example, do not leave policy administration to bureaucrats. Politicians are involved with technical aspects of the policy process, and bureaucrats with the political realities of policymaking. Almond and Powell, for example, see overlapping functions for these two sets of actors.

> Both types of structures (political parties and bureaucracies) provide direct links between a large number of interest groups and the decisionmakers, and yet are capable of aggregating interests as well as articulating and transmitting them.[3]

They see the civil servant as clearly involved in the policy process.

> Much of the substance of policy is a matter of decision by bureaucrats, and the effectiveness of policy is the consequence of the spirit and will of bureaucrats.[4]

While this "convergence thesis" is advanced by many writers, there are also writers who recently are reemphasizing the importance of expertise among elites and the distinction between the technocrat and the politician, as Putnam has recently reminded us. Thus Jean Meynaud writes of "the rise to power of those who possess technical knowledge or ability, to the detriment of the traditional type of politician."[5] This, he says, is linked to "a latent anti-parliamentarism and concern that the technician preserve his independence with regard to politics."[6] Suzanne Berger's conclusion about France, which may be applicable elsewhere, is that

> in most areas of policy, with the exception of defense and foreign policy, case studies of decisions made fifteen years ago and today suggest that the power of the technocrats has increased relative to that of the politicians.[7]

Further, Robert Putnam has emphasized the different recruitment channels of politicians and bureaucrats and the different tests of functional competence expected of them.[8] We should be cautious, therefore, in dismissing too easily the earlier theoretical contributions of Max Weber.

In our interviews with M.P.'s and senior bureaucrats we found views expressed that emphasized different aspects of elite roles, sometimes reflecting the Weberian conception of separation of roles, sometimes suggesting that such roles were mixed or overlapping. Thus one bureaucrat said:

Civil servants are advisors of the minister, directly if they are at the top or less directly if they are on a lower level. . . . They should advise their ministers as well as possible. They should do that perfectly objectively . . . regardless of their personal views, political ideas, or social opinions, whatever they are. They are solely advisors of the ministers.

Another senior civil servant, however, suggests a wider range of policy influence for the bureaucrat.

Essentially the cabinet of course has to decide what the policy is. If that is policy with which the body of civil servants cannot agree, then they (civil servants) have the tools to, let's say—to slow down. You always are able to come up with technical problems and difficulties which make it desirable that a certain decision of the minister is postponed for half a year . . . I do not want to use the word sabotage, but. . . . The influence of certain higher civil servants can be fairly large.

An M.P. also espouses this more expansionist view of the senior bureaucrat's role.

The higher civil servants are of course, the ones who prepare law proposals in a technical sense, and policy in general. I think it is the task of those people to do that as well as possible, only with two notes: (1) I think that they actually should present alternatives . . . , and (2) the task for the civil service is not to work only for the government, but also much more for Parliament.

These quotations illustrate the variations in views of elites on one aspect of their roles—the policy contributions and influence of civil servants. There are many other role perceptions that we could illustrate from our interviews. For example, on the role of M.P.'s, we note the following alternative positions.

Views of Civil Servants:
A member of Parliament has to listen to his voters, pressure groups, and other people who want to talk to him. A member of Parliament stands closer to common people (than the civil servant) if he is doing this job well. . . .

A member of Parliament should of course have a broader knowledge and intuition of the political possibilites and that is what is missing in the civil servant, just because he is so terribly specialized.

I see two main tasks for M.P.'s: ombudsman, that is direct contact with the population, the analysis of complaints and problems and to make translations of these. A second task is in my opinion to develop a vision, a senator-like vision on middle- and long-term policy.

Views of M.P.'s:
I think that you are able as a civil servant in spite of all the contacts with society. . . . to emphasize the rational aspects more so than the politician in his direct contact with the voters.

Members of Parliament have to be able to convince people, to make people enthusiastic. . . .

A civil servant is mainly working in the privacy of the department, whereas the member of Parliament is working under the flashlights of public opinion.

Keeping in mind these differences in viewpoints, we will present in this chapter a summary of our data on mutual role perceptions, attempting to discuss the following questions:

1. To what extent is there congruence in these perceptions? Do bureaucrats and politicians agree on each other's roles, or not?
2. Are these roles, as perceived, distinct or overlapping—in a sense, does the Weberian distinction between the bureaucratic and political roles hold up in the data? A corollary of this is the question of how conflicting are the role images and expectations of bureaucrats and politicians.
3. How do roles as perceived by Dutch elites compare to elite perceptions elsewhere in Europe—in what ways are the Dutch distinctive?
4. If we operationalize some of Weber's key concepts for the bureaucracy, how Weberian does the higher civil service appear to be? What are the characteristics of those who are Weberian and those who are non-Weberian?
5. To what extent do such variables as party, type of ministry, age, length of service, as well as other orientations seem to be linked to role perceptions of M.P.'s and civil servants?
6. What consequences may there be from different role perceptions for other attitudes and orientations of civil servants and M.P.'s and in their mutual acceptance and trust of each other?

The Basic Patterns of Role Images

In our interview we asked respondents to describe the traits and qualities that they thought the administrator should have and those that the politician should have. Open-ended coding of their responses resulted in the use of twelve traits for administrators, and ten for politicians. These might be called the "prescriptions," which also are a product of "role perceptions."

We find remarkably high agreement by these elites as to the traits and roles of top bureaucrats (table 22). Both M.P.'s and civil servants place major emphasis on policymaking, the advisor-counselor role, and intellectual traits—64 percent to 87 percent mentioned these. At the other extreme, very few think bureaucrats should be charismatic leaders, advocates, or representatives. The conception of the bureaucrat as "neutral-executor," which is traditional for the Dutch image of the depoliticized civil servant, does persist (54 percent of bureaucrats mentioning it and 46 percent of M.P.'s). Technical skills are mentioned by 41 percent of the civil servants (but by only 24 percent of the M.P.'s). So two types of images persist.

There are different emphases (as in the importance of organizational skills), but by and large the role perception of the bureaucrat as involved in policymaking seems to prevail. Above all, there is high congruence—a coefficient of agreement of 0.84—in the specification of traits by the two sets of elites.

TABLE 22. Traits Linked to the Role of Administrator

	Mentioned by Bureaucrats		Mentioned by M.P.'s	
	Percentage	Rank	Percentage	Rank
Policymaking	86	1	71	3
Organizational skills	81	2	49	5
Advisor, counselor	80	3	87	1
Intellectual ability	64	4	73	2
Sociability, interpersonal relations	64	4	29	7
Neutral executor	54	6	46	6
Character, conscience	41	7	55	4
Technical skills	41	7	24	8
Mediating, bargaining	31	9	2	12
Representational	20	10	22	9
Ideologue, advocate	11	11	5	10
Charisma, leadership	7	12	5	10

Note: Figures record items mentioned as "very important" or "important." The average difference between M.P.'s and bureaucrats = 14.7. Spearman Rho coefficient on agreement between bureaucrats and M.P.'s = 0.84.

In order to secure an overall judgment of these role perceptions we asked our coders to indicate for each respondent, on the basis of his total discussion, whether the civil servant's role was seen as active or passive (see table 23). Clearly, both sets of elites, with similar proportions, see the senior civil servant as an activist. Only a minority of 10 percent or less, of M.P.'s as well as bureaucrats, view the senior civil servant as passive. While the content and nature of the role is not precisely specified, the character of the policy role as perceived by elites is evident.

As for the traits of M.P.'s, there is again high congruence in the rank orders of the two sets of elites. Policymaking is at the top of the list for both, mentioned by 76 percent of M.P.'s and 64 percent of senior bureaucrats. Comparing tables 22 and 24, however, one notes that civil servants are more likely to specify a policymaking role for themselves than for M.P.'s. The representative role and intellectual skills of M.P.'s are high on the list of both leadership groups. And no one really sees M.P.'s as mediators or bargainers. Surprisingly, M.P.'s do not see themselves also as advocates (only 10 percent), while over a third of the senior bureaucrats see M.P.'s as advocates. On the other hand, M.P.'s talk about their leadership traits (49 percent) while senior bureaucrats deemphasize that (only 18 percent mentioning it). On balance, with these differences (which are not serious), there is a high level of agreement on what traits are tied to M.P. roles (a coefficient of agreement, again, of 0.84).[9]

At the conclusion of the coding of the whole interview, and based on all the attitudes expressed, the coders characterized our respondent's view of what *his own role* in fact was. We used here nine different role characterizations (table 25).

As in our previous analysis, there is a heavy emphasis here again on policymaking, for both M.P.'s and senior bureaucrats. Both elites are also seen by themselves as "trustees" (representatives of the na-

TABLE 23. Perception of the Senior Civil Servant's
Role in Policy (in percentages)

	Senior Civil Servants	M.P.'s
Very active	26	29
Moderately active	43	46
Pro/con	8	10
Moderately passive	7	10
Very passive	4	0
Not ascertained	12	5

tional interest or of the state). The focus on legal roles is also similar. Basic differences, however, stand out. A large proportion (59 percent) of the senior civil servants refer to their technical-expertise role, a larger proportion than earlier had mentioned this as a necessary quality or trait of a civil servant, which suggests that actual perceptions deviate from prescribed roles. Other differences: M.P.'s see themselves as "mobilizers" (fighting for causes and representing group interests) and "ombudsmen" (concerned with specific problems of constituents and clients). Senior civil servants see themselves as "brokers" (mediating and resolving conflicts of interest) much more than do

TABLE 24. Traits Linked to the Role of M.P.

	M.P.'s		Bureaucrats	
	Percentage	Rank	Percentage	Rank
Policymaking	76	1	64	1
Representation	68	2	45	3
Intellectual ability	54	3	54	2
Charisma, leadership	49	4	18	7
Technical skills	44	5	33	5
Sociability	37	6	19	6
Ideologue, advocate	10	7	38	4
Organizational, managerial	5	8	1	9
Mediating, bargaining	2	9	7	8

Note: Figures record items mentioned as "very important" or "important." The average difference between M.P.'s and bureaucrats = 14.2. Spearman Rho coefficient for agreements between M.P.'s and bureaucrats = 0.84.

TABLE 25. Role Self-Characterizations of M.P.'s and Senior Bureaucrats

	Percentage Focusing "Very Much" or "Somewhat" on Role	
	M.P.'s	Senior Civil Servants
Policymaker	83	90
Mobilizer	69	24
Ombudsman	59	1
Trustee	54	57
Legalist	34	52
Partisan	44	0
Technician	33	59
Facilitator	32	7
Broker	7	40

Note: Spearman Rho coefficient between bureaucrats' and politicians' role orientations = 0.31.

M.P.'s. From these summary codes, then, we see considerable distinctiveness in role orientations for seven of the nine roles. The coefficient of agreement was relatively low, 0.31.

A Comparison: Dutch, British, and German Elites' Role Perceptions

The role perceptions of Dutch elites differ in certain specific and interesting respects from those of other western European countries. Since the same question and codes were used in our international project, we can illustrate these differences here with similar data (table 26). Senior bureaucrats in Britain, for example, have basically the same role images—emphasizing the policymaking, advisory counselor, organizational, and neutral executor roles as most important, but also with a minority of two-fifths mentioning technical expertise. The main difference is that British civil servants talk more about a mediational role (53 percent compared to 31 percent of the Dutch). The same is true of German senior bureaucrats (60 percent mention mediation), who also place more emphasis on their technician role (73 percent see it as important). German senior bureaucrats are much less self-conscious about an advisor-counselor role than either the Dutch or British. The similarities that exist, then, are in the emphasis on policymaking, advising, and neutral executor role perceptions, particularly between the Dutch and British.

The contrasts in perceived M.P. roles are perhaps more striking (table 27). Dutch, British, and German M.P.'s all place high importance on policymaking and representation. After that, however, they differ considerably. The emphasis on the mediational role of M.P.'s is virtually nonexistent in the Netherlands (2 percent referring to it), but relatively important in Britain and Germany (43 percent and 60 percent respectively). Also, Dutch M.P.'s do not see themselves as ideo-

TABLE 26.   Comparison of Bureaucratic Role Self-Perceptions (in percentages)

	Netherlands	Britain	Germany
Policymaker	86	73	80
Advisor, counselor	80	89	48
Neutral executor	54	57	40
Technician	41	37	73
Mediation	31	53	60

Note: Figures record roles mentioned as important.

logue-advocates, but British and German M.P.'s do. On the other hand, many Dutch M.P.'s consider themselves technical experts in particular policy areas (44 percent), but this is not true in Britain (5 percent) and much less so in Germany (25 percent). Thus, the Dutch M.P. still has role images that seem to reflect the consociational past. He is preoccupied with representative and policymaking roles (and for many the development of a special expertise in policy is important), while British and German M.P.'s see themselves less as policy specialists and more as involved in conciliating different interests and in pressing for particular causes. This lack of mediating emphasis among Dutch M.P.'s may have to do with the institutional structure, in which the Social Economic Council (SER) has an important role in mediating between social and economic groups and the government. The government is partially represented by top civil servants in these bodies. The higher mediating-role definitions of civil servants may refer to this relationship.

Weber and the Dutch Higher Civil Service

The classical view of bureaucracy, exemplified in Max Weber's writings, operationalized precisely the elements in the bureaucrat's role. Although these were part of an ideal type, they are useful for guiding investigation. Indeed, Weber himself indicated that "in its conceptual purity, this mental construct cannot be found empirically anywhere in reality." Yet he also says that "historical research faces the task of determining in each individual case, the extent to which this ideal construct approximates to or diverges from reality."[10]

In order to test that part of Weber's conception of bureaucracy that deals with the role attributes of the civil servant, we have selected three elements that are critical to his theory and on which our data are relevant. We are dealing here of course only with that part of the theory that is concerned with role expectations, and the attitudes of

TABLE 27. Comparison of M.P. Role Self-Perceptions (in percentages)

	Netherlands	Britain	Germany
Policymaker	76	79	87
Representative	68	69	62
Mediator	3	43	60
Ideologue, advocate	10	58	51
Technician	44	5	25

Note: Figures record roles mentioned as important.

our respondents towards their roles, not their actual behavior. The three elements we focus on here are:

1. the technical knowledge and expertise that bureaucrats have because of their education, skill training, and continuity in positions that emphasize and demand specialized competence;
2. the hierarchical status of the bureaucrat, and his subordination to a superior, and consequently the requirement for him to serve, advise, and be loyal to that superior whoever he may be;
3. the policy analysis style of the bureaucrat, in which he conceives of problems as technical ones, converts or defines problems in technical terms, and believes that technical criteria in the solution of problems are superior to political criteria.

These three elements are the core of Weber's role conception. He clearly sees the bureaucrat in this ideal type model as part of a "mechanism," a "community of functionaries" who are technical specialists taking orders and serving an official at "the very top." They should not be making political decisions (although Weber was worried that they would). They should be subservient to political authority. In his ideal type he sees them as engaging in "impartial administration." Above all, because of their training and very special competence they would dislike the application of political criteria to the solution of problems and would prefer the use of technical criteria. To decide what is "proper" for Weber was the task of the lawyer, "but not at all . . . that of the civil servant."[11] Karl Mannheim's summary proposition is particularly apt: "The fundamental tendency of all bureaucratic thought is to turn all problems of politics into problems of administration."[12]

Our aim here, then, is to test to what extent Dutch higher civil servants reveal these elements in Weber's construct in the attitudes they expressed. Three separate indices measure each of the three elements. First, to determine the extent to which *technical expertise* and knowledge is a role expectation, we used three types of evidence:

1. the spontaneous mentioning of technical expertise in the discussion of tasks;
2. the rating by coders of the importance of technician traits to the respondent in this discussion;
3. the overall assessment by the coder of the degree to which the respondent expresses a "technician-inventor" role orientation toward the solution of problems facing the society (i.e., focuses on the application of specialized knowledge to the solution of policy problems).

The distributions on these items were as follows: 24 percent mentioned technical expertise in discussions of tasks and traits; 41 percent saw technician traits as "important" or "very important" (22 percent chose "very important"); 59 percent gave "very much" or "some" evidence of being technician-inventors (33 percent for "very much"). From this one can see considerable variation in the incidence of this Weberian element, but a sizable minority appear as consistently concerned about the place of technical expertise. We constructed an index using these three pieces of evidence, concluding that 28 percent of the senior civil servants were "technically oriented" (on two or more of these items), and the remainder were not consistently thus oriented. Yet in this latter group there are 31 percent who scored as technical on one indicator.

Second, we were interested in a measure of the extent to which there was recognition of the *hierarchical* status of the bureaucrat and the need, therefore, for loyalty to a superior. Different types of evidence were available to us from the interviews: their references to governmental loyalty (18 percent), to impartiality (13 percent), the importance of the neutral executor role attribute (54 percent), and their willingness to work with a superior when a new government (and thus for them a new minister) comes into office. We asked on this latter point whether they had difficulty in implementing a policy at variance with that of a previous government, particularly if they personally disagreed with the new policy position. The distributions on this latter question were as follows:

	In General	Personal Disagreement with New Policy
Great difficulty	11%	12%
Difficult to a certain extent	15	12
Pro/con	8	12
No important difficulty	18	24
No difficulty	46	37
Don't know	3	4

The majority of Dutch senior civil servants say they are loyal supporters of a minister and government irrespective of a change of policy, but one-fourth to one-third had at least some difficulty with their implementing role, or had some reservations about it. Personal disagreement with a policy did not necessarily produce greater conflict, however.

We again constructed an index of hierarchical loyalty, scoring the respondents on each of the items used. Those who were consistently loyal on all measures numbered 37 percent, and the remainder were divided between a large middle group who were probably loyal but did not meet our test on all measures, and a small group who did not stress hierarchical loyalty, about 23 percent.

Third, in operationalizing Weber's emphasis on the bureaucrat's conceptualization of problems in technical (rather than political) terms and his belief that technical considerations should predominate in the solution of these problems, we again used different types of evidence: (1) their agree-disagree response to the statement, "Nowadays in dealing with social and economic problems more weight should be given to technical considerations than to political factors"; (2) the extent to which they felt "political feasibility" was important in solving governmental problems;[13] and (3) in their discussion of national economic planning, the extent to which they construed this as a technical (rather than a political) problem. The distributions on these measures are again interesting: 32 percent agree that "more weight should be given to technical considerations than to political factors"; 25 percent feel that political feasibility is not important; 20 percent believe that national economic planning is basically a technical problem; and 22 percent think such planning is both a technical and a political problem. If we combine these stems into an index of the superiority of technical over political approaches we again can place the respondents on a scale ranging from strong feelings of the superiority of technical approaches to strong feelings of the superiority of political approaches. We find that 25 percent of the senior bureaucrats are consistent technocrats, approximately 32 percent are at the other end of the continuum—politically oriented—and the remaining 43 percent seem to fall in the middle.

Using all three sets of variables, we can classify all senior bureaucrats on these Weberian role dimensions (table 28). The pure Weberian type includes only 5 percent of all bureaucrats, that is, those who fulfill all the requirements in our data for that type. On the other hand, 40 percent of the senior bureaucrats reveal none of the attitudes or orientations that would be expected of Weberian civil servants. Depending on which requisites one wants to emphasize, one can deduce from table 28 the proportion of Dutch senior civil servants that approximates the classical model. If emphasis on either hierarchical loyalty or technical expertise is alone used (the first three rows in the table), the Weberians constitute 53 percent; if loyalty alone is used, it is 37 percent; if belief in the superiority of technical approaches is used (the first column), 25 percent are Weberians. Whatever requisites one wishes to apply, it is clear that in utilizing *all* three types of variables Dutch senior civil servants tend to be non-Weberian in their total perspectives.[14] There are pockets of classical bureaucratic orientations in the civil service, however, and therefore it is useful to look for the location of these pockets with the use of other indicators.

Factors Linked to Bureaucratic Role Orientations

There is no consistent relationship between age, or number of years in the service, and these bureaucratic role orientations. That is, older bureaucrats (over fifty-seven years old), or, those who entered the service before 1950 and have been in the civil service a long time, are not necessarily those who have developed Weberian role orientations. It is true that older bureaucrats and those entering the service very early tend to emphasize technical expertise, but they are not necessarily the most Weberian in other respects. Indeed, the younger civil servants with less years in office tend to emphasize hierarchical loyalty more. There is, thus, absolutely no evidence that being in the Dutch civil service over time leads to more Weberian technocratic orientations, and some evidence that length of service may lead to less such technically oriented task perceptions.

University education may be more relevant. We have grouped our respondents into three broad disciplinary categories in table 29 and then looked at their role orientations. Clearly, those trained in law emerge as "generalists." Only a small minority (approximately 10 percent) em-

TABLE 28. Weberian Role Patterns for Dutch Senior Bureaucrats (in percentages)

	Believes Technical Approaches are Superior to Political	Believes Political Approaches are Superior to Technical	Total[a]
Stresses hierarchical loyalty and technical expertise	5 (pure Weberian)	7	12
Stresses hierarchical loyalty but not technical expertise	5	20	25
Stresses technical expertise but not loyalty	7	9	16
Stresses neither loyalty nor technical expertise	8	40 (pure non-Weberian)	48
Total	25	76	101

a. N = 76.

phasize technical expertise or insist that technical approaches to policy-making are superior to political approaches. They also stress hierarchical loyalty less. Those from natural science disciplines are inclined to emphasize technical expertise (39 percent, compared to 33 percent for economics and only 13 percent for law). But they are not at all antipolitical in their views about the policymaking process. Here it is those trained in economics who predominate, over 50 percent asserting the superiority of technical approaches to policy. University training, then, is indeed an influence that appears to condition the bureaucrat's views about administration long after they have left the university.

Another factor that seems related is the party preference of senior bureaucrats (table 30). The differences are not always large, but they

TABLE 29. University Curriculum as Related to Bureaucratic Role Orientations (in percentages)

Curriculum	Emphasizes Technical Expertise	Stresses Hierarchical Loyalty	Believes Technical Approaches Are Superior to Political	N
Law	13	30	7	30
Natural sciences	39	31	15	13
Economics	33	52	57	21

Note: There was one civil servant trained in social science who we have included here with law. Each percentage is the proportion of each curriculum category who held a given orientation. The rows do not, therefore, add up to 100 percent.

TABLE 30. Party Affiliations as Related to Bureaucratic Role Orientations (in percentages)

	Emphasizes Technical Expertise	Stresses Hierarchical Loyalty	Believes Technical Approaches Are Superior to Political Ones	N
Left-wing (PvdA, PSP, PPR, D'66)	25	25	10	20
Confessional	29	35	29	17
Right-wing (VVD, DS'70)	33	43	33	30
No preference	11	44	22	9

Note: Party preference was based on respondent's stated identification with a party; when no identification was given or could not be ascertained (30 percent of the sample), voting report for the 1972 election was used. Each percentage in the table is, again, the proportion of the party preference group who hold a particular role orientation.

are consistently in one direction. That is, bureaucrats supporting left-wing parties are less Weberian, confessional party supporters are more Weberian, and the supporters of right-wing parties are the most Weberian in their views. The difference is particularly notable on hierarchical loyalty and in their beliefs about the superiority of technical over political approaches. On the average, over one-third of those with right-wing partisan sympathies are classical bureaucrats, while this is true on the average of only 20 percent of those of left-wing partisan persuasion. The rationale for this set of findings may be that left-wing parties are more favorable toward governmental intervention in the society, and thus bureaucrats supporting such parties themselves see their roles in activist terms. Ideological position, then, may be a crucial intervening variable, a matter which we will explore subsequently in our chapter on ideology.

One other socialization variable seems important in this connection—the ministry in which the bureaucrat has been working. The function or type of administrative activity may determine role images. It has been argued, for example, that bureaucrats in social service ministries would be more political and activist in policymaking than those in traditional or maintenance type ministries. There is some confirmation of this in our study. Ministries do differ in the incidence of Weberian orientations. One must be cautious here because of the low number of respondents in our sample who were senior bureaucrats from any one ministry, obviously for one reason because there are not many *directeuren-generaal* and *directeuren* (our sampled population) in many of these ministries.[15] Keeping that caution in mind, we note the ministries on our three measures that did not reveal any evidence of Weberian technocratic orientations and those which were consistently high, in figure 9. When we find none of the senior civil servants in certain ministries emphasizing technical expertise, hierarchical loyalty,

No Evidence	Minimal Evidence	Moderate Evidence	Much Evidence	Consistently High Evidence
Transport Culture	Education Health Surinam and Antilles Social Affairs	Housing Finance General Affairs	Agriculture Justice	Economic Affairs Interior

Fig. 9. Indications of Weberian role orientations by ministry

or the superiority of technical approaches, while up to 55 percent in other ministries assert such role orientations, we can only deduce that there is in some ministries an "indoctrination" process going on over time that leads to such perspectives.

Our analysis strongly suggests that the pockets of Weberian orientations towards role can be located primarily (1) in certain ministries, (2) among bureaucrats supporting confessional and right-wing parties, and (3) among those not trained in law. There is certainly some overlap in the incidence of these variables. For example, it is interesting that over two-thirds of the bureaucrats in the ministries where we found officials *low* in Weberian perspectives were trained in the law, while only 40 percent of the remaining bureaucrats took university degrees in law. But there is some moderate evidence of Weberianism in most sectors of the civil service, despite party backgrounds and university training. Leftist partisan preference and legal training reduce the likelihood of classical Weberian views on the administrator's role, but do not eliminate it.

What can we conclude from this empirical exploration into the reality of Max Weber's ideal type bureaucrat for the senior bureaucrat in the Netherlands? First, in its pure form it is virtually nonexistent. Second, in a moderate form it exists among perhaps no more than 25 percent of the bureaucrats. Third, there is a very high congruence in the perceptions of M.P.'s and higher civil servants, agreements that the senior bureaucrat is involved in policymaking and that this is not primarily, certainly not exclusively, a technical function. Fourth, age and length of years in the service generally do not help explain what Weberian orientations exist. Fifth, within certain ministries there is indeed a socialization to accept either traditional bureaucratic orientations or the opposite, more modern and less technocratic orientations. But in quite a few ministries it is unclear that any such socialization process is going on. Sixth, the economists and natural scientists are most inclined to be technocrats, while the lawyers are not. And seventh, leftism in politics is apparently associated with non-Weberian orientations towards bureaucrats' roles.

Factors Linked to M.P. Role Orientations

In attempting to understand the attitudes that M.P.'s take toward their roles, it is much more difficult to identify key factors, but party and university education also seem to be important, as with civil servants. We find that M.P.'s of the Left overwhelmingly stress representative roles, (81 percent) more than confessional (64 percent) and, particularly, right-wing deputies (50 percent). Further, leftist M.P.'s emphasize technical expertise and charismatic leadership more. The M.P. of the Left therefore appears to have a composite role image that is both specialist and populist, while the role images of confessional and right-wing M.P.'s are more difficult to generalize about.

The university-trained M.P. also tends to see himself as the representative, the leader, and the technical specialist. The nonuniversity-educated M.P. seems much less certain of his role self-images; he is not inclined to emphasize technical expertise or a charismatic leader role, as is the university-trained M.P.

The Consequences of Role Orientations for Other Elite Attitudes

How important is perceived role for understanding the ways in which elites think about politics? Is role as important as position (in the Parliament or in the bureaucracy), or party affiliation, or ideology, or other basic orientations? This is an argument that many scholars have pursued, both theoretically and empirically, but relatively little has been done comparatively to test the impact of role orientations within the bureaucracy. We have noted the different "role" and "trait" emphases emerging from our discussion with senior bureaucrats, reporting considerable agreement in the descriptions of role. Nevertheless, we have noted differences, in particular differences in emphasis on the importance of technical expertise, hierarchical loyalty, and the superiority of technical approaches over political approaches to policymaking. We thus identified a subset of bureaucrats whose role orientations seem to be Weberian in the classical sense, in contrast to those who are moderately Weberian and non-Weberian. This distinction we will use here to test the relationship between role orientations and other elite attitudes.

Among the many attitudes we might seek to link to bureaucratic role orientations is, first, the level of satisfaction these civil servants have toward their jobs. As table 31 reveals, both Weberians and non-Weberians like their jobs very much and, paradoxically, the Weberians are happier with the political aspects of their jobs than are the non-Weberians. Despite their basic role orientation, with its emphasis on technical expertise, they are not on balance dissatisfied with the nontechnical aspects of their work. Only a small minority (17 percent) really dislike politics in administration.

In more general terms, however, a second observation one can make is that the Weberian bureaucrats are the ones who are more inclined to be critical of partisan politics and group conflict, of the politician, and of too great participation in the system by citizens. They are not extremely negative, but rather dubious, while the non-Weberian bureaucrats are much more positive about the politician and party politics. Thus, 62 percent of the non-Weberians have positive feelings towards party politics, compared to 38 percent of those Weberian in role orientations. This contrast appears also in an analysis we made of the views of bureaucrats about citizen participation.

Those non-Weberian bureaucrats who see themselves as having an active policy role are much more interested in increasing the influence of voters in the political system (58 percent in favor) than those Weberians who see themselves as passive in the policy process (25 percent).[16]

Among the many other attitudes of senior bureaucrats that interested us, their view of the "rule of anonymity" was particularly interesting, because this is an important element in the discussions about a politicized bureaucracy: the more politicized, the less anonymity. The rule is that civil servants should not publicly express their opinions on matters concerning their work nor be personally identified publicly

TABLE 31. Bureaucratic Role Orientations as Related to Other Attitudes of Senior Civil Servants (in percentages)

	Non-Weberian (N = 34)	Moderate Weberian (N = 18)	Strongly Weberian (N = 18)
Attitudes toward political aspects of the job			
Likes political aspects very much	18	28	39
Likes political aspects somewhat	29	22	17
Pro/con	47	39	28
Dislikes political aspects	5	11	17
Overall assessment of job of civil servant			
Likes it	82	54	95
Uncertain	15	43	5
Dislikes it	4	0	0
Feelings about politics generally			
Positive	62	37	38
Neutral	35	52	62
Negative	3	11	0
View on the relaxation of the anonymity rule			
Favors relaxation	26	26	5
Pro/con	23	26	21
Opposes relaxation	51	48	74

with a position, since the minister as political head is responsible and solely answers for decisions and actions. The rule of anonymity has been widely discussed in and outside the civil service and in 1974 was a topic for discussion in Parliament with the minister of interior. The debate pits the socialists and liberals who assert the bureaucrat's freedom of speech against the confessionals who argued for the loyalty of the civil servant to the minister and who suggested that it would be proper for the bureaucrat to seek the advice of his superior before breaking the rule.

On the whole our civil servants are in favor of the anonymity rule (56 percent approving it outright and another 21 percent "sitting on the fence"). It is interesting to note that despite the roles of the liberals and confessionals in the Parliament, *in the bureaucracy* it is the liberals (VVD and DS'70) who overwhelmingly (70 percent) oppose a change in the rule, while close to 60 percent of both the leftist partisans and the confessionals favor relaxation. We found also that the older bureaucrats with more years in the civil service were most likely to be opposed to changing the rule—only 29 percent of those with less than twenty years experience opposed relaxation compared to 71 percent of those with thirty-two or more years of service.

Where do our Weberian and non-Weberian civil servants stand on this issue? As indicated already (table 31, p. 88), the Weberians are the most likely to oppose a relaxation of the anonymity rule—74 percent oppose change. Close to 50 percent of the non-Weberians, however, also oppose change, so that it is not an all-or-none finding. Yet the data are in the direction that our theory would expect. This confirms again that the basic Weberian/non-Weberian distinction is useful for understanding the perspectives senior civil servants have towards their work. Clearly there remain great differences of opinion on the matter, but perhaps the tide of opinion may be shifting in favor of more publicity. One still hears the classical view, such as this opinion of a senior bureaucrat:

He [the minister] is responsible, we civil servants are not. He is responsible, politically responsible towards Parliament. He has to get all information with all our opinions, then he has to decide. . . . You have to be able to say controversial things to the minister, but these do not have to be shown to the outside. . . ."

But perhaps this attitude is now changing.

One final point might be made concerning the linkage of civil servant attitudes to role perceptions—the non-Weberians are much more likely to feel that the civil servant's job has changed over time than are the Weberians. One-half of the Weberian civil servants see very little change in the civil service, but 80 percent of their colleagues who are more political in their role conceptions view the civil service as changing a great deal, and many of these emphasize changes in the policymaking function. As one respondent says: "Policymaking is more comprehensive; it takes more factors into account, and . . . is applied to more areas than previously, due to greater governmental intervention in the economy and society." While others also mention organizational changes ("there is a necessity to work under great pressure" and there is "more *inspraak,*" or participation from the lower echelons), the former concerns predominate. A large number of top civil servants stress increased demands in the policymaking area, a concern particularly of the non-Weberian bureaucrats.

The role orientations of M.P.'s also seem in some respects linked to other orientations. But the distinctions within the M.P. elite group are not as clear as in the bureaucracy. Our major finding: M.P. attitudes towards parties seem linked to role images. We can illustrate this by focusing on the two role codes we have that emphasize the M.P.'s relationship to the public. One of these we call the mobilizer role (fighting for or representing the interests of a social group, class or cause, or protesting injustice) and the other we call the ombudsman role (protecting and defending the interest of individual constituents or clients). From 40 to 50 percent of our M.P.'s considered either or both of these roles as "very important." If we contrast these M.P.'s with those who considered such roles "not very important" we note one major difference between these two sets of M.P.'s. The mobilizers and ombudsmen are very proparty in their perspectives, whereas the others are more critical of parties and party leaders (even though they themselves are party leaders). Two separate measures can document this difference (table 32). Those who see their roles as working with and for the public, or who see themselves as activists for causes or groups or constituents, are the M.P.'s who are not worried about partisan conflict and who feel partisan politics and the party leadership should have a major role in the system. There is much concern about the nature of party conflict in the Dutch system, even by M.P.'s. But this concern is much less salient among M.P.'s who see themselves as tribunes of the people.

Concluding Observations

We have presented here data on the task prescriptions and role perceptions of Dutch senior bureaucrats and M.P.'s. We see in these data no basic cleavages or overt conflicts between these elites, though potentially they could exist. There certainly does not appear to be a serious conflict between M.P.'s and civil servants over senior bureaucratic roles, nor over M.P. roles. There is in fact high congruence and much consensus.

Further, the bureaucracy at the top appears to be a structure that is adaptive, or at least undergoing some modifications in elite views of administration. It is not the older civil servants who are "traditional" and the younger ones who are more "activist." Rather, at all ages, and despite the generational era of career origin, Dutch senior bureaucrats seem to have taken on roles that are positively linked to the policy process, and roles that are changing as the polity and society are changing. For the majority of civil servants role images still emphasize the neutral executor function while also stressing involvement with policy. This is not an involvement with policy in narrowly conceived technical terms. This composite role image is one in which M.P.'s for the most part concur. We do indeed find pockets of the classical Weberian orientation toward bureaucratic roles. And many of the Weberians hold views that are at times as predicted, namely, they are negative about politics, more elitist, and less interested in citizen involvement in politics. However, the Weberians with such classical views are a relatively small minority.

Dutch M.P.'s seem to be much aware of their roles as public representatives, communicators with the masses, supporters of interests and causes, and servants of constituents. This is particularly so of

TABLE 32. M.P. Role Orientations as Related to Attitudes toward Parties

M.P. Role Orientations	Percentage Who Feel Parties Exacerbate Conflict Unnecessarily	Percentage Who Feel National Organizational Leaders of Parties Should Have Much Influence on Decision Making
Mobilizer role		
Sees role as very important	35	60
Sees role as less important or not at all important	72	38
Ombudsman role		
Sees role as very important	33	67
Sees role as less important or not at all important	63	36

deputies on the Left. This reveals an interesting development in the Dutch system, which previously was not considered to be so populist in its role orientations. Along with the policymaking role, which both M.P.'s and senior bureaucrats place at the highest priority these M.P. roles in relation to the public are frequently emphasized. It is the representative function, however, not the ideological advocate function, nor the mediational function, which stands out in these data for M.P.'s. Thus, *within* the Parliament as *within* the bureaucracy one finds new and emerging images articulated. *Role orientation* as well as *position,* therefore, must be taken into consideration in understanding the elite actor's beliefs about his political world and how problems in that world are to be solved.

NOTES

1. H. H. Gerth and C. Wright Mills, eds., *From Max Weber: Essays in Sociology* (New York: Oxford University Press, 1960), p. 95.
2. Ibid., pp. 233–34.
3. Gabriel Almond and G. B. Powell, *Comparative Politics: A Developmental Approach* (Boston: Little, Brown & Co., 1966), p. 101.
4. Ibid., p. 154.
5. Jean Meynaud, *Technocracy,* trans. Paul Barnes (New York: The Free Press, 1969), p. 31.
6. Ibid., p. 219.
7. Suzanne Berger, "The French Political System," in Samuel H. Beer et al., *Patterns of Government: The Major Political Systems of Europe,* 3d ed. (New York: Random House, 1972), p. 426.
8. Robert Putnam, "Bureaucrats and Politicians: Contending Elites in the Policy Process," in *Perspectives on Public Policy-Making,* ed. George C. Edwards and William B. Gwyn, Tulane Studies in Political Science, vol. 15 (New Orleans: Tulane University, 1975), pp. 179–202.
9. For an earlier study of the "qualities" of M.P.'s, see Jan Kooiman, *Over de Kamer gesproken* (The Hague: Staatsuitgeverij, 1976), pp. 19–22.
10. Max Weber, *The Methodology of the Social Sciences* (Glencoe, Ill.: The Free Press, 1949), p. 90.
11. Max Weber, "Politics as Vocation," in Gerth and Mills, eds., *From Max Weber,* p. 95.
12. Karl Mannheim, *Ideology and Utopia,* trans. Louis Wirth and Edward Shils (London: Routledge and Kegan Paul, n.d.), p. 105.
13. A "political feasibility index" was constructed from two variables, one dealing with bureaucrats' feelings on the solution of problems generally, the other dealing with the solution of economic planning problems.

14. The views of Dutch M.P.'s on the role attributes of senior civil servants confirm this basic interpretation. An analysis, using the same types of variables employed here, reveals that M.P.'s are, if anything, less inclined to perceive senior civil servants as Weberian.

15. The number of cases in our sample range from Health and Surinam and Antilles (two); General Affairs, Justice, Transport (three or four); Agriculture, Culture, Education, Interior (five or six); to Social Affairs and Housing (eight), Finance (eleven), and Economic Affairs (twelve).

16. We used a nine-point scale in asking our respondents to indicate how much influence they wished various actors to have in the system (such as ministers, M.P.'s, churches, etc., including voters). The percentages used here are for the top three scale positions, 7-9.

CHAPTER 5

Elite Styles: The Way Leaders Think about Politics

The operators of a political system think constantly about the problems they face and how these can be resolved in the context of the interests, institutions, and processes of that system, as well as in the context of their own beliefs. How political leaders approach their problems—on what aspects they concentrate their attention, how they reason their way to a conclusion, and how their cognitive orientations are structured (rigidly and dogmatically or flexibly and openly)—may help us understand leadership behavior.

What the most useful and relevant components of political "style" are has been discussed by many scholars. Robert Putnam has cryptically defined political style as "not *what* men think about politics and policy but *how* they do so—this is the essence of political style." Putnam goes on to interpret "ideological politics" in stylistic terms, arguing that "an ideological politician is . . . a politician who analyzes policy in a particular way . . . one who focuses on general principles rather than specific details, who reasons deductively rather than inductively, who stresses the role of 'ideas' in politics."[1] Certain aspects of this view of style will be employed in the analysis presented here.

Dutch parliamentarians and high civil servants were asked a variety of open-ended questions that invited them to discuss their views on the key problems facing society, the nature of the political process and the role of conflict in the system, the place of political parties and other groups in the influence structure, and similar matters. This gave us the opportunity to see how they think about politics, how they discuss, reason, and argue about politics.

It is obvious in reading the typescripts of these interviews that these leaders are quite different in how they discuss these matters. The responses to the "conflict question" illustrate some of the differences nicely. (The question was: "Some people say there will always be conflicts and opposing interests, while others contend that the group-ings and classes of the population have much in common and have the same interests. What is your opinion about that?")

One M.P. discussed the question at a very abstract level:

> Politics in my opinion is nothing else than conflict. Conflicts are not reconcilable really. Nor do I believe in an *eindfase* [final phase] of a development in society in which everyone very harmo-niously and peaceably gets along together with everyone else. . . . Conflicts are useful. All power and inventive energy must be brought to bear to find solutions. . . .

Quite in contrast, another M.P. immediately attacked the question much more pragmatically and specifically:

> It is clear that the different population groups have different sorts of interests. You don't have to think only of employers and em-ployees, but you can look also at the middle class, farmers, people who live in special jurisdiction (or area). . . . There are indeed very different interests and you must look at these and see how you can arrive at a special solution. . . . That is what politics is very busy with, how to weigh these against each other . . . and how to reach a solution for one problem while realizing that you may make another problem more difficult.

What impresses one in statements such as those above is the varia-tion in starting points in such discussions, and in the reasoning process, aside from the substantive focus. The civil servant who talks about the class conflict between employers and workers as irreconcilable, and reasons about politics from that point on, is in sharp contrast to one who reasons inductively by looking first at the interests of various groups in the system and then concludes the discussion by contending that "people have so much in common." The leader who begins with a discourse on the difficulty of the decision-making process, and then strongly and passionately argues that it is an "illusion" to think of citizen participation as being very helpful, is quite different from one who is interested at the outset in all the citizen input he can get and in the discussion communicates that he is very tolerant of others' ideas.

There are many ways we might characterize and differentiate the styles of politicians. Indeed, the literature is rich with suggestions as to which dimensions are most useful. Putnam discusses many of these in his study of British and Italian M.P.'s, and he develops particularly an "ideological style index" as one syndrome.[2] Milton Rokeach uses two "ideal types": the ideological or rational type, and the pragmatic or

empirical type, one distinguishing characteristic of which is the "openness" of the cognitive orientation of the individual.[3] Borrowing from
these students as well as considering what stylistic dimensions might be
most relevant for understanding leadership in the Dutch political system, we will present here first a variety of stylistic characteristics and
then pursue more intensively two dimensions that interest us particularly—cognitive generality and cognitive openness.

First we can take a look at some ways in which Dutch bureaucrats
and politicians differ in their thinking patterns. Table 33 provides the
marginals for some of these responses. It is interesting to see in such a
simple dimension as "practicality" (the reference to technical and ad-

**TABLE 33. Distribution of Elites on Selected Stylistic Dimensions
(in percentages)**

Style Characteristic Shown in Discussion of Problem Solution	Bureaucrats	M.P.'s
Emphasis on practicality		
Definitely	15	46
Somewhat	17	15
Not	68	38
Unclear	0	1
Reference to tradition		
Yes, central	7	20
Yes, but not central	13	22
No, not referred to	80	58
Optimism level		
Definitely optimistic	18	5
Somewhat optimistic	37	37
Pro/con	25	21
Somewhat pessimistic	16	18
Definitely pessimistic	4	18
Tolerance of others ideas		
Very intolerant	1	3
Somewhat intolerant	32	41
Tolerant	66	54
Unclear	1	3
Conceptual schema		
Consistent use of a single simplified conceptual schema	7	39
Much evidence of such use	17	10
Frequent use, but not in all discussions, not highly integrated	33	29
Limited use of such a schema	13	7
No evidence of a conceptual schema	19	7
Unclear: difficult to code respondent	11	7

ministrative matters in policy formulation) the considerable difference between M.P.'s and civil servants, with the former much more likely to reveal such practical concerns—46 percent compared to 15 percent. The same is true with reference to financial practicality (the costs involved in alternative policy positions). Whereas 68 percent of the M.P.'s make some such reference (42 percent clearly and definitely), only 29 percent of the higher civil servants do.

On many other stylistic dimensions the civil servant and parliamentarians are very similar in their distributions. The level of optimism about problem resolution is similar, and fairly high. And the reference to tradition is relatively low for these elites, much lower for the bureaucrats than one might have expected. On the other hand, the fact that 42 percent of the M.P.'s refer to tradition at all (20 percent seeing it as central to the analysis of policy) is noteworthy. It is a higher proportion than for any other group of western European M.P.'s. It stands in contrast also to the finding of Putnam for British and Italian M.P.'s, 90 percent of whom did not mention tradition at all.[4]

On two other stylistic dimensions the Dutch bureaucrats are rather different from those in other countries (table 34). They place much less emphasis on technical and administrative practicality (15 percent consider it very important, while 42 percent consider political feasibility very important), which is by far the lowest in these western European countries except Sweden. On the other hand, they place great emphasis on the representation of group interests in policymaking (38 percent seeing this as central), while the civil servants of other countries tend to play down the group focus (except again Sweden). Dutch M.P.'s, however, rate practicality highly (46 percent strongly emphasizing it), while also viewing groups as rather important in the policy process.

The above discussion illustrates the differences and similarities with which Dutch bureaucrats and M.P.'s cognitively approach political problems. Sometimes the contrast is considerable, for example, in the emphasis on practical considerations. Sometimes the differences are minimal or nonexistent, for example in the group focus of these elites in their discussion of the policy process. In probing for basic distinctions in cognitive style, two emerged on which we now wish to concentrate our attention. They are (1) cognitive generality and (2) cognitive openness.

Generalizers and Particularizers among Dutch Elites

In identifying and operationalizing the basic cognitive orientations elites have in dealing with political problems, we focus first on what we call

TABLE 34. Comparative Elite Differences on Selected Style Dimensions (in percentages)

Style Dimension	Top Civil Servants						Parliamentarians				
	French	Dutch	British	German	Italian	Swedish	French	Dutch	British	German	Italian
Emphasis on practicality											
Strong	40	15	54	39	51	4	25	46	24	12	39
Somewhat	48	17	28	29	25	12	35	15	32	28	36
None	12	68	18	32	24	84	40	38	44	60	25
Group focus											
Central	11	38	16	20	20	29	30	39	37	25	27
Intermediate	9	16	16	16	19	29	11	16	15	12	21
None	80	46	68	64	61	42	59	45	48	63	52
Emphasis on tradition											
Central	7	7	0	3	0	2	8	20	6	1	4
Somewhat	12	13	8	2	5	5	16	22	15	4	13
None	81	80	92	95	95	93	76	58	79	95	83

here "cognitive generality." By this we mean the tendency for leaders to utilize a general theory or set of principles as the basis for their reasoning, or, on the other hand, to work with details and the specifics of the policy situation without engaging in much generalization. Related to this is the existence (or absence) of a basic conceptual schema that is clearly and consistently utilized. This style dimension is related to but not the same as the "ideological style index" used by Putnam. He includes in his operationalization the reference to a particular ideology and to a "future utopia," elements which emerged from his factor analyses as linked to the generalization component.[5] Our usage here is more simply in terms of the inclination of a leader to be a generalizer (or particularizer) and to employ (or not employ) a basic conceptual schema in his reasoning about politics. At four points in our interview these leaders provided us with discussions of politics that permitted us to analyze and code their responses in terms of the above components, thus generating our "index of cognitive generality."

We found that civil servants consistently use a simplified conceptual schema much less frequently than do M.P.'s (39 percent for M.P.'s compared to 7 percent for civil servants—see table 33, p. 96). Bureaucrats are somewhat more likely to be preoccupied with details than are M.P.'s and thus were coded as particularizers, although actually the majority of bureaucrats are generalizers. Only 5 percent of our M.P.'s were classifiable as consistent particularizers. Combining these two sets of data, we finally classified all of our elite respondents as follows:

	High Civil Servants (N = 75)	M.P.'s (N = 41)
Extreme particularizers	7%	0
Moderate particularizers	23	15%
Generalizers	47	29
Extreme generalizers	24	56

These findings attest to the broad conceptual tendencies in political style in the Netherlands. Both sets of Dutch elites are clearly inclined to be generalizers, but this is particularly the case for M.P.'s, only 15 percent of whom really do not discuss politics as generalizers (i.e., not using frequently a general theoretical or conceptual standpoint) and 56 percent of whom are "extreme generalizers."[6]

Dutch elites scored highest in western Europe (and the United States) in their tendency to generalize and use conceptual orientations. For example, while 80 percent of the British civil servants, 65 percent of the German, and 71 percent of the Swedish show no real evidence of utilizing a conceptual scheme, only a third of Dutch top civil servants do not.

The linkage between these conceptual styles and other orientations to politics are important to note. For both M.P.'s and civil servants we note that the extreme generalizers have distinctive views about the role of conflict in the system, the importance of political solutions to problems, and the desirability of important (even radical) changes in the system (table 35).

We find among the top bureaucrats a group of generalizers who do, as the M.P.'s do, approve of conflict much more than the particularizers do. They are less likely than M.P.'s to talk about radical change or the importance of political considerations, but they do emphasize politics and change more than the particularizers in the bureaucracy do. When asked about the traits and qualities that are important in the civil service, the extreme generalizers are also more likely to talk about policymaking aspects of the bureaucratic job.

M.P.'s, even more than top bureaucrats, show a consistent picture of orientations linked to the generalizing-particularizing styles (see table 36). On many orientations, thus, this stylistic long-term dimension in leaders' approach to politics seems to be relevant. The M.P. generalizers are program oriented in their thinking, are more willing to take extreme positions, and tend to be liberal ideologically. One gets the image of them as liberal interventionists who believe in conflict, who indeed feel that polarization is not all that bad in a society like that of the Netherlands, if it is associated with broad perspectives, basic program concerns, and changing the system. The image of the particularizers, on the other hand, is that of the conservative, status

TABLE 35. Linkage of Style to Other Political Orientations
         (in percentages)

Elite Orientations	M.P.'s		Civil Servants		
	Extreme General-izers	Others	Extreme General-izers	Moderate General-izers	Particu-larizers
Conflict is good for the system	62	35	59	31	38
Major or radical changes needed	52	11	33	3	5
Political rather than technical considerations are more important in dealing with social and economic affairs	65	29	33	30	14

quo oriented leader who has short-term goals, is much more worried about conflict, opposes extremism, and believes much less in politics than in technology and technocracy for the solution of problems. This is not to say that either type is more or less able to come up with specific proposals for dealing with problems, nor that one or the other type is more successful at governance, nor that one or the other type is more competent. When in power, leaders of each style may be effective representatives or administrators. But their approaches to problems seem to differ considerably. They work with different views about the system and they reason about political problems in strikingly different ways.

What background variables correlate with differences in style—do social and political environments seem to be at all related? Our data suggest that for M.P.'s the type of milieu to which they have been exposed may be very important. Most obvious is the tendency for M.P.'s of the partisan Left to be extreme generalizers—73 percent compared to about one-third for the deputies of confessional and right-wing parties. Further, age seems to be a factor (60 percent of the younger groups are generalizers compared to 40 percent of the older cadre). Most interesting is the finding that the Catholic deputies are least inclined to be generalizers—11 percent compared to 75 percent of the Protestants and 60 percent of those professing no religion. There are some clear distinctions, thus, by age, party, and religion among M.P.'s. This is by no means so for the bureaucrats. Differences by age cohort do not exist, party affiliation seems irrelevant, and although Catholics again are the most infrequent generalizers, religious differences are very minimal. Above all, one notes that for all social background subcatego-

TABLE 36. Linkage between M.P. Political Style and Other Attitudes toward Politics (in percentages)

Attitudes	Extreme Generalizers	Less Inclined to Be Generalizers
Talk in general terms only about the solution to the most important problem	52	29
Emphasize the program of the government rather than its efficiency	90	56
Inclined to see politics as concerned with long-range, rather than short-term, goals	95	44
Take the conservative position on the issue of state intervention in the society and economy	5	47
Feel that one should avoid extreme positions in political controversies	37	76

ries (except Catholicism) M.P.'s are much more frequently generalizers than bureaucrats, suggesting the superior importance of position and career for socialization to these cognitive styles.

The generalizers among both the politicans and administrators are somewhat more in contact with citizens, party leaders, interest group representatives, and other political leaders, but the differences are not large. Among the bureaucrats contacts with M.P.'s are more likely for generalizer civil servants than for the particularizers (28 percent compared to 10 percent). Similarly, 39 percent of the extreme generalizers see client group representatives weekly, while only 5 percent of the particularizers do. On the other hand, being a particularizer is related to more frequent interaction within the bureaucracy. Interestingly, our data also reveal that M.P.'s who are extreme generalizers are less likely to have weekly contacts with civil servants (23 percent) than do those inclined to more particularizing (41 percent), suggesting again that styles may be associated with interaction subcultures.

Does being a generalizer mean that a political or administrative leader is not concerned with practical matters? Not necessarily. At various points in the interview our respondents could discuss policies in terms of technical, administrative, or financial practicality, or the political feasibility of solutions to problems. We constructed an index based on these responses, classifying each leader as not concerned with practical considerations, somewhat concerned, or definitely concerned. If we cross-analyze this with the stylistic dimension used here, we find the distributions set forth in table 37.

It is significant that while they are generalizers (or extreme generalizers), the majority of Dutch elites are also mindful of practical considerations. The "fantasts," or theoreticians, with no concern for the pragmatic aspects of politics are relatively few in the bureaucracy, but

TABLE 37.   Cognitive Generality and the "Practicality" Dimension (in percentages)

	Bureaucrats			M.P.'s		
	Particu- larizers	General- izers	Extreme General- izers	Particu- larizers	General- izers	Extreme General- izers
Practical in orientation	22	40	20	10	10	37
Not concerned with practical considerations	7	7	4	5	19	19
			100%			100%

more numerous among the M.P.'s. The pragmatic generalizers outnumber them, however, in the Parliament 47 percent to 38 percent,
and in the bureaucracy 60 percent to 11 percent. This is one contrast
important to note in comparing the two elite structures. The other
contrast is intrastructural—the existence of pragmatic particularizers
and practical-minded generalists, as well as nonpragmatic theoreticians
within each elite structure. Within the Parliament these differences in
style and orientation seem particularly apparent.

Dogmatists and Compromisers among Dutch Elites

A second basic cognitive style dimension is the rigidity and intolerance, or flexibility and tolerance, with which one holds one's beliefs
and relates one's own positions to those of others. As Rokeach has put
it, this is the question of "open mind" versus the "closed mind." While
many specific characteristics and components of these stylistic oppo-
sites have been identified, for our purpose we will concentrate here on
two primarily, although three codes were employed:

1. *Tolerance of ideas:* the willingness to entertain opinions contrary to one's own.
2. *Inclination to compromise:* whether "in a case of conflict or
   disagreement in which one side seems to you in the right and
   the other side wrong," the side which is in the right should
   "stick to its guns" or be inclined to compromise.
3. *Compromise impossible:* whether the respondent ever referred
   to questions where compromise is impossible as a matter of
   principle.

These variables reveal significant stylistic divisions in both the bureaucracy and Parliament. About one-third of the top civil servants
and two-fifths of the M.P.'s are classified as "somewhat intolerant"
(only 1 and 3 percent, respectively, are considered "very intolerant").
As to the inclination to compromise, the distributions were:

	Bureaucrats	*M.P.'s*
Definitely compromise	35%	6%
Leans towards compromise	38	31
Pro/con	10	29
Leans toward "sticking to guns"	13	14
Definitely "sticking to guns"	4	20

Finally, only 20 percent of the civil servants mentioned questions on
which compromise was impossible, while 40 percent of the M.P.'s did.

Clearly, all three sets of data suggest that the members of Parliament were much more likely to be intransigent, intolerant, and rigid in their positions. When we combined all three types of information for all respondents into an "index of cognitive openness" we found this basic distribution:

Index of Cognitive Openness (maximum score = 12)	Bureaucrats (N = 71)	M.P.'s (N = 38)
Closed (scores 1–6)	13%	34%
Moderately open (scores 7–10)	39	37
Very open (scores 11–12)	48	29

The Dutch bureaucracy appears from this to be a relatively "open-minded" structure, certainly giving much more evidence of flexibility in opinions and willingness to recognize the need for compromise, and the *possibility* of compromise, than is the case for Dutch M.P.'s. A third of the latter appear to be "closed," dogmatic, inflexible types. Almost universally we find in our international project that bureaucrats are more likely than politicians to support compromise and to be more tolerant of the ideas of others. This runs counter to the image of the dogmatic, rigid, closed-minded bureaucrat that presumably existed in the past. On the basis of our evidence, this type of higher civil servant is in the majority in most of these countries, and in the Netherlands.

The linkage of this cognitive style dimension to other orientations is again highly suggestive. In table 38 we first look at the relationships for M.P.'s. It is significant to note that 60 percent of those M.P.'s whom we call "closed" (one-third of our sample) disagree with the

TABLE 38. Linkage between M.P. Cognitive Styles and Other Orientations (in percentages)

Orientation	Closed and Dogmatic	Moderately Open	Very Open and Tolerant
Thinks compromise is dangerous	42	21	0
Feels extremes should be avoided	41	43	80
Agrees that parties needlessly increase conflict	33	43	83
Approves of conflict in politics generally	54	54	36
Fears state intervention in the society and economy	17	14	30
Favors important or radical changes in the system	45	14	45
Strongly emphasizes partisan role	46	7	0
Emphasizes practical considerations in policymaking	85	36	45

statement that extreme positions should be avoided. They also see
compromise as dangerous more frequently. Further, a majority tend to
see conflict as necessary, normatively approve conflict, and do not see
parties as needlessly exacerbating conflict. On the other hand, 80 percent of the most open-minded M.P.'s see party conflict as dangerous.

In addition, the closed-minded M.P.'s are somewhat more likely
to be liberals on an issue such as state intervention in the society, and
45 percent are also interested in important or radical changes in the
system. The most open-minded M.P.'s are also interested in major
changes in the system but they are not as likely to be liberals. The
dogmatic M.P. reveals a somewhat special pattern—opposed to compromise, not worried about extremism, approving of conflict and party
conflict particularly, taking liberal policy positions, and supporting
radical change as enthusiastically as will the open-minded M.P. Further, the closed-minded M.P. emphasizes his partisan role a great deal.
Finally, one should note also that the closed M.P. is very practical
minded in his discussion of problems. He is, then, often a liberal,
partisan dogmatist who may be very pragmatic about political problem
solving.

These findings do point consistently in the direction of more dogmatism among those who are more liberal in their ideological positions. It is not the conservatives in the Dutch Parliament who exhibit
the greatest intransigence and inflexibility in cognitive style (table 39).
It is true, again, however, that in the top bureaucracy it is not the
conservatives in ideological orientation who are the *most likely* to be
closed-minded.

On certain other orientations one finds open-minded civil servants
to reveal distinctive positions compared to the dogmatists (table 40).
In some respects these are not the same as for M.P.'s. For example,
the closed-minded civil servants do not feel that "extreme positions
should be avoided"—both closed and open types favor compromise

**TABLE 39. Linkage between Liberal and Radical Ideology and
Cognitive Style of M.P.'s (in percentages)**

Cognitive Style	Position on State Intervention in Society and Economy			Position on the Need for Change in the System		
	Liberal	Inter-mediate	Conser-vative	Radical	Inter-mediate	Status Quo
Closed	43	27	29	46	29	25
Moderately open	43	40	29	15	53	37.5
Open	14	33	42	39	18	37.5

and wish to avoid extremism (at the 80 to 90 percent level). On the other hand, the dogmatists among the top civil servants are very concerned about conflict, more so than the open types, which again is at odds with the findings for dogmatist M.P.'s, a majority of whom welcomed conflict.

What stands out for the top bureaucrats is the linkage of their open or closed cognitive style to their relative view of the civil service vis-à-vis the party system and the Parliament, as well as their own role perceptions. The closed bureaucratic types are the ones who still see the civil service as the saving grace of the system—78 percent arguing for its priority over parties and Parliament, compared to 38 percent of the open types. The closed types are also more elitist in opposing citizen participation and in being critical of parties as needlessly increasing conflict (100 percent of the closed types espoused this position). They also emphasize the trustee role (representing national interests) in their bureaucratic role perception. One must note finally too that they are inclined to be practical minded, proposing specific solutions to problems, a finding which was also generally true for the closed-minded M.P.'s.

We have, then, two sets of dogmatists (and two sets of open-minded types) among Dutch elites in the bureaucracy and Parliament.

TABLE 40. Linkage between Cognitive Styles of Bureaucrats and Other Orientations (in percentages)

	Closed and Dogmatic	Moderately Open	Very Open and Tolerant
Feels civil service more important to effective policymaking than the parties or Parliament	78	40	38
Opposes increased citizen participation	56	32	35
Sees conflict as dangerous	67	52	59
Feels parties uselessly exacerbate conflict	100	68	74
Presents specific proposals or alternatives to deal with the problems facing country	50	25	24
Emphasizes the trustee role (as representative of the national interest) as very important	44	18	29

The dogmatists in the Parliament are more numerous. They are liberal, often radical, favor conflict, emphasize the role of parties in the system, and do not argue strongly for compromise. The dogmatists in the bureaucracy are less inclined to be liberal (although the relationship is a poor one here), they are not radical, are very much in favor of compromise, and desire to avoid extremism. Above all, the civil servant dogmatist is critical of conflict and parties, and views the role of the civil service as superior to that of Parliament.

Basically, it appears that these two sets of dogmatists developed different orientations as a result of their conditioning and socialization in their different institutional milieus. Being open in cognitive style, or being dogmatic and closed, tends to mean something different in the bureaucracy than in the Parliament. And yet the constellation of linkages of orientations to styles does seem to have a rationale meaningful for that institutional milieu. The antiparty attitude of bureaucratic dogmatists compared to the proparty attitude of the parliamentary dogmatists is understandable, as is the procompromise view of the open bureaucrat compared to the relatively skeptical attitude to compromise of the open M.P. The dogmatists in both institutional settings represent perhaps in a sense the extreme types—the zealot parliamentarian and the Weberian bureaucrat.

What types of environments or backgrounds seem relevant for explaining dogmatism or the lack of it in elites? Our data suggest that party, age, and length of elite career may have some influence. Thus, we find that leftist partisans and the confessionals are least dogmatic among the M.P.'s—20 percent to 30 percent, compared to 50 percent of right-wing deputies. Bureaucrats who support left-wing parties also tend to be less dogmatic, but the differences are not as great. Young M.P.'s tend to be much more dogmatic than older M.P.'s—a striking contrast of 50 percent for those below the age of thirty-eight compared to none for the oldest cadre, who were fifty-one years old and over. But length of service seems to be the most consistent factor for both sets of elites: of the M.P.'s who have joined the political elite in the past few years, 55 percent could be classified as closed-minded, while only 22 percent of those who have held elite status for many years fit into this category. Among civil servants, 11 percent of the newcomers are closed-minded, as compared to 7 percent of the "old timers." This suggests that socialization to role in both Parliament and the bureaucracy may lead to more open-mindedness and tolerance. In the discussion of roles earlier we noted this tendency also for civil servants, since our oldest bureaucrats were not inclined to hold the most rigid Weberian conceptions of their roles. However, a constraint on this obviously is partisanism, with leftist partisans, particularly in the Parliament, tending to be ideologues, extreme generalizers (as we saw earlier), and open-minded; right-wing partisans are more likely to be particular-izers, moderate ideologues, and more closed-minded. Experience in a role, therefore, may lead to more open-mindedness, in the absence of strong partisan and ideological controls.

The finding that increasing open-mindedness in elite style may correspond to length of elite experience appears to be salutary for a consociational system which places a heavy premium on tolerance. Our findings on elite sociometric networks of those who were dogmatists and tolerant in style also suggest that over time there are forces at work that tend to open up the Dutch system rather than close it. Thus, we find that the contact patterns of the dogmatist M.P.'s are as activ-ist, if not more so, as the contacts of those who are open-minded already. Four-fifths of the M.P. dogmatists are in weekly contact with party leaders (including those of other parties than their own), 50 percent are in weekly contact with interest group leaders, and 75 per-cent normally are in contact with citizens (true of almost all M.P.'s). These proportions (aside from citizen contact) are 30 percent higher than for the open-minded M.P. Thus, the young, ideological, closed-minded M.P. is subjected to a great diversity of interactions with other actors of the system and is not closed off from the system. This condi-tion would appear to be functional to the achievement of integration and other operational goals of consociationalism.

The Overlapping Relationship of the Two Style Dimensions

Having analyzed two basic political style concepts and noted their incidence and relationship to other orientations, we might now com-bine the data for the two dimensions and observe the presence of stylistic types in the Dutch elite population. When we do this for M.P.'s we see the basic distribution revealed in figure 10. Dutch M.P.'s tend to cluster somewhat, but there is a fairly even distribution except for the bottom row of extreme generalizers, who are closed or moderately open. The preponderance is not in the direction of ex-tremely open and extremely generalizing—only 13 percent fit this cate-gory. On the other hand, the very dogmatic particularizers are few in number also, only 8 percent. There is a significant group of dogmatic generalists, however, who may be more of a problem for the resolution of conflicts. They constitute 26 percent and are perhaps the potential (or actual) polarizing elements in the Parliament.

Perhaps the crucial group in functional terms consists of the four groups in the lower right-hand section of the figure, the moderately open and very open generalizers, who constitute 58 percent of the total M.P. group. These are deductive types who work with theories, reason about political problems on the basis of principles, and who also are tolerant of others ideas and are willing to compromise. These are more likely to be the accommodationist politicians in the classic sense which, according to the view of scholars of the system, the Dutch system has needed. It is interesting to note in this connection that the open-minded M.P.'s take views about the resolution of conflict that seem to be accommodationist also. For example, as compared to those M.P.'s classified as closed-minded generalizers, twice as many very open-minded generalizers believe extremes should be avoided (80 percent versus 41 percent); over half see conflict as reconcilable (54 percent versus 36 percent); but only half as many see conflict as bad for the system (18 percent versus 31 percent), and only half as many see consensus as typical (9 percent to 17 percent). Added to the basic distributions presented for the two style dimensions, these data suggest a set of M.P.'s who tend to see conflict as typical, reconcilable, and probably good for the system, and who utilize basic theories and principles in developing solutions to problems and resolving conflicts. Above all, these M.P.'s seem to be open to other ideas, to compromise, while they interact very regularly with a wide variety of actors in the system. For approximately 60 percent of the M.P.'s these stylistic tendencies and approaches seem applicable, approaches which to a large extent meet the requirements of elite accommodation that a consociational democracy needs.

COGNITIVE OPENNESS DIMENSION

	Closed	Moderately open	Very open
Particularizers	8%	5%	3%
Generalizers	5%	8%	13%
Extreme generalizers	21%	24%	13%

COGNITIVE GENERALITY DIMENSION

N = 38 (100%)

Fig. 10. Stylistic variations among Dutch M.P.'s

The basic distributions on the two style dimensions for the Dutch top bureaucrats are in certain respects different. The picture appears as figure 11. There are actually fewer dogmatic particularizers among bureaucrats than among M.P.'s (4 percent) and more at the other extreme who are very tolerant generalizers (15 percent). The total number of particularizers, as noted earlier, is larger, however (28 percent compared to 16 percent for the M.P.'s). One notes also that there is no sizable group of dogmatic generalizers in the bureaucracy (only 9 percent), and thus the probability of polarization in the top civil service by theoreticians unwilling to listen to, work with, or compromise problems with colleagues, in the bureaucracy or outside it, is minimized.

Again, one must note the critical four groups in the lower right-hand section of the figure. There we find the 63 percent of the top bureaucrats who are generalizers, but generalizers who are open-minded and tolerant in their interaction with others. Again, the linkage of conflict perceptions with the openness dimension supports the view. All top bureaucrats are very aware of conflict, and almost 90 percent of the open types see it as more typical than consensus. Further, the open-minded bureaucrat is inclined to see conflict as reconcilable—only 24 percent say conflicts are definitely irreconcilable. Although bureaucrats are more concerned than M.P.'s about political conflict, they do feel solutions can be found. This is particularly true of the open-minded types. We have here in the Dutch bureaucracy, therefore, a set of fairly tolerant deductive types or generalizers who are reality oriented about conflict and bring to its resolution theoretical

COGNITIVE OPENNESS DIMENSION

	Closed	Moderately open	Very open
Particularizers	4%	17%	7%
Generalizers	6%	17%	25%
Extreme generalizers	3%	6%	15%

COGNITIVE GENERALITY DIMENSION

N = 71 (100%)

Fig. 11. Stylistic variations for senior bureaucrats

schema and approaches while accepting the need for compromise and being willing to listen to others. This also suggests that if accommodationism is necessary in the bureaucracy it apparently exists in the Netherlands. Indeed, in contrast to Parliament, where there is a sizable minority of liberal and closed-minded generalizers who are interested in radical change and not interested in compromise, the Dutch top bureaucracy looks less polarized in these stylistic terms.

We have here two structures with two sets of elites employing a variety of cognitive styles in their approaches to Dutch problems. There are dogmatic inductive types and open-minded generalizers, there are intolerant generalizers of both liberal and conservative persuasion, and tolerant particularizers. But predominantly we find in these two elite structures open-minded generalizers who, although they do not agree on many aspects of the Dutch political process, seem to approach the resolution of problems in stylistically similar ways of thinking. And these open-minded generalizers appear also to be the performers who are most frequently in contact with other system actors, from the citizen level to the ministerial level. Overall, despite polarization potentialities, this does appear functionally salutary for whatever Dutch accommodationism is still needed today.

NOTES

1. Robert D. Putnam, *The Beliefs of Politicians: Ideology, Conflict, and Democracy in Britain and Italy* (New Haven: Yale University Press, 1973), p. 35.
2. Ibid., pp. 34–35.
3. Milton Rokeach, *The Open and Closed Mind* (New York: Basic Books, 1960).
4. Putnam, *Beliefs of Politicians*, p. 41.
5. Ibid., p. 43.
6. Because of this skewed distribution of M.P.'s, we will dichotomize the group for further analysis, combining all who are moderate particularizers and moderate generalizers into one group and contrasting them with the extreme generalizers.

CHAPTER 6

Ideology and Values: Views about Society and Politics

Modern Western societies have been engaged in a continuing series of critical decisions about growth, change, and development since World War II. The increase in national wealth, industrial production, and standard of living, as well as changes in the social structure, have stimulated much controversy over the direction and content of desired societal development as well as over the involvement of the government in such development. Concerns about the role of government usually are focused less on *whether* the state should take a primary role in promoting change, than on the *extent* of such intervention, the *goals* of interventionist policies, the *pace* of the development, and the *process* by which decisions are made. Furthermore, the conflict that such controversy has triggered between interest groups, regions, classes, and parties is linked to the values that the public and the elites have about the ends of political action and public policy. These values are changing. There are important disagreements then, about the role of the state and the nature of policy goals, about the meaning and consequence of political conflict. In this sense there is no "end of ideology."

Dutch society in the postwar period reflects this basic image. It has been known in the past as accommodative—deeply divided at the mass and group interest levels, but united because of a historically based capacity for consensus building among its elites. But this society has been changing, in its segmented structure and in the character of its consensus. Since World War II it has had to cope with most of the same basic decisions on social and economic policy as other Western societies, in the process rebuilding a country devastated by the war. Since the sixties, in contrast to its historic consensual politics, it has witnessed the appearance of more open conflict and ideological debate, at both the mass and the elite levels, conflict that is less easily managed now with the decline of the politics of accommodation.

The attitudes and values of Dutch elites about policy options are basic to understanding how that political system has been responding to its crises, and they provide indications as to how they will be handled in the future. In the functioning of the body politic, elites are the main producers of ideas. Above all, their basic views, their ideological positions, and their values form the framework for the roles they adopt and the behavior they engage in. Consequently, our analysis aims at understanding them as top actors whose beliefs influence authoritative decisions about rules of the game and about substantive policy questions.

Our major queries in this chapter are:

1. What are the basic ideological positions of Dutch leaders in three respects: the extent of acceptance or rejection of the social order; the extent of support for an expanding or contracting role of government in the economy and society; and the degree of tolerance or intolerance of social and political conflict?

2. What is the value hierarchy of Dutch elites? What goals for the political system rank highest with them? Do value concerns overlap with ideological orientations, or are they today distinct from them?

3. How much convergence or polarization is there in the beliefs of administrators and M.P.'s?

4. What background and career variables seem to be linked to ideological and value positions?

5. What are the consequences of elite beliefs for other orientations that elites have toward politics, political groups, or other actors in the system?

Our use of the term *ideology* here is not complicated. By the political ideology of elites we mean their attitudes towards the *present* social and political order and process—attitudes based on an analysis of how the system *is* performing as well as their evaluative preferences as to how it *should* function. We assume these beliefs are integrated, comprehensive, coherent, that they have a structure, and that they can be characterized in a dimensional sense (on a continuum from left to right, liberal to conservative, or similar types of dimensions.) We assume that they derive from a basic commitment and/or philosophy, but this may indeed be more latent than manifest. We also assume that their beliefs about how the society *should* function are linked to their perceptions about how it *does* function and their evaluations about *how well* it functions.

Values as discussed here refers to the goals for society for the

future that they as leaders personally prefer, that they think should
rank highest in the concerns of society and politics because they represent the greatest needs of people in the system. These are their priorities (such as material welfare, or social justice, or liberty, etc.). These
comments about ideology and values are similar to those of other
scholars. Some are more inclined to emphasize "moral beliefs" (Shils),
or the actions and practices of elites (Apter), or the styles of thinking
about political matters (Sartori and Putnam).[1] We focus primarily here
on *what* elites think about their political world in preferential terms—
should the system change, and if so, how radically; should the government intervene more or less, and plan more or less for such change (if
it is desired); how conflictual does the governing process have to be? If
the system should change, toward what goals? These are basic ideological and value questions and concerns facing elites. They probe
fundamental normative orientations about societal and governmental
form and action.

Attitudes toward Society Generally

We begin our discussion by analyzing the views of these elites concerning the social order—the extent to which they accept the present social
order as well as the manner in which they would go about changing it.
One might assume that as elites they are part of this order and would
defend it heartily. But, on the other hand, they are also leaders, have
connections to parties and groups that function in a society in a period
of great change, and they are by no means wedded to the status quo.
These latter expectations are to some extent borne out by the data
(table 41). Our coders were asked to interpret each interview in terms
of the degree of acceptance of the social order, the amount or level of
change desired in the system, and the mode of change.

Senior administrators are much less critical in their views about
the present social order than are M.P.'s. Whereas one-third of the
M.P.'s are so critical as essentially to reject their own social and political order, this is true of only 7 percent of the top civil servants. This is
a striking difference. And it is corroborated when one codes the
amount of change desired in the structure of society and government—
51 percent of the M.P.'s advocate important or major changes, compared to 25 percent of the senior administrators. These are not revolutionary elites, however. The mode of change desired is not by revolution but, for almost 30 percent of the M.P.'s, by radical action within
the present system. Civil servants are neither revolutionary nor radical;
they prefer change, if it is necessary, by moderate means. In short, a

minority of 25 percent to 40 percent of Dutch senior civil servants want some change in the social and political order, but they advocate moderate approaches. A majority of Dutch M.P.'s, however, desire significant changes, and up to 30 percent want radical action to achieve social change.

These types of findings are paralleled in our findings for other countries. For example, on the question of the acceptance or rejection of the social order (item A in table 41), bureaucrats are generally more supportive of the social order in Germany (100 percent), England (95 percent), and the Netherlands (93 percent) and M.P.'s in the three countries are more critical (75 percent, 69 percent, and 64 percent, respectively).

These differences among elites are clearly linked to party preference (table 42). It is a consistent and striking finding that those on the Left are critical of the social order and seek reforms in it. This is particularly so in Parliament, where 59 percent of the left-wing M.P.'s are outspoken critics, whose discussions about the problems facing the government clearly occurred in a context of rejection of the current system. On the other hand, very few of the confessional and right-wing deputies were outspokenly critical, although 50 percent wished to see reforms in the system.

TABLE 41.   Views of Elites on the Social and Political
            Order (in percentages)

	Bureaucrats	M.P.'s
About present social order		
Passionate rejection	0	7
Rejects; reforms proposed	7	29
Accepts; reforms proposed	36	42
Accepts; no reforms proposed	57	22
Passionate affirmation of		
existing order	1	0
About amount of change desired		
Major change	0	12
Important change	25	39
Minor change	21	27
No change	54	22
About mode of change preferred		
Revolutionary	0	2
Radical (major, rapid, directed)	4	27
Moderate action	57	54
Laissez faire (natural social forces the		
primary mechanism for change)	19	2
No change desired	20	15

Among bureaucrats, only 30 percent of the Left were unquali-
fiedly supportive, compared to 65 percent and 70 percent of the confessional and right-wing partisans, respectively. This Left versus Right
contrast suggests a polarization *within* these elite structures as well as
between them. The rightist partisans in Parliament and the bureaucracy
are very congruent. The confessionals in Parliament are less supportive
of the system overall, but the difference at the level of rejection is not
large. The leftist partisans, while the most critical in both structures,
reveal a considerable difference at the rejection level. That is, 59 percent of the left-wing M.P.'s take the basic position that there is something fundamentally wrong with the social order, while only 15 percent
of the leftist administrators do. The socialism which prevails among
bureaucratic elites is of a much more moderate version than one finds
in Parliament.

Attitudes toward the Role of Government

Historically and today, a central ideological test is the individual's
belief about the proper role of government. This is a fundamental issue
in political theory and presumably also in popular and elite orientations toward politics. The issue is: To what extent, if at all, should the
state intervene in the social and economic order in the solution of
society's problems? In the Netherlands, as elsewhere, the controversy
over the expansion of governmental action, the inclusiveness of governmental concern, and the extensiveness of the impact of governmental policy has continued since World War II. The issue is not *whether,*
but *how much,* since few would argue that we should revert to a free
enterprise regime with minimal governmental intervention. Debates

TABLE 42.   **Party Preference as Linked to Attitudes toward the Social
Order (in percentages)**

	Bureaucrats			M.P.'s		
**Attitude toward
the Social Order**	Leftist
(N = 20)	Confes-
sional
(N = 17)	Right-
wing
(N = 30)	Leftist
(N = 22)	Confes-
sional
(N = 11)	Right-
wing
(N = 8)
Rejection[a]	15	6	0	59	18	0
Acceptance; reforms
needed	55	29	30	36	45	50
Acceptance; no
reforms needed	30	65	30	22	11	8

a. "Rejection" classification includes both those who do and those who do not advocate reforms
in the present order.

over subjects such as tighter control of investment in industry, over land acquisition and utilization, over the structural aspects of social inequality, and others bring out this basic difference of opinion. In a recent discussion three representatives of three different streams of opinion in the Netherlands—socialist, confessional, and liberal—illuminated the partisan differences in thinking about this basic ideological question.[2]

> *Confessional politican:* The west-European type of mixed economic order, such as has evolved in the last thirty years, has as its great advantage that it has been able to develop and accept a great variety of economic forms of organization necessary for a modern polity.

> *Liberal politician:* The most desirable economic order can best start from individually owned and profit-oriented production; this form of production should be continuously adapted to the circumstances and demands of a changing society.

> *Socialist politician:* It would be a miracle if a market economy, with profit as its main motive and inequality in standard of life as the result, could in the future serve as a basis for an economic order without growth in production and material austerity.

During our conversations with leaders they communicated their philosophies about the proper role of government in a variety of ways. They discussed the most important problem (as they identified it) facing the society and were pressed to present their ideas on its resolution. We specifically discussed with all respondents the role of government in planning. In addition we asked them to express their agreement or disagreement with a series of short answer items, one of which was: "Many of the doubts and fears about state intervention in the economy and society are justified." Finally, throughout the interview comments were often made concerning the desired role of the government in solving the problems of Dutch society. All of these constituted the basis for our interpretation of their positions.

M.P.'s are much more frequently and consistently interventionist in their attitudes to governmental action than are the senior bureaucrats (table 43). They not only are overwhelmingly in favor of the government's role, but a large proportion wish to see it expanded. Thus, 80 percent of M.P.'s favor more state involvement compared to 47 percent of the bureaucrats. The pattern was similar for elite views on the expansion of the government's role in planning for the society— 78 percent and 42 percent. This does not mean that bureaucrats tend to oppose a positive role for government in economic and social regulation. Only a small minority of perhaps 10 percent do want to return to laissez-faire. But a not insignificant minority of senior bureaucrats have fears and doubts (32 percent) about such intervention, favor the present balance of state regulation (43 percent), or are not clearly in favor of the role of government in planning (28 percent). These senior civil servants are, therefore, much more divided than are M.P.'s on this ideological question. On an index measuring state intervention in society, constructed from the items in this analysis, 25 percent of the M.P.'s were strongly and consistently in favor of an expanded government role while only 9 percent of the bureaucrats were. There is only a minority of M.P.'s (15 percent) who oppose the level and extent of governmental intervention.

The attitudes of Dutch elites must be seen in comparison with those of other countries. If we calculate the proportion of these elite

TABLE 43.   Beliefs about the Role of Government in
            Society (in percentages)

Attitude Item	Bureaucrats	M.P.'s
"Many of the doubts and fears about state intervention in the economy and society are justified."	(N = 72)	(N = 42)
Strongly agree	3	7
Agree	29	14
Disagree	51	38
Strongly disagree	17	41
Extent of state involvement in society	(N = 72)	(N = 38)
For much more state involvement	8	29
For some more	39	51
Favors present balance	43	10
For some more free enterprise and individual initiatives	7	7
For much more free enterprise	3	0
Role of government in planning	(N = 68)	(N = 68)
Enthusiastically supports	35	74
In favor, but some reservations	37	17
Pro/con	19	3
Moderately opposed	6	0
Strongly opposed	3	6
Expansion of the role of government	(N = 72)	(N = 42)
Favor expansion	42	78
Pro/con	1	0
Favor contraction	18	7
Leave as is	14	10
Uncertain or not applicable	25	5

samples who favor more state involvement, we find it to be 80 percent of M.P.'s in the Netherlands, 58 percent in Italy, 48 percent in England, and 35 percent in Germany. Among bureaucrats, we find 47 percent of Dutch civil servants favor more involvement, compared to 34 percent in Italy, 27 percent in England, and 13 percent in Germany. The level of support for state involvement is highest in the Netherlands. There is consistently less enthusiasm among bureaucrats for an expanding role of the state, but Dutch bureaucrats are most supportive. Yet, on the surface at least, the conflicts between M.P.'s and senior bureaucrats may be greater in the Netherlands.

The role of political party affiliation in explaining these attitudinal positions is presumably central, because these are the main themes parties concentrate on and with which they seek to make themselves distinctive. The differences between M.P.'s and bureaucrats stand out again, however (table 44). In the bureaucracy, affiliation with Left parties is not the basic determinant of liberal ideologies. In Parliament, although the socialist M.P.'s are certainly the most interventionist ideologically, only 30 percent are consistently at the high end of our index continuum. The confessional M.P.'s are more liberal than confessional civil servants. Among both confessional and rightist party M.P.'s there are sizable minorities who rank high on our index—about one fifth fall at the interventionist end of the continuum. This suggests considerable ideological diversity by party among M.P.'s, but also indicates that both the Right and the Left want governmental involvement, though not necessarily for the same purpose.

Party differences in elite attitudes for the Netherlands, in comparison to other European nations, are distinctive. As an illustration, if we look at the responses of elites to the same item used cross-nationally on governmental intervention in the society, we note the following comparisons:

	Percentage Favoring More Intervention	
	M.P.'s	*Civil Servants*
In the Socialist party:		
Netherlands	94	92
Britain	80	82
Germany	77	72
In the Conservative party		
(or groups of parties):		
Netherlands	50	71
Britain	7	51
Germany	19	23

TABLE 44. Relationship between Party Affiliation and Position on Government Intervention (in percentages)

Position on Government Intervention Index	Bureaucrats				M.P.'s			
	Leftist	Confessional	Right-wing	Total	Leftist	Confessional	Right-wing	Total
High (favors government role)	10	0	13	9	30	17	22	25
Middle	70	47	57	51	70	58	44	60
Low (opposes government role)	20	53	30	40	0	25	33	15
Total	100	100	100	100	100	100	99	100

Socialist M.P.'s are interventionists, and the ideological distance between them and the conservatives is great. But in aggregate terms the Dutch elites seem less polarized than in Britain and Germany. Among civil servants, however, the distance by party affiliation is not as consistently large, and there is a surprising interventionism among civil servants of conservative party orientation in two countries (Netherlands and Britain). The importance of party varies therefore both by elite position and by system.

Orientations toward Conflict

A basic question is whether the political elites look at the system in terms of a consensus model or a conflict model. Historically the Dutch political culture has manifested elements of both types of models. The socialist Left, for example, operated with a class conflict model prior to World War II, but in the aftermath of the war embarked on a more cooperative program of participation with the other parties in reconstruction. Both the political Center and Right have demonstrated at times tendencies reflecting both models. Although there are structures like the Social Economic Council, which facilitated political and social cooperation, in recent years there is evidence of the decline of a commitment to these forms of consensus. One notices today more direct confrontation between labor and management, new political parties challenging old parties, and evidence of more polarization between political leaders and groups. There are those who have argued that in recent years conflict is more prominent in political life than consensus or harmony.[3] Keeping these general observations in mind, what does our study reveal on this question?

Our first observation is that respondents speak rather freely about conflicts, with a heavy emphasis on conflict between socioeconomic classes or interest groups. At least 70 percent of the senior civil servants mention class and group conflict, with a third focusing almost exclusively on class conflict. Further, large proportions of both M.P.'s and civil servants see conflicts as necessary. But whether necessary or not elites clearly operate with a conflict model of how the political system does in fact function (table 45). There is a small minority (15 to 17 percent) that argues that consensus is more typical, and another minority (about one-fifth) sees the process as a mix of consensus and conflict. But the majority of both sectors—54 percent of bureaucrats and 63 percent of M.P.'s—accepts as reality the "conflict whole." While there is evidence of skepticism among elites on the reconcilability of conflict, only one-fourth to one-third are pessimists. The optimists in the senior bureaucracy outnumber the pessimists but not by much; the optimists and pessimists in Parliament are evenly divided. Dutch elites are indeed preoccupied with political conflict, perceptually and normatively. Many are concerned about whether such conflict is healthy or functional. We asked them to agree or disagree with this statement, for example: "Only by social conflict can progress be achieved in modern society." The emphasis in this statement was on the essentiality of conflict for progress. M.P.'s and bureaucrats reacted differently (item C, table 45). M.P.'s tended to be supportive of conflict, but two-thirds of the bureaucrats did not see conflict as functional to social progress, a finding that is rather distinctive for the Netherlands, if comparisons are made with British and German bureaucrats. Of bureaucrats questioned, those opposed to the view that conflict is linked to progress totaled 68 percent in the Netherlands (44 percent moderately opposed, and 24 percent strongly opposed), 45 percent in Britain (30 percent moderately, 15 percent strongly), and 28 percent in Germany (19 percent moderately, 9 percent strongly). Similarly, Dutch M.P.'s are also more skeptical of the utility of conflict than are German and British M.P.'s. Only 30 percent of the latter responded negatively, compared to 49 percent of the Dutch.

If, again, we analyze conflict beliefs by party membership or affil-

TABLE 45. Attitudes toward Conflict in the System (in percentages)

	Bureaucrats	M.P.'s
Perception of conflict		
Consensus is typical	15	17
Pro/con (both are common)	22	20
Conflict is typical	54	63
Evaluation of conflict		
Conflict is very healthy	9	14
Conflict is healthy (with reservations)	39	47
Pro/con	37	22
Conflict is sick (weakens society)	12	14
Conflict is very sick (dangerous)	3	3
Views of conflict in relation to social progress		
Conflict is functional (strongly in favor)	6	10
Conflict is functional (moderately in favor)	26	42
Conflict is not functional (moderately opposed)	44	32
Conflict is not functional (strongly opposed)	24	17
Views on reconcilability of conflict		
Irreconcilable	27	36
Pro/con	19	22
Reconcilable	54	42

iation, the contrast between the socialist M.P.'s and those of the Center or Right is striking. Thus, over 70 percent of the Labor party deputies feel conflict is healthy and functional, while one-fourth or less of the conservatives do, with approximately one-third of the confessionals supportive of conflict. The differences among civil servants are not very great, however. Dutch civil servants of whatever party are not inclined to see conflict as functional.

The Relevance of Ideology for Other Attitudes

The findings on elite ideology are fairly straightforward. We found differences both *within* and *between* the elite sectors, sometimes sizable contrasts. Thus, concerning the attitude of M.P.'s toward the social order we find a confrontation between socialists, who were critical (59 percent), and right-wing partisans, all of whom accept the system. Even among civil servants it is a contrast of 70 percent (socialists favoring reforms) to 30 percent (right-wing supporters favoring reforms). Not all the findings are as striking as these. On the role of the government in the economy there is less extreme disagreement in the bureaucracy. And as to elite views on conflict, the conflict model is the perceptual reality for the majority of both elite groups, while, on the other hand, both elites split internally in their normative evaluations of conflict.

Elite ideological views, in the three senses in which we have used that term here, seem to be linked to some of their other attitudes. We can illustrate that with a look at their views about citizen participation in the political process (table 46). In both sets of elites those who approve

TABLE 46.   Elite Ideology as Related to Attitudes about Citizen Role

| | Percentage Supporting the Idea of Increased Citizen Participation | |
	Bureaucrats	M.P.'s
Evaluation of conflict		
Healthy	50	68
Pro/con	20	75
Harmful	30	33
View of state intervention in society		
Favor strongly	73	79
Favor	38	60
Oppose	13	33

of political conflict and are interventionists as to the role of the state
are most likely to favor the increased involvement of citizens in the
political process. The differences are considerable here (a 46-point
difference for M.P.'s and a 60-point difference for civil servants).

There is a cluster of attitudes here that at least occur together.
One is tempted to infer from these findings that the type of attitude
illustrated by the question of citizen participation is a derivative of a
more basic liberal or conservative ideological position about society
and politics. Another part of this cluster is a leader's attitude toward
interest group conflict and party conflict. Those who are liberals in
their philosophy about state intervention in the society are also more
sanguine about group conflict. We find as follows:

	State Interventionism Positions		
	Favors Strongly	*Favors*	*Opposes*
Group conflict harmful			
civil servants	8%	11%	43%
M.P.'s	0	6	67
Parties unnecessarily			
conflictual			
civil servants	17	35	50
M.P.'s	0	13	56

Again, a clear linkage exists between basic ideological positions and
other more particular normative views about the functioning of subsystems in the polity. Ideology is suggested by these data as probably
central for elite perceptions and behavior.

Finally, it is worthwhile noting that Dutch elites do not differ
fundamentally from elites in other Western systems. Dutch M.P.'s
seem rather more liberal in the interventionist role for government,
and Dutch civil servants seem more negative about the functionality of
conflict. But, as elsewhere, M.P.'s are consistently more critical of the
social order, more interested in the expansion of the government's
role, and less worried about conflict than senior bureaucrats. These
general observations appear to have cross-systemic validity.

The Value Priorities of Dutch Elites

The basic goals and values of elites, and citizens, are as important as
their ideologies, their views of society, or any of the other perspectives
that we discussed earlier. Indeed, there are those scholars who would
argue that values are possibly more important in understanding human

behavior than other orientations.[4] Certainly if the value priorities of elites were in sharp conflict or diverged radically from those of the public, one should be alert at least to the possibility of conflictual and unrepresentative approaches to the solution of problems. For senior bureaucrats and legislative politicians one might well expect divergent value priorities due to different political and social backgrounds, role socialization, and contacts in the elite setting. Our elite interviews were coded to determine "the implicit top priority of the respondent throughout the entire interview." That is, we sought on the basis of our discussions of the critical problems facing the society and their resolution, as well as in the discussions of various aspects of the political process (the role of parties, the nature and consequences of conflict, the position of citizens in the system, etc.), to derive the dominant value of each person. These could be called "situational" value priorities since they dealt with immediate normative considerations. The coders used a set of value categories based on earlier research.

One of the most distinctive findings for Dutch elites is their emphasis on a value that we called "belongingness" or "community." Both the M.P.'s and senior civil servants utilize this value orientation much more than in other countries (table 47). Approximately one-third of Dutch elites do, compared to a mean of 4 or 5 percent in other European countries. As an isolated finding this might be considered questionable. But when we place that finding alongside other differences in value priorities a pattern emerges that has some consistency. First, in table 47 one notices that the value of "material welfare" is much more prevalent for elites in other European systems than in the Netherlands, and on the other hand "social justice and equality" receive more emphasis in the Netherlands. Further, political institutional "reform" is a priority preoccupying other European elites much more. If one combines the two "bourgeois" values and contrasts them with so-called "postindustrial values" as well as "reform," one sees the distinctiveness of the Dutch elite data.

A direct comparison with the British elite data highlights the contrast. British senior civil servants are committed to material welfare values—56 percent compared to 7 percent for the Dutch; British M.P.'s are somewhat less so but still much more than the Dutch—35 percent compared to 3 percent. On the other hand, there is less commitment to social justice and equality—5 percent of the bureaucrats and 22 percent of the M.P.'s in Britain place this value highest in their value hierarchy, as compared to 12 percent and 38 percent in the Netherlands.

A second point that should be made is that these elite differences

TABLE 47. Value Priorities of Dutch Elites Compared to Other Western European Nations (in percentages)

Value	Bureaucrats			M.P.'s		
	Netherlands (N = 68)	Europe[a] (N = 723)	Difference[b]	Netherlands (N = 37)	Europe[a] (N = 377)	Difference[b]
Material welfare	7	38 ⎫	−21	3	18 ⎫	−13
Security, safety	18	8 ⎭		8	6 ⎭	
Institutional reform	3	23	−20	8	28	−20
Social justice, equality	12	9	+ 3	38	26	+12
Knowledge	12	8		3	4	
Morality	7	3		5	4	
Liberty	4	6		3	10	
Belongingness, community	37	5	+32	32	4	+28

a. These are means for elites in Britain, France, Germany, Italy, and Sweden.
b. Plus (+) means Dutch rate value higher; minus (−) means they rate it lower.

by nation seem to be reflections of, or congruent with, the differences in mass value and goal preferences. The data from Inglehart's earlier study suggest again that the Dutch public is in certain respects different from the rest of Europe (table 48). Dutch citizens in 1973 (the time we did our elite study) were less interested in economic goals than Britain, Germany, or indeed for European countries on the average. They were more interested in postmaterialist goals. While 19 percent fewer Dutch citizens mentioned economic aims, 27 percent more than the European mean mentioned postmaterialist aims. The correspondence of these data with elite data is indeed striking.

While national differences seem significant, *positional* differences within a nation are significant also. Note the differences between Dutch M.P.'s and top civil servants in table 49. Both sets of elites are very similar in emphasizing "belongingness" but in the emphasis on other values they diverge considerably. M.P.'s are less bourgeois than bureaucrats and more likely to be committed to social justice and equality. These findings are similar, in the same direction, as the positional differences found for the elites in all other European systems included in our international project. The bureaucracy produces individuals (or recruits them) who consistently have value priorities differing from legislative

TABLE 48. Values and Goals of the Public in the Netherlands and Other Western Systems, 1973 (in percentages)

	Netherlands	Britain	Germany	Mean for Nine European Countries
Economic				
Fight rising prices	26	50	44	39
Stable economy	16	25	39	22
Security, safety				
Maintain order	18	11	18	19
Fight crime	26	17	21	22
Strong defense forces	4	6	5	4
Post-materialist aims				
Less impersonal society	26	12	11	16
More say on job	24	15	12	17
More say in government	14	15	9	12
Protect free speech	13	11	11	11
More beautiful cities	10	6	4	7
Ideas count	10	4	3	7

Source: Ronald Inglehart, *The Silent Revolution: Changing Values and Political Styles Among Western Publics* (Princeton, N.J.: Princeton University Press, 1976) chapter 3.

Note: These are percentages of adults in national samples who chose the given goal as first or second most important of the eleven goals.

politicians. The basic goals that motivate their work tend to differ, or to put it more precisely, at least one-third of the M.P.'s do not share value priorities of senior bureaucrats, and for most of these the conflict is over bourgeois versus postindustrial values.

When we divide M.P.'s by party affiliation we see precisely where values of both types are located in Parliament (table 50). While M.P.'s of the Center and Right hold what little bourgeois orientation exists among deputies, the M.P.'s of the Left are overwhelmingly the holders of postindustrial values (62 percent compared to 6 percent of the Center and the Right). In the bureaucracy value preferences are not as distinguishable by party preference, although those affiliated with confessional and rightist parties are inclined to be more "bourgeois" (12 percent of the Left, 50 percent of confessionals, 29 percent of the Right).

One other variable that may have utility in explaining elite values (or describing elites who hold certain values) is their contact patterns. We found this to be particularly true for M.P.'s. The activist M.P.'s, those who are in frequent contact at the elite and mass level, are distinctive, holding to postbourgeois values of social justice, equality, and reform of the system much more frequently (84 percent) than do M.P.'s who are less active (32 percent). Whether it is their values that motivate them to such linkage behavior or their contacts that socialize them to acquire certain values, or whether a mutual reinforcement of values and contacts is occurring, is really an argument of no great consequence. The major point is that the M.P.'s who are interacting with other leaders and with citizens hold these types of values. The implications of this for the political system are considerable.

Do elite values have consequences for their views of politics? We could test their relevance by analyzing their linkage to a variety of other attitudes. In table 51 we have selected two sets of attitudes to demonstrate the way in which values are associated with their other

TABLE 49. Summary of Differences in Values of Dutch Elites (in percentages)

	Bureaucrats	M.P.'s	Difference
Bourgeois values (material welfare, security)	25	11	14
Postindustrial values (reform, justice, equality)	15	46	31
Knowledge	12	3	9
Morality, liberty	11	8	3
Belongingness	37	32	5

TABLE 50. Values of M.P.'s and Bureaucrats as Linked to Political Party (in percentages)

	M.P.'s		Bureaucrats			
	Leftist	Confessional and Right-wing	Leftist	Confessional	Right-wing	No Party Preference
Material welfare	0	6	6	17	5	7
Security, safety	0	19	6	33	24	7
Institutional reform	14	0	0	0	5	7
Social justice, equality	62	6	19	17	10	7
Knowledge	0	6	13	0	14	20
Morality	0	13	13	0	5	7
Liberty	0	6	0	8	5	7
Belongingness	24	44	44	25	33	40

perspectives on politics: their views about the role of citizens in the system, and about the influence that certain interest groups should have. As one might have hypothesized, those elites committed to social justice are more consistently favorable to citizen participation. For bureaucrats the contrast between those committed to social justice values and the bourgeois value holders is fairly impressive.

The linkage of values to the influence preferences of M.P.'s is interesting. As expected, those ranking social justice highest are much more interested in giving influence to labor unions and action groups, but *not* to employer groups. A large proportion (50 percent) of those committed to "belongingness," however, desire *both* unions and employer groups to have influence, but *not* action groups. And the remainder of the M.P.'s are not interested in giving much influence to any of these groups. For senior civil servants it is difficult to discern any relationship between values and group influence preferences. But

TABLE 51. Relationship between Elite Values and Other Attitudes
(in percentages)

	Value Priorities						
	M.P.'s			Senior Bureaucrats			
Elite Attitudes	Social Justice, Equality, Reform (N = 17)	Belong-ingness (N = 12)	Other Values (N = 8)	Social Justice, Equality, Reform (N = 10)	Material Welfare Security (N = 17)	Belong-ingness (N = 24)	Other Values (N = 16)
Citizen participation							
Favor increase in citizen say	69	50	29	78	53	33	31
View of interest groups							
Desire high influence for action groups	53	25	0	33	14	23	29
Desire high influence for labor unions	65	50	14	44	43	26	43
Desire high influence for employer groups	12	50	14	33	43	17	50
Feel group conflict is harmful	18	58	29	22	73	63	44

Note: We had too few cases for M.P.'s of those committed primarily to material welfare and security values to permit a separate analysis. They are included under "other values," therefore.

the basic attitude of both sets of elites towards group conflict is distinctive in value terms. Both bureaucrats and M.P.'s who value "social justice" are not worried about such conflict being harmful. But the "material welfare" bureaucrats and those holding to the value of "belongingness" are very much more negative about group conflict.

Conclusions: The Overlap of Values and Ideology

Value priorities can therefore have consequences for, or with, other attitudes and behavior. For Dutch elites value hierarchies seem distinctive compared to other countries, and also differ internally by political party and by position. Values may be a central key to understanding their views of politics and their policy preferences.

Two major questions relevant to our analysis here have been posed in recent years: (1) Is there a decline in the importance of ideology in the conflicts of modern societies, manifest particularly in the attitudes of elites? and (2) Has the old Left-Right dimension, based on attitudes towards state intervention in the society, which presumably captured the essence of the conflict in our societies in the postwar period, given way to another dimension based on different and new value conflicts, which has been called the materialist (or bourgeois) and postmaterialist (postbourgeois) dimension? This is a complicated argument that preoccupies quite a few scholars these days, and one that we cannot discuss here in great detail. We can use our Dutch elite data, however, to suggest what the answers are recently in that system.

The issue for us is not really one of the "end of ideology," because our data clearly show that there is considerable elite conflict, indeed considerable indication of polarization within elite sectors, in their orientations towards the political system, the need for change, the desirability of conflict, and on similar questions. Rather, the question here is which of the two dimensions of conflict seem to describe elite dissonance the best—the old Left-Right dimension based on attitudes towards the intervention of the government in the economy and society, or the dimension linked to basic materialistic-nonmaterialistic value orientations?

In fact, we find a considerable, but not perfect, overlap. If we combine the M.P.'s and civil servants into a single group, we find a strong association. A minority (15 percent) of the liberals who favor state intervention also explicitly support the materialist value position. The remaining 85 percent espouse nonmaterialist values: 40 percent emphasize the value of "belongingness," 30 percent look for social justice, equality, and reform, and 15 percent seek knowledge, morality, and liberty.

The pattern is somewhat similar among conservatives who favor state intervention. Twenty-eight percent hold materialist values, while 72 percent support nonmaterialist goals: 27 percent value "belongingness," 12 percent value social justice, equality, and reform, and 33 percent value knowledge, morality, and liberty.

Thus, there appears to be a high coincidence between the two dimensions if we combine M.P.'s and bureaucrats. Similarly, if we employ another test, the extent of support for increased citizen participation, we find the results as presented in table 52. Clearly, on the question of citizen involvement, presumably an important issue in the bourgeois-postbourgeois conflict, there is little difference among elites if we divide them on these two dimensions. Materialists and conservatives tend to be slightly less supportive, but there is no major difference in the extent of support for either dimension.

One must be careful, however, before assuming that the Left is all of one piece. It is true that Dutch elites appear to be clustered at the liberal end of both dimensions. But, as figure 12 demonstrates, this is less so for bureaucrats than for M.P.'s—a contrast of 78 percent (M.P.'s) and 55 percent (civil servants). There are indeed two types of liberals in the Dutch bureaucracy—materialists (16 percent) and nonmaterialists (55 percent)—plus a group of nonmaterialist conservatives (22 percent). There are few conservative materialists (8 percent). Therefore, what we find on the Left among Dutch administrative elites are (1) those who are the old Left—who are still primarily economic-welfare oriented *and* desire governmental action, and (2) a much larger group of those who are not economic-welfare oriented and desire governmental action for postbourgeois goals. Among bureaucrats, thus, we have two value groups on the Left, a sizable nonmaterialist group on the Right, and a much smaller group of old style right-wing ideologies.

TABLE 52. Coincidence in Support for Citizen Participation by Ideology and Values Dimensions (in percentages)

Attitude toward Citizen Participation	Liberal on State Intervention (N = 81)	Conservative on State Intervention (N = 18)	Non-materialists (N = 82)	Materialists (N = 32)
Favor	65	59	67	56
Oppose	35	41	33	44

VALUE DIMENSION

	Materialist	Nonmaterialist	

<table>
<tr><td rowspan="14" style="writing-mode:vertical">IDEOLOGY ON STATE INTERVENTION</td></tr>
</table>

IDEOLOGY ON STATE INTERVENTION		Materialist	Nonmaterialist	
	Liberal	11%	63%	All elites
	Conservative	7%	19%	
			N = 99	
	Liberal	3%	78%	M.P.'s
	Conservative	6%	15%	
			N = 35	
	Liberal	16%	55%	Senior civil servants
	Conservative	8%	22%	
			N = 64	

Fig. 12. Distribution of Dutch elites by ideological and value dimensions

Within the Parliament, however, the elite conflict is different. We have the battle joined over the *purposes* for which governmental intervention should be used, and *whether* the government should intervene. Thus, 90 percent of M.P.'s are nonmaterialists, not primarily preoccupied with economic security and welfare. But one-fifth want little (or less) governmental intervention, and the remainder differ over the proper goal perspectives for governmental action. But there are few M.P.'s who still place economic security and welfare at the top of their hierarchy of values. The elite conflict pattern thus differs in these two elite sectors, but the value basis of the conflict is more obvious, explicit, and intense in the bureaucracy than in the Parliament. In the Parliament the conflict is an ideological battle among nonmaterialists.

NOTES

1. Edward Shils, "The Concept and Function of Ideology," *International Encyclopedia of the Social Sciences,* vol. 7 (New York: Crowell Collier and

Macmillan, 1968), pp. 66–75; David E. Apter (ed.), *Ideology and Discontent* (Glencoe, Ill.: The Free Press, 1963); G. Sartori, "Politics, Ideology, and Belief Systems," *American Political Science Review* 63 (1969): 398–411; Robert D. Putnam, *The Beliefs of Politicians: Ideology, Conflict, and Democracy in Britain and Italy* (New Haven: Yale University Press, 1973).
2. W. Albeda, et al., *Stelsels ter sprake* (Scheveningen: Stichting Maatschaapijen Onderneming, 1974), pp. 17, 53–54, 66.
3. J. Pen, *Harmonie en conflict* (Amsterdam: Bezige Bij, 1962).
4. Ronald Inglehart, *The Silent Revolution: Changing Values and Political Styles Among Western Publics* (Princeton, N.J.: Princeton University Press, 1977).

CHAPTER 7

The Linkages of Elites
with the Political System

The associations, interrelations, and exchange relationships that elites
have with each other, with the public, and with other actors are considered central for a functional analysis of the political system. Almond
was particularly concerned, in his 1956 study, that in European systems
political elites were too constrained by ideological differences to bargain and to engage in exchange behavior, a position to which others
such as Sidney Tarrow have taken exception.[1] Dutch scholars, on the
other hand, have argued that is was the capacity for Dutch political
elites at the apex of the system, despite their ideological differences, to
interact politically and to bargain effectively (while the bureaucracy
was depoliticized and protected from such conflict resolutions) that has
made such a consociational system viable.[2] The importance of elite
contacts has been discussed, therefore, from different perspectives,
and theories of the functional relevance of elite interaction have been
effectively argued.

The key question that concerns us here is "elite integration," or
"mutual access" in elite communication linkages. As stated in the
introductory chapter, the density of elite contacts is important to investigate and analyze if we are to test the basic elite theories of elite class,
elite conflict, or elite convergence. Further, we wish to know what are
the patterns of distance and balance in these contacts. This leads to a
variety of specific questions. To what extent do senior bureaucrats and
M.P.'s see each other? What is the frequency of their contacts with
other actors—Ministers, other civil servants, party leaders, interest
group representatives, and citizens? Which elites are well balanced in
relationships? On the other hand, are there communication specialists
in the elite system who maintain only particular types of contacts?
What types of elites are activists and who are the isolates? Above all,
are elite contact patterns linked to attitudes and orientations about

politics? Finally, if we can unravel these contact patterns, the question that interests us is "So what?" That is, what seems to be their relevance for system performance?

The theorists of elite class place emphasis on the closeness of elite networks and the ease of elite access to each other, hypothesizing that the contacts among elites are common and are (as Michels claimed) more dense at the top of the system. Further, the theory states, contacts produce or solidify friendships, as well as encouraging concerted action (if not conspiracy), exchange of information, similar perspectives, and shared values. Distance in elite views presumably diminishes with contacts, while imbalance in contacts will be reflected in particularistic orientations. In short, what you believe is a function of whom you associate with. Those disagreeing with this formulation may argue any of the following positions: (1) elite networks are not common or dense, and many elites in certain systems are quite isolated; (2) elite contacts are highly selective, suggesting that perspectives were shared before contacts were initiated; or (3) despite elite interaction patterns (whether mutual or minimal) elites reveal patterns of congruence in views that suggest autonomous convergence unrelated to elite contacts. Further, there are those who argue that elite contacts are *consequences* of the basic characteristics of the political institutions and traditions of the system. For our study, this would mean that the positions or roles of the M.P. and the top civil servant determine the nature of the contacts. It is therefore in a state of considerable theoretical uncertainty and with some disputation that we undertake this analysis of elite linkages in the Dutch system.

The Contact Patterns of Senior Bureaucrats

What theoretical expectations might we have when we investigate the contacts of Dutch bureaucrats with other actors in the Dutch system? Generally, scholars are inclined to emphasize one of two theoretical foci. There are those who are inclined to see the bureaucrats as encapsulated in their own elite social system and culture, skeptical of politics and politicians, by no means favoring public contacts and citizen involvement with the system, and, at most, maintaining certain special clientele relationships with interest groups. A second model is found in the thinking of scholars who see bureaucrats as much more politicized, as involved with policy and seeking contacts with other actors in the system. Earlier our discussion of bureaucrats' role orientations demonstrated the existence of both of these models, Weberians and non-Weberians as well as an intermediate group with a combination of role traits. The elements distinguishing these models are the extent to which higher civil servants reveal in their patterns of associations:

1. an inward departmental or ministerial orientation;
2. clientelistic contacts with interest groups;
3. arm's-length relationships (or nonrelationships) with politicians such as M.P.'s;
4. elitist rejections of contacts with the public;
5. limited contacts with party organization politicians, linked to cynicism or hostility to the party system.

The issue here, narrowly stated, is whether bureaucrats are conservative in the sense of noninvolvement with politics outside their own department, are concerned primarily with their own jobs and tasks, and see no responsibility to the larger system, or whether they are cosmopolitan, that is, interested in developing or maintaining relationships with other actors in the system, linkages that are perceived as assisting them in coping with major problems facing the society. In the broader perspective the question is whether these bureaucrats are performing the functions of maintaining elite communication with the infrastructure of the system, with other elite sectors, and with the public, and thus being continuously informed of the content of demands and alternative proposals that have relevance for policy, while also legitimating in such communications downward and laterally the structure and decisions of the system's bureaucratic elite. We have then both narrow and broader theoretical propositions to keep in mind as we present the data on Dutch senior bureaucrats.

Dutch higher civil servants, as table 53 reveals, are a professionally communicative elite. Very few are out of touch with professional colleagues. Many are in frequent contact with their ministers (45 percent at least weekly), as well as with other superior officials in their own ministry and other ministries.[3] If we combine our data on top level contacts we find over two-thirds (69 percent) of our top civil servants had frequent contacts with officials above and below them; 27 percent had frequent contact with lower civil servants only. Our small sample of high flyers (those civil servants at a much lower level of the ministry) revealed much less likelihood of communicating upward in the system, and thus were much more isolated; only 36 percent had frequent contacts with both high and low civil servants, while the same percentage had contacts only with those on a lower level. Not only did higher civil servants interact frequently in the bureaucracy, but 62 percent said they belonged to a civil service association. There is clear evidence here, then, of continuous, professionalized exposure of the civil servant to the cultural norms and expectations of his professional subsystem, of his own ministry, and of the bureaucracy of which that is a part.

It is interesting to note how civil servants report the substantive content of their contacts with other civil servants. There appears to be a predominance of communication about technical and professional matters (55 percent report such contacts), but there is considerable interest also in political subjects (35 percent); a minority (10 percent) reported contacts of both types. When civil servants discussed their contacts with their *staatssecretaris*, 45 percent indicated the contact dealt with technical matters, 42 percent said political matters, and 13 percent said both were discussed.[4]

If the Dutch civil servant's pattern of professional communication seems to be very active and wide ranging, his contacts with the political environment are more limited and particularized. As table 54 reveals, the descending order of importance in these contacts is clear. Dutch civil servants are relatively isolated from political party leaders in and outside Parliament, and only a third are in regular touch with citizens. Their contact with organized interest groups, often probably the clientele groups for their ministries, is high, however. And this seems to be the major exposure to external stimuli for the majority of higher civil servants. Yet we must note that few of these civil servants (no more than 2 percent) are completely withdrawn from political, as opposed to

TABLE 53. Professional Contacts of Higher Civil Servants (in percentages)

	Frequency of Contact			
	Weekly or more	Less than Weekly but Regularly	"Now and Then"	Seldom or Never
Contacts in				
own ministry				
Own minister	45	28	15	11
Staatssecretaris	33	19	23	25
Secretaris-generaal	44	27	22	7
Directeur-generaal	80	11	6	3
Contacts outside				
own ministry				
Other ministers	3	18	33	46
Other staatssecretarissen	0	16	30	54
Other high civil servants	55	36	8	1
Civil servants at the provincial or municipal level	9	16	31	43

professional, associations. A majority have *some*, though infrequent, contact with M.P.'s and citizens. It is only party organization leaders outside Parliament who are almost completely outside their orbits of association.

The Dutch senior civil servant's political contacts, if seen in a comparative perspective, are rather restricted. Our data for other countries reveal this (see table 55). The British and Dutch bureaucracies seem very similar, with limited political contacts. They fit a model of exclusiveness and relative isolation, while the German and American systems are quite different, their bureaucracies having much more extensive and frequent contacts, particularly with M.P.'s (but in the case of American bureaucrats, with citizens as well).

The special character of contacts for higher civil servants can be seen from the correlations between different types of contacts. Those civil servants who see M.P.'s also are inclined to see party leaders (0.544) and citizens (0.484). But those who have a high incidence of contacts within the bureaucracy do not ordinarily see M.P.'s (0.149) or party leaders (0.081) or citizens (−0.033).

TABLE 54. Political Contacts of Higher Civil Servants (in percentages)

	Frequency	
Contacts	Regularly or More Often	Seldom or Never
Representatives of organized interest groups	64	14
Citizens	29	37
Members of Parliament	16	39
Executives of political parties	4	80

TABLE 55. Comparative Differences in Bureaucrat Contacts with M.P.'s and Citizens (in percentages)

Contacts	Britain	Germany	United States	Netherlands
M.P.'s (or members of Congress)				
Weekly	1	30	43	1
Regularly	4	44	21	15
Total	5	74	64	16
Citizens				
Weekly	4	15	54	13
Regularly	5	14	14	17
Total	9	29	68	30

Those civil servants who concentrate primarily on intrahierarchical interactions in the bureaucracy, or who focus on contacts with interest groups, are specialists and many of them engage in no other types of interactions. When we cumulate our information concerning the contact patterns of these civil servants, we see that few are engaged in diversified and active political subsystem interactions. The distributions are as follows:

	Percentage of higher civil servants	Percentage of lower level "High Flyers"
"Activists"—in communication with 2 or more external sectors, weekly or more often	6	6
"Moderate Activists"—in communication with one political sector weekly, fairly regular for another sector	22	29
"Specialists"—in contact with only one sector, but fairly frequently (usually organized interest groups representatives)	71	65
"Isolates"—no contact with any actors	2	—

Although civil servants are not removed from exposure to the political arena, only a minority of 28 percent are classified as "activist" or "moderately activist" in their political relationships. Figure 13 demonstrates the specialized nature of these contact patterns.

Factors Associated with Linkages of Civil Servants

What types of civil servants are more likely to be political in their contact patterns, which civil servants are more bureaucratic, and which seem to be most isolated? Factors such as party preference or religious background did not turn out to be very useful. We noted some class bias in contact patterns—those with lowest family class origins revealing more propensity for contacts with citizens and interest groups. Though an interesting finding, it is perhaps less significant than age differences (table 56).

The oldest civil servants are less in contact with other political sectors than their younger associates. They seem particularly to be out of touch, almost completely, with members of Parliament. It is the younger and middle-aged civil servants who tend to maintain what associations there are with citizens, party leaders, and M.P.'s. On our index of activism in contacts, the age cohort fifty-six to sixty-five years old included 20 percent who were active and 40 percent who were relatively isolated, compared to 37 percent active in the younger cohort, while only 26 percent of the young bureaucrats were isolated. One must remember, however, that at all age levels, contacts with other civil servants and with organized group representatives are high. These are the two key subsystems Dutch bureaucrats relate to.

The type of ministry theoretically might structure the pattern of political contacts, because of its "mission" or "culture." And we do, on inspection of the data, find some interesting differences by ministry. An illustration of this is found in the data about civil servant contacts with organized groups (table 57). We dichotomized ministries on the basis of our expectation that they were oriented (or not) to maintain close relations with organized groups. Our data partially support such a distinction. We do find that in the traditionally, internally oriented ministries (such as Finance and General Affairs), civil servants show much less frequency of contact with the representatives of organized groups—39 percent regularly compared to 76 percent of the traditionally clientelistic ministries (such as Agriculture and Education). But

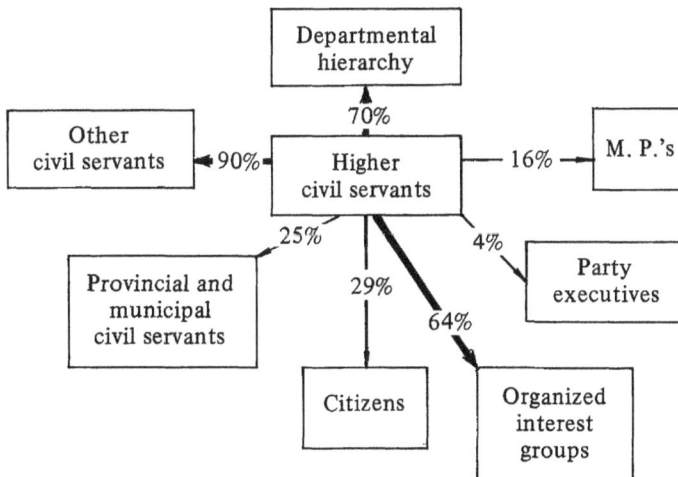

Fig. 13. The specialized nature of civil servant contacts in the Dutch political system. Each percentage is the proportion of higher civil servants who see other actors "regularly."

there are exceptions. We do not find that civil servants in Transport and Health are in very frequent contact with interest groups. And there is some evidence that in Justice senior servants do not conform to this image of the older ministries. Nevertheless, it appears as if a type of ministerial culture, function, or policy orientation develops that expects and encourages contact with interest groups, or that discourages such contact.[5]

If we take the relationship of higher civil servants to M.P.'s, we note again variations by ministries. The civil servants in three of the ministries are more inclined to see M.P.'s than in others. These are Economic Affairs, Agriculture, and Cultural Affairs, whose senior bureaucrats report that they see M.P.'s regularly. In the other ministries, regular contact is at the 10 percent level or lower. Similar observations can be made concerning ministerial differences in civil servant contacts with citizens. Less than 30 percent see citizens regularly, but the varia-

TABLE 56.   Age Differences in Civil Servant Contact Patterns (in percentages)

	Age (in years)		
Contacts	37–46 (N = 10)	47–56 (N = 32)	57+ (N = 33)
M.P.'s (regularly)	20	29	3
Other civil servants (weekly or better)	100	94	81
Contacts with citizens (regularly or more often)	40	31	24
Contacts with organized groups (regularly or more often)	70	70	58

TABLE 57.   Variations in Civil Servant Contact Patterns with Interest Groups, by Type of Ministry

Interest Group Contacts	Ministries Theoretically Less Involved with Client Relations (N = 21)	Ministries Theoretically Clientelistic (N = 49)
Weekly or more frequently	10	31
Regularly but not weekly	29	45
Less regularly but with some frequency	28	18
Seldom or never	33	6

Note: Ministries included in the first column are: General Affairs, Surinam and Antilles, Justice, Interior, Finance; in the second column: Education, Housing, Transport, Economic Affairs, Agriculture, Culture, Social Affairs, Health. One should remember that the ministries of Foreign Affairs and Defense were excluded from our comparative survey.

tions by ministries are again considerable. In certain ministries, regular citizen contact is reported by 50 percent or more of the senior bureaucrats; in others the percentage having regular contact is 10 percent or less. The classical ministries referred to earlier are noticeably less in touch with citizens. Yet this is not the basic dividing line. There are other ministries that seem exclusive in this regard.

Contact networks for senior civil servants therefore vary considerably by department, although the rationale for this is not completely clear. Certain traditional ministries are low in contact; certain client ministries are high in contacts. But the conditions of the department or the functions of a ministry that lead to activism in bureaucratic contacts are not completely clear. Of the factors we have looked at here, age and ministry seem to be best associated with the interaction patterns of bureaucrats.

Contrasting Contact Patterns for M.P.'s

When we look at the M.P.'s in our sample, the patterns of interaction are quite different from those of senior bureaucrats (table 58). The M.P. is in frequent contact with ministers, national, regional, or local party leaders, and citizens. Our data reveal the percentage of M.P.'s who saw the following groups or individuals once a week or more,

TABLE 58. M.P. Contacts with Elites and the Public (in percentages)

Contacts	At Least Weekly	Less than Weekly but Regularly	"Now and Then"	Seldom or Never
Civil servants and ministers				
Ministers	47	29	17	7
Higher civil servants	29	37	24	10
Civil servants at the provincial and local level	12	38	29	12
Party leaders				
National (own party)	63	26	12	0
Provincial and local (own party)	45	47	7	2
National (other parties)	5	16	30	49
Regional and local (other parties)	0	9	30	61
Interest groups and the public				
Representatives of national group	30	51	19	0
Representatives of regional group	21	44	28	7
Citizens	72	16	12	0

Note: Each percentage is a proportion of all M.P.'s.

arranged on descending order of frequency of contact: individual citizens (72 percent); national party leaders (63 percent); ministers (47 percent); provincial or local party leaders (45 percent); representatives of national interest groups (30 percent); higher civil servants (29 percent). The magnitude of M.P. contacts is clear. Not only are large proportions of M.P.'s very frequently in contact with a variety of political actors or groups, but only a very small proportion are generally out of touch—10 percent or fewer.[6]

One notes that M.P.'s are as frequently in touch with ministers as are the higher civil servants—about 45 percent weekly or more, and about 75 percent regularly. One also notes that M.P.'s are in touch with civil servants at both the national and lower levels of the system to a remarkable extent. Half of the M.P.'s even more frequently contact representatives of national interest groups (81 percent report regular contact) than they do higher civil servants (64 percent). In addition, M.P.'s keep in touch with regional groups; two thirds do so regularly. Contacts with citizens are extremely frequent for most M.P.'s; 70 percent meet with citizens weekly or more often, compared to 13 percent for higher civil servants.

This contrasts strikingly with what we know about civil servants. Eighty-eight percent of M.P.'s reported regular contacts with citizens, while only one-third of both higher and lower civil servants did so. A very small number (4 percent of higher civil servants, and 6 percent of lower) had regular contacts with party organization leaders outside of Parliament, in contrast to 88 percent of M.P.'s. And while two-thirds of both higher and lower bureaucrats regularly saw representatives of organized interest groups, 81 percent of M.P.'s did the same. In addition, 66 percent of the M.P.'s tell us that they regularly see certain civil servants and only 10 percent say that they seldom or never see civil servants. Clearly, the Dutch M.P. is an active and multifocused communicator in his contact with his political system, while the civil servant lives in a world of political relationships that is much more constricted.

Dutch M.P.'s are as active in linkages to other elites as is the case for other countries. The following comparative findings reveal percentages of M.P.'s having weekly contact with the groups listed:

	Britain	Germany	Netherlands
Citizens	95%	87%	72%
National interest groups	12	20	30
National leaders of party organizations	69	56	63
Senior civil servants	10	38	29
Ministers	58	39	47

There is great cross-national uniformity in these findings. One notes the low frequency of the British M.P.'s contacts with senior civil servants and interest groups, but the Dutch are not much different than the British in both respects. Generally, Dutch linkage relationships are very similar to that of the German and the British M.P.'s.

The intercorrelation matrix for M.P. contacts documents the fact that the M.P. is at the hub of the system in Holland. M.P.s who are in touch with ministers are also inclined to see senior civil servants (0.429), and such contacts are in turn fairly well correlated with citizen contacts (0.457) and interest group contacts (0.554). M.P.s in touch with national interest groups also see local interest group representatives (0.520), and local interest group contacts are linked to contacts with local civil servant contacts (0.741). Correlations are low between M.P. contacts with national party leaders and civil servant contacts (−0.111). Thus, though M.P.'s are very active and have frequent contacts in a variety of sectors, even among them some specialization in contact patterns occurs.

The Dutch M.P. is obviously an active interactor. If we combine our data on contacts, we find 66 percent are activists in bureaucratic contacts (that is, they regularly see more than one type of civil servant) and 77 percent are activists in political contacts (that is, they regularly see two or more of the categories of party leaders, organized groups, and citizens). On the other hand, by their own indication 15 percent are fairly isolated from the bureaucracy, but only 2 percent are isolated in political contacts.

Figure 14 illustrates the centrality and complexity of the Dutch M.P. contacts in contrast to the bureaucrat. The Dutch M.P.'s patterns are characterized as more extensive, more diverse, and much more frequent and regular than are the contacts of higher civil servants. Clearly, in interaction terms the M.P.'s are at the hub of the system, or at least one of the centers of the system. The multilevel, multidirectional nature of M.P.'s interactions stands out in contrast to the rather focused and limited set of interactions for the bureaucracy.

Factors Associated with M.P. Linkages

Although M.P.'s are activists in linkage terms, there are variations in extent and focus of contacts among M.P.'s. The factors explaining these differences could be many. Indeed, the literature on this matter suggests that such factors as type of party, social background, political career, ideology, and political attitudes may be important, as well as others on which we find it difficult to collect data. Among these might be the "structure of opportunities" within which elites function; that is, the limiting or facilitating exchange environment of the system. Another relevant factor might be the perceptions of mutual advantage that an elite actor holds and that conditions his efforts to make contacts. Certainly a political leader's view of the political system and the role of elites in that system, on which we do have data, are variables that theoretically should influence political contact efforts.

Does party constrain or expand the political relationships of M.P.'s? Our data suggest that differences do exist. The basic pattern seems to be that M.P.'s of parties of the Left (PvdA, PSP, PPR, D'66) are consistently inclined to emphasize political contacts but to interact with civil servants less frequently (table 59). Thus we note that 60 percent of the M.P.'s of parties that are Center and Right see ministers and other civil servants at least weekly, while less than 40 percent of our Left M.P.'s do. This differential of 25 percentage points is noticeable also in the other direction, when one looks at contacts with interest groups, citizens, and national party leaders.[7] It is the M.P.'s of the Left who are particularly active in these contacts. The differential is greatly reduced, however, for citizen contacts. Most M.P.'s are very

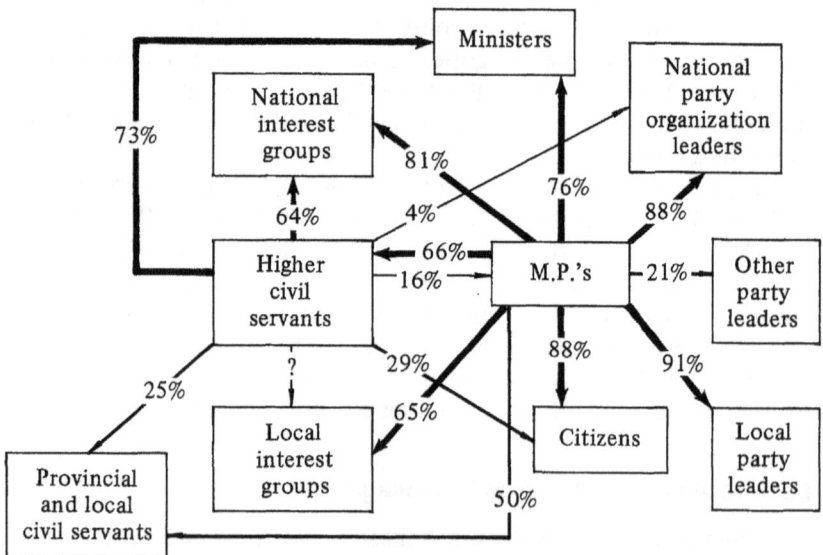

Fig. 14. The complexity and diversity of elite contacts in the Dutch system. Each percentage is the proportion of M.P.'s or higher civil servants who see others "more than weekly," "weekly," or "regular—but not weekly."

much involved with citizens, regardless of party direction or type. An imbalance exists thus in M.P. contact relationships—M.P.'s of the Left are more externally (politically) oriented than lateral (bureaucracy oriented) than are their colleagues at Center and on the Right. One explanation is that the socialist M.P. was in the opposition in 1973 and thus expanded his political contacts and was less inclined to see the need to work closely with the bureaucracy. However, there may also be an explanation in the developing attitudes of party groups to changes in the Dutch system.

The previous career of an M.P. in politics or government tends to predispose him or her to a subsequent pattern of behavior. This is strikingly demonstrable for those M.P.'s who in the past had party positions. A large number (over 50 percent) of M.P.'s held such positions. Over 70 percent of the M.P.'s with some party experience were in weekly contact with their own national party leaders (table 60). And the chances that they maintained contact at the local and regional party organization level was more likely with a party career background that also had been regional or local. Thus 68 percent of the M.P.'s who had held local party office were still in weekly contact with local party leaders, while only 11 percent of M.P.'s without such experience were so frequently in contact with the local party. Quite clearly, the Dutch system is one in which there are close, functional links between the party organizations on all levels and the day-to-day parliamentary scene through elite contacts.

The influence of previous career was also noticeable in contacts of M.P.'s with interest groups and citizens. Contacts with *regional* (not

TABLE 59. Relevance of Party in M.P. Contacts (in percentages)

	Party of M.P.	
Frequent Contacts	Left-wing (N = 22)	Center-Right (N = 19)
Bureaucratic and ministerial contacts		
Civil servants	39	67
Ministers	35	63
External political contacts		
Interest group leaders	48	17
National party leaders	87	56
Citizens often	78	67

Note: Each percentage in this table is a separate proportion of the M.P.'s in each party category who see others often (weekly or more).

national) interest groups were more probable for those with prior party experience. For example, 88 percent of M.P.'s with previous experience in *regional* party organizations were in regular contact with *regional* interest groups, compared to 37 percent of those without such previous experience. And the same finding was true, although not as strikingly, for contacts by M.P.'s with citizens—100 percent compared to 73 percent.

We found much less evidence that certain other types of previous career experience were relevant for explaining M.P. contact patterns. There was no evidence that previous legislative experience in the Provincial Estates or in the national civil service itself (true for about one-fourth of our sample) had any significance for contact relationships after they become M.P.'s. This is somewhat surprising. One could have expected previous bureaucrats to seek out bureaucrats.

The roles of social background variables as determinants of M.P. contact patterns are very interesting, and more clearly relevant than for the contacts of higher civil servants.[8] We find considerable age differentials, with the younger (and middle-aged) M.P.'s more in contact with citizens and national party leaders than older M.P.'s. Thus, 70 percent of the age group under thirty-eight years old and 76 percent of the cohort between thirty-eight and fifty years old have weekly contacts with national party leaders, but only 33 percent of the older M.P.'s do. The latter are more in contact with citizens—67 percent weekly compared to 80 percent for the youngest cohort. This age difference is not apparent for M.P. contacts with civil servants, but it tends to be true also for interest group contacts.

Similarly, when we look at the time when these leaders entered Parliament and contrast the newcomers from the old-timers we note the same type of differences. Those who entered Parliament recently

TABLE 60.   Relevance of Previous Party Career for M.P. Contact
                 Patterns (in percentages)

| | Previous Party Organization Experience | | | | | |
| | National Executive | | Regional Party | | Local Party | |
Weekly Contact	Yes	No	Yes	No	Yes	No
With national party leaders	73	52	75	47	76	44
With regional and local party leaders	50	38	63	21	68	11
With interest group representatives	36	24	25	37	32	28

(1971–73) are inclined to be slightly more energetic in contacts with party leaders, citizens, and interest groups, but not more energetic (though still high) in contacts with ministers. Yet it is important to note that these newcomers immediately become active.

Another interesting variable is father's social class position. Those with lower-class family backgrounds seem to continue a greater interest in citizen contacts (83 percent have weekly contacts, while for those from upper-class family backgrounds the figure is 47 percent), greater interest in contacts with party leaders (78 percent versus 53 percent), and a slightly greater interest in contacts with interest group representatives. There does seem to be some carryover influence from the class milieu of the family.

Another background factor of relevance is the particular type of occupation that the respondent had just before entering Parliament (table 61). Those who were previously in governmental office of some kind were much more likely to be in contact with ministers weekly (64 percent), and they also were high in contacts with party leaders. Their weekly interest group contacts were low (18 percent). Those coming from educational positions into Parliament were unique in that they were surprisingly high in weekly contacts with party leaders (92 percent) and with citizens (83 percent), but their contacts with ministers and civil servants, while not negligible, were less frequent. Those from other professions (upper and middle types) were fairly low in a relative sense in bureaucratic and political contacts, although they did marginally better in contacts with interest groups.

The interesting picture that begins to emerge from this is that the younger elites, with early backgrounds that were lower in social class, are the most active among both bureaucrats and M.P.'s. We earlier noticed that the higher civil servants who were in the younger age

TABLE 61. Relevance of Previous Occupation for M.P. Contact Patterns (in percentages)

Weekly Contact	Office Holders (Including Civil Service) (N = 11)	Educators (N = 12)	Professionals and Related Positions (N = 13)
With ministers	64	33	38
With senior civil servants	36	25	15
With national party leaders	73	92	23
With interest group representatives	18	33	38
With citizens	64	83	69

bracket and who came from relatively lower-class backgrounds were interacting much more with M.P.'s. The younger, lower-class M.P.'s, we now notice, are interacting more frequently with civil servants. And both M.P.'s and higher civil servants who are at the younger age levels and lower class in both elite groups, are more likely to be in touch with citizens and interest groups. While party and minority differences are important for M.P.'s and bureaucrats, respectively, this image of how elites are communicating with citizens, groups, and other leaders is very suggestive. "New elite politics" has been emerging, at least in terms of elite contact behavior.

Interparty Linkages

The exchange relationships of leaders between parties in any political system are important for communication. For some scholars this is the key test of the integrative character of the system. In the Dutch system they may be critical for the politics of accommodation or of conflict resolution. It is therefore particularly interesting to note from our limited data on Dutch M.P.'s the extent of cross-party contacts. Our M.P. respondents were asked to inform us of the frequency of their contacts with the leaders of other parties at the national, regional, and local levels. The emphasis was on party executives outside of Parliament. We found the following basic distribution among forty-three M.P.'s:

	Contacts with National Leaders of Other Parties	Contacts with Regional or Local Leaders of Other Parties
Weekly	5%	0
Regularly but not weekly	16	9%
Now and then	30	30
Seldom or never	49	61

A fifth of Dutch M.P.'s are in regular contact with other party organization leaders (outside of Parliament), and another 30 percent see such leaders occasionally. While only 12 percent said they *never* saw such leaders, the fact is that a minority of M.P.'s have *regular* contact across party lines. Combined with their high frequency of interaction within their own party, this suggests that interparty integration activity may be low.

In attempting to identify what types of M.P.'s do engage in such interparty contacts we looked at three factors: the M.P.'s own party, age, and religious background (table 62). While M.P.'s from parties of the Left are more inclined to interact with the leaders of other parties, a large minority of the confessional M.P.'s do so also. Only right-wing M.P.'s (VVD and DS'70) are less inclined to see other party leaders. One notes also that religious background is no barrier to interparty elite associations—30 percent of both Catholic and Protestant M.P.'s are in regular contact with other parties. And, finally, it is the young M.P.'s who are rather more inclined to be the integrators, to "see the opposition"—40 percent regularly for those below thirty-eight years of age, while none of the M.P.'s over fifty regularly contact other party leaders. This may indicate a developmental tendency in the Dutch system—a break away from *verzuiling* (pillarization).

The Association between Elite Contacts and Elite Attitudes

It is an important element in elite theories that elite interactions may be linked to their views of politics, either as cause or effect. That is, one may see the particular contacts of elites as a consequence of their perspectives and beliefs, or, on the other hand, one may argue that elite interactions themselves have consequences for the attitudes of elites. Of course, one may also hypothesize that there is no significant relationship at all and that elite attitudes are developed irrespective of their associations with others. But our position here is otherwise. We see administrative and parliamentary elites, although constrained by

TABLE 62. Factors Associated with Interparty Contacts of M.P.'s (in percentages)

	Contacts with Other Party National Leaders		
	Regularly	Now and Then	Seldom or Never
Own party background			
Left-wing	26	35	39
Confessional	18	27	55
Secular right-wing	0	25	75
Religion			
Catholic	30	30	40
Protestant	31	25	44
None	6	38	56
Age			
Below 38 years	40	30	30
38–50	24	33	43
51+	0	25	75

Note: Each percentage is the proportion of M.P.'s in each background category who engage in contacts, by the frequency of such contact.

the institutional characteristics of the system (by the nature of the bureaucracy and of the parliamentary structure), as capable of initiating and developing contacts with others in the system. Such contacts are the product of a variety of considerations, among which may well be their basic orientations towards politics, their role perceptions of self and others, their preferences for involvement with others, or their images of the political process. In turn, the contacts that elites engage in have consequences for their beliefs; figure 15 presents a diagram of this model. To test this and to do it with complete confidence in the results is virtually impossible without longitudinal data; one needs measures of pre- and postcontact attitudes. We only can suggest here the nature of these relationships, using data in conjunction with the logic of the associations of variables.

To illustrate the possibility that elite orientations may lead to contacts with others, we will use here, first, senior civil servant role perceptions. As we noted earlier, these bureaucrats differed in the way they defined their involvement in the policy process, the majority conceiving an active role and a minority feeling that theirs was a passive role. We now find this difference in role perceptions related to their contact patterns (table 63). Those bureaucrats who seem themselves as having a very active role in the policy process are more inclined to have contacts with other elites or other sectors of the system. As the civil servant tends more towards a passive role perception for himself, he is more likely to be isolated from other actors. What the causal direction of this relationship is we cannot say with certainty, but at least these two factors are associated, an important finding in itself.

An orientation of possible relevance in explaining civil servant contacts with M.P.'s and others outside the bureaucracy is their evaluative reactions to politics, particularly their tolerance of partisan politics and their elitism in attitudes toward citizen participation. We used

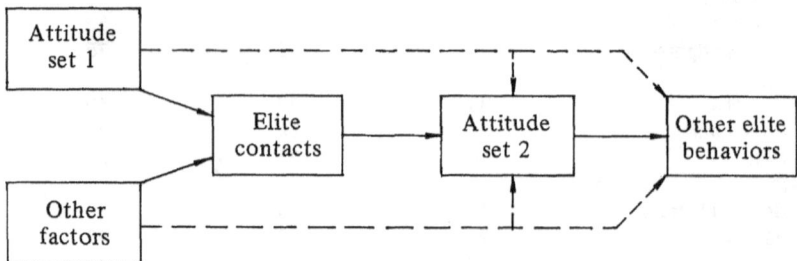

Fig. 15. Model of the relevance of elite interactions for elite attitudes

an index of tolerance of politics to differentiate bureaucrats on the first basic dimension and an index of elitism for the second dimension.[9] Bureaucratic contacts were linked to both basic dimensions. On the first, we found a 20 percentage point differential in the frequency of bureaucrats' contacts with M.P.'s, depending on their tolerance of politics. Those most tolerant were more likely to have such contacts. Again, with the second dimension we found that 82 percent of those least elitist on our index had some contact with M.P.'s, while slightly more than 50 percent of those scored at the elitist end of the scale had some such contact—a 30 percentage point differential.

Other basic orientations seemed to be more useful in explaining M.P. contact patterns. We found three types of such possibly relevant orientations: ideological positions on policy, political value preferences, and normative views about the desirability of conflict in the system. Those M.P.'s who were the liberals—approving regulative intervention in the society and economy, who were preoccupied with reforming the system and seeking social justice, and who did not feel conflict in the system was dysfunctional—these were the M.P.'s who were somewhat more inclined to have a high frequency of citizen contact. For example, M.P.'s ranking high on social justice and reform of the system had very frequent contact with citizens (82 percent) while those ranking economic security and material welfare high in their value hierarchy were less likely to (53 percent).

Elite Contact Behavior and Its Attitudinal Consequences

Presumably, elite contacts should have some impact on the attitudes and beliefs of elites. Implicit in much of the theoretical work on elites is the expectation that this is likely. The classical Weberian bureaucrat

TABLE 63.   Relationship of Role Perceptions to Contact Patterns for Civil Servants (in percentages)

Contact Patterns (Index of Contacts Outside the Bureaucracy)	Perceptions of Role in the Policy Process		
	Very Active Role (N = 19)	Moderately Active Role (N = 32)	Limited or Passive Role (N = 14)
Extensive and frequent contacts	42	22	21
Specialists (with interest groups primarily)	37	44	36
Relatively isolated	21	34	43

interacting with his colleagues and isolated from politicians presumably has certain attitudes reinforced by this association that would be altered if he spent much time with politicians. Similarly the politician who interacts frequently with leaders of other parties, and also those who maintain frequent citizen and interest group contacts, would theoretically develop different views (not necessarily more favorable views) of these subsystems, and possibly also of the political process generally. Dutch consociational theory would certainly see elite contacts as functional to system performance, partly because these contacts would influence attitudes of elites about each other. More generally, but relevant also for the Dutch system, is the importance of elite contacts with interest groups and the public, for in such a two-way interaction flow (in the Dutch system within and across the "pillars"), presumably specific veiws and basic understandings are communicated. We can only test here the possible impacts of elite contacts on the elites of our study, one part of this interaction process.

Our data strongly suggest, first, that the contacts of senior bureaucrats with M.P.'s may be relevant for bureaucrats' attitudes toward politics (table 64). There is a variety of evidence indicating that senior bureaucrats in contact with M.P.'s are less Weberian (not emphasizing technical aspects of the policy process) and more willing to accept significant change in society. Conflict is an aspect of politics that usually worries civil servants. But those who interact with M.P.'s are more tolerant of conflict and less pessimistic about its resolution. They are

TABLE 64. Orientations of Bureaucrats by Frequency of Contacts with M.P.'s (in percentages)

Senior Bureaucrats' Attitudes	Interactors (Frequent Contacts)	Isolates (Few or No Contacts)
Technical considerations are more important than political	17	34
Major or important change in society is necessary	47	24
Social conflicts are functional to progress	42	29
Parties uselessly exacerbate conflicts	25	40
The welfare of the country is endangered by the clash of interest groups	8	24
Conflicts are irreconcilable	15	46
Enthusiastic about citizen participation	58	30

also less critical of parties and interest groups as generators of conflict and positively support citizen participation in the system. In short, there is a convergence of perspectives in the direction of more support for politics, suggesting that bureaucratic elites *may* be influenced by their contacts with politicians. This is a useful finding in its own right, even though one must emphasize "may," since no causal connection is established here. It is interesting that the attitudes of those senior bureaucrats with the highest frequency of contact with other civil servants are generally a reciprocal of the findings in table 64. That is, we find that extreme activists within the bureaucracy reveal a greater preoccupation with technical expertise, with efficiency, and less programmatic commitment than those senior bureaucrats somewhat less in contact with other civil servants.

The contacts of M.P.'s with civil servants reveal some evidence of an influence in the direction of so-called bureaucratic orientations. Those M.P.'s who interact frequently with bureaucrats are somewhat more inclined to emphasize the importance of technical considerations in the solution of policy problems, and also to reveal more of the bureaucratic concern about conflict. But the evidence is much less consistent and the differences small. Thus, one must conclude that, although there is a convergence in attitude linked to contacts, it is more a convergence in the direction of acceptance of the views of the parliamentarians than of the bureaucrats.

Turning to another set of contact relationships—of elites with citizens and interest group representatives—the findings are somewhat paradoxical and in certain instances contrary to expectations (table 65). Elite contact with citizens does not seem to be conducive to greater enthusiasm about citizen participation in the political process. Most M.P.'s are of course rather supportive of citizen involvement. But those less in contact with citizens, interestingly, among both M.P.'s and senior bureaucrats, are *more* supportive of the citizen's role

TABLE 65. Elite Contacts with Citizens and Their Basic Attitudes toward Citizen Participation (in percentages)

Support of Citizen Participation	M.P. Contacts		Senior Bureaucrat Contacts		
	Weekly (N = 30)	Less Frequently (N = 12)	Regular (N = 20)	Occasional (N = 23)	Seldom or Never (N = 25)
Very enthusiastic	17	40	11	5	12
Somewhat enthusiastic	40	30	11	33	24
Total	57	70	22	38	36

than those seeing citizens frequently! On the other hand, there is evidence to indicate that M.P.'s (not bureaucrats) in contact with citizens are more liberal ideologically (less likely to be opposed to state intervention in the society) and less concerned about political conflict.

There are many other attitudes and orientations of elites that can be analyzed in terms of their contacts and linkages. Many of them seem to be significant. We find, for example, that M.P.'s most frequently in contact with ministers are the most respectful of them and most likely to think they should have considerable influence in the system (a 25 percentage point difference by frequency of contact). And we find that M.P.'s fairly frequently in contact with the national leaders of other parties manifest a pattern of orientations that are often distinctive. For example, M.P.'s who maintain more frequent contacts with other party leaders are more likely to believe that conflict is a typical part of the political system, and are less likely to be inclined to compromise.

Those M.P.'s in regular contact (20 percent of the sample) combine an interesting set of attitudes. They are more likely (76 percent) to be concerned that conflict is typical, but they personally are not inclined (11 percent) to compromise with their partisan adversaries. Those not in contact with the other party leaders are less likely (44 percent) to feel conflict is necessary, typical, or reconcilable. But they are more likely (53 percent) to be compromisers. Contact does not, therefore, seem to lead to an attitude of personal compromise, but it is linked to a realistic view about the inevitability of conflict.

As for the perception of differences between parties, those M.P.'s in fairly regular contact see these differences as extensive (84 percent see party differences as great or important, compared to 58 percent of those infrequently or never in contact), and they also tend to be less critical of party differences and to see them as not harmful. Practically none (11 percent) of those M.P.'s in regular contact feel that parties uselessly exacerbate conflict, while 62 percent of those infrequently in contact take that position. Thus, the interparty elite exchanges seem indeed to be related to elite attitudes and to attitudes very important for the functioning of the Dutch system.

In concluding the discussion of the linkage of elite contacts with their attitudes, major emphasis should be placed on a finding that stands out in most of our data. We note the emergence of attitudes basically facilitative of accommodation, *even though contacts often are infrequent.* That is, it is quite obvious that other factors are determining elite attitudes, as well as the elite contacts we have been discussing in this section. A good example of this is the attitudes of the senior bureaucrats. A large proportion of them are isolated from M.P.'s and other party leaders *and* still take a modern or nontraditional bureaucratic view of the role of the M.P. and the nature of the policy process. Figure 16 suggests the distribution of all the bureaucrats using the two dimensions of contacts with M.P.'s and their classical views of politics. Clearly, although the large majority of bureaucrats are not interactors with politicians, they have taken on modern orientations—they are not narrow technocrats, nor extremely hostile to politicians. This convergence of bureaucratic and parliamentary elite attitudes, even in the absence of contact, may well be one of the saving graces of the system. Another saving grace, as pointed out earlier, is the interparty pattern of elite contacts and the utility of these contacts for making leaders realistically aware of the nature and basis of party differences and the development of confidence in their resolution.

Conclusions

We were concerned in this chapter with elite integration, primarily from the viewpoint of elite interaction and contact patterns. In evaluating these data it is important to recall that the backgrounds of these leaders revealed considerable diversity of social origins, social status, and political milieu. They came from Catholic, Protestant (of different types), and nonreligious families. They came primarily from upper- and middle-class backgrounds, although a sizable minority had fathers with lower-class occupations. And they came from diverse political party careers and experiences. For some of these elites, these backgrounds were constraining, for others not. But their contacts must be

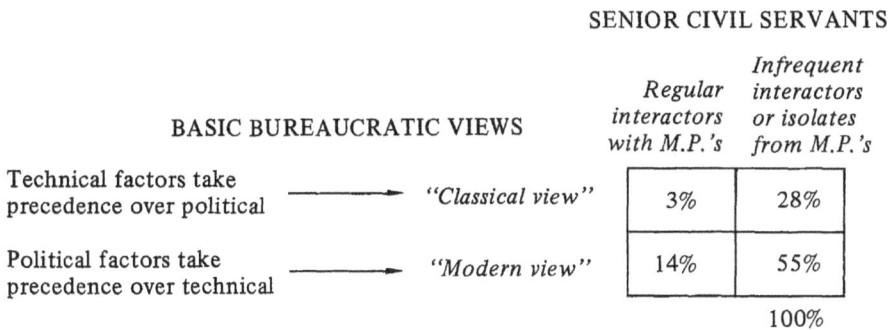

SENIOR CIVIL SERVANTS

BASIC BUREAUCRATIC VIEWS		Regular interactors with M.P.'s	Infrequent interactors or isolates from M.P.'s
Technical factors take precedence over political	⟶ *"Classical view"*	3%	28%
Political factors take precedence over technical	⟶ *"Modern view"*	14%	55%

100%

Fig. 16. Total distribution of Dutch senior civil servants in "classical" and "modern" orientations, by contacts with M.P.'s

seen as bridging social status, family type, and political party preference differences.

There are two major senses in which one can speak of elite integration in interactional terms. On the one hand, one can be interested in the extent to which elites associated with each other and constitute a coherent, closed, self-conscious elite class. One of the complaints against elite theorists such as Pareto, Mosca, and Michels was that they never empirically demonstrated such elite coherence. It is clear from the data presented here for the Dutch M.P.'s and higher civil servants that their interactions are too skewed, specialized, and one-sided for them to be viewed as a close-knit, interactional, monolithic set of leaders. The other meaning of elite integration, and one used throughout this chapter, is the contact patterns of these elites with other sectors or actors in the system. Data concerning such contacts speak to the integration of other sectors of the *system* with elites, not just the integration of *elites*. The detailed analysis of our findings begins to indicate what the extent of this integration may be.

Dutch top civil servants have very specialized linkages to the system. On the one hand, they are very preoccupied with the bureaucracy itself, conservative in this sense, and outside the bureaucracy they concentrate their attention primarily on contacts with interest groups. They are clientelistic in this respect. Only 16 percent see M.P.'s regularly and less than a third are in frequent contact with citizens. Only 4 percent see party organization leaders regularly. This suggests an arms-length, elitist, and antiparty perspective, so far as contacts are concerned. Nevertheless, the top civil servants are by no means completely isolated; indeed, they do engage a great deal in interest group contacts. Dutch top civil servants appear to be as Daalder described them at one time, as possibly functioning as "points of brokerage between highly differentiated subgroups of society." With respect to their functional value for integrating interest groups this seems true. But their role as "brokers between officials and politicians and between various parties," a historic role which Daalder also suggested for Dutch bureaucrats, is much more questionable, based on our limited data.[10] They just do not see party leaders enough, nor do they emphasize such contacts.

Dutch M.P.'s are, on the basis of our empirical evidence, much more integrated with the Dutch political system. This is based on a variety of evidence. First, M.P. contacts are *multisector* contacts. M.P.'s see ministers, other civil servants, party organizational leaders, and interest group representatives with a high degree of frequency. Second, M.P. contact patterns are *multilevel,* suggesting that M.P.'s are at the center of a system of contacts with national level elites, middle level subelites such as interest groups and party leaders at regional levels, civil servants at the regional and local level, and citizens. They are truly integrative in terms of maintaining contacts with activists and group representatives at all levels of the system. Third, M.P. contacts are only minimally *cross-party*, only 20 percent maintaining regular contact with party leaders of opposition parties at the national level and 10 percent regularly at the regional or local level. We would have to know much more about such contacts, as well as contacts among M.P.'s, before concluding that these were adequate accommodationist exchanges. Finally, we have earlier noted that there is a certain amount of *cross-time* sequential overlap in the careers of M.P.'s in relation to the careers of their families. Indeed, one can find no significant gap in the political distance of M.P.'s and other political sectors. From whatever motivations, they appear to be very attentive to the need for communication with citizens, groups, parties, administrators, and ministers.

It is important to note that religion and party do not seem to constrain or influence the contacts of M.P.'s. This is not a segmentalized, pillarized elite. Indeed, M.P.'s from religious parties seem to be more active in contacts than M.P.'s of parties without a religious orientation.

A variety of factors were discovered to be related to the contact patterns of elites. For civil servants age, social class background, and ministerial subculture are most useful. For M.P.'s, factors that may help explain varieties in contact patterns are party, previous party experience, age, time of entrance into Parliament and social class background. These findings suggest that relatively younger Dutch elites, still influenced to some extent by lower- and lower middle-class backgrounds, but obviously also influenced by the political milieu within which they were trained and specialized, whether ministerial or party organizational, are the most actively involved in politically relevant contacts in the system. This suggests also that if there is any one leadership type that is attempting to maintain political communication and adapt to the needs of the changing Dutch society it is an emerging administrative and political elite that is younger, experienced, diversely partisan and religious, and energetically in touch with all levels of the system. This is more true of the politicians than the bureaucrats, but a minority of the latter are also involved.

Finally, the key question concerning the relevance of these contacts for attitudes was explored at some length here. We found some interesting and significant evidence of a linkage between elite contacts and their orientations to politics. Elite interactional behavior is a meaningful aspect of Dutch politics. These elites are often not only system integrated but often also attitudinally adaptive and responsive. This suggests at least that they are politically integral in the transitional Dutch polity.

NOTES

1. Gabriel Almond, "Comparative Political Systems," *The Journal of Politics* 18 (1956): 391–409; Sidney Tarrow, "Italy: Political Integration in a Fragmented Political System" (Paper delivered at the Annual Meeting of the American Political Science Association, San Francisco, 1975).
2. Arend Lijphart has written at great length and at many different places on his interpretation of the Dutch system, beginning with his *The Politics of Accommodation: Pluralism and Democracy in the Netherlands* (Berkeley: University of California Press, 1968). See also, for example, his "Consociational Democracy," *World Politics* 21 (1968–69): 207–25. Hans Daalder has also discussed the Dutch system in these terms at length. See particularly his "On Building Consociational Nations: The Cases of the Netherlands and Switzerland," *International Social Science Journal* 23, no. 3 (1971): 355–70.
3. One should note that ten of our seventy-six civil servant respondents indicated that they had no *directeur-generaal* and twenty-eight that they had no *staatssecretaris*. The remainder who did have such superior officials saw them frequently.
4. See our earlier article, "Elite Perceptions of the Political Process in the Netherlands, Looked At in Comparative Perspective," in *The Mandarins of Western Europe*, ed. Mattei Dogan (New York: John Wiley & Sons, Halstead Press, Sage Publications, 1975).
5. Joel D. Aberbach and Bert A. Rockman found in their American study, which is a part of this project, that the social service agencies in the United States had bureaucrats with attitudes distinct from those in the other agencies and cabinet departments. See their "Administrators' Beliefs about the Role of the Public: The Case of American Federal Executives" (Paper delivered at the Annual Meeting of the American Political Science Association, San Francisco, 1975).
6. Jan Kooiman presents data from an earlier study of Parliament in his book, *Over de Kamer gesproken* (The Hague: Staatsuitgeverij, 1976). He reports that M.P. contacts with voters are "regular" for 40 percent of M.P.'s, less than regular for another 40 percent, and seldom or never for 20 percent. He also discusses the content of these contacts, reporting that three out of four of them deal with personal problems. See his discussion of this and other M.P. contacts (with interest groups, for example), ibid., pp. 112–32.

7. In a small subsample of eleven Center-Right M.P.'s, those with Anti-Revolutionary and Catholic affiliations, we actually see certain of these contact differences accentuated even more. The religious party M.P.'s are more in touch with civil servants (80 percent weekly or more often), but they conform to other Center-Right M.P.'s in other contacts.
8. It is difficult to demonstrate that religious background helps explain M.P. contact patterns. Catholics appear to be somewhat more active than Protestants, and both religious groups of M.P.'s more active than those with no religion, but the differences are neither large nor consistent for all contacts.
9. See appendix 1 for a description of these indices.
10. See Hans Daalder, "Parties, Elections, and Political Developments in Western Europe," in *Political Parties and Political Development*, ed. Joseph La Palombara and Myron Wiener (Princeton, N.J.: Princeton University Press, 1966), pp. 60–61.

CHAPTER 8

Elite Views on the
Functioning of Parliament

The perceptions and evaluations of political elites about their institutional environment provide important insights into the character and
effectiveness of the political system. The key institutions we mean here
are: the Parliament, the bureaucracy, the party system, the interest
group system, and the mechanisms and processes for citizen involvement in the system. These constitute the focuses of the political world
of elites. Their attitudes concerning the functions, the performance,
and the influence roles of these key institutions are central for understanding the differences in the way elites behave in different systems.
Thus, if M.P.'s and bureaucrats have congruent perceptions about the
functions of Parliament, for example, what these are and what these
should be, a balanced bureaucratic-M.P. relationship is probable, with
minimal hostility. But when the perception of these elites diverge, as
to the power (actual or proper) and performance of Parliament (or the
bureaucracy, or the party system, etc.), then an imbalance in elite
orientations and relationships may develop. If there are basic disagreements concerning the roles and performance of these key institutions,
elite distrust and hostility may interfere with the cooperative and efficient working of the policymaking process. And worse, it may lead to
the historic confrontation between bureaucrat and politician that Max
Weber suggested was inevitable.[1]

For the operation of the Dutch consociational system this is particularly relevant. As we pointed out in the introductory chapter, there
have been fairly precise expectations as to what the role of Parliament
should be, as well as that of the bureaucracy, of parties and interest
groups (as major components of the pluralized, segmented society),
and also of citizens. Because the system has been changing since 1967,
the question is whether the type of national level elites we interviewed
have begun to reveal new perceptions of how these institutions and

actors should and do perform. And it is particularly important whether the M.P.'s and bureaucrats *agree* in these perceptions and evaluations. We begin this part of our analysis with a discussion of Parliament. In succeeding chapters we deal with the other political institutions.

Our first question is: "What do you think of Parliament, how well does it perform its tasks, and how important to the system is Parliament compared to the civil service?" The focus of our concern here is Parliament as an institution of governance. One must remember that Dutch elites work in special parliamentary and bureaucratic cultures. Parliament is a small body (150 members in the lower house), and highly fragmented (fourteen parties in 1973). Its relationship to the bureaucracy is one of formal separation and independence. Ministers run ministries (the bureaucracy), but they cannot be M.P.'s. Parliament in the past has had a circumscribed institutional status in policy-making. Nevertheless its legislative role is important, as is its representative function. Its debates over cabinet policy are a central feature of the national political arena. They are important episodes in the weighing of governmental proposals. Further, under the system of cabinet responsibility, we should not forget that Parliament can bring a government to resign.

The basic question posed here, then, is how Dutch senior civil servants and M.P.'s feel their parliamentary system is performing. While theoretically the Dutch bureaucracy has been politically neutralized, its involvement with political decision-making tasks has certainly here, as in all systems, led bureaucrats to develop views of the working of Parliament vis-à-vis the bureaucracy. Has this institutional relationship of formal separation but actual policy involvement led to attitudes of estrangement or support, of criticism or defense, of Parliament? And for M.P.'s (70 percent of whom see ministers regularly, and two-thirds of whom say they are in contact with some civil servants fairly often), what are their views of the Parliament, and of their relationships with the bureaucracy? Above all, what patterns of congruence or dissonance do we find when we compare the views of these elites?

Our interviews were rich with ideas and imagery about Parliament and the contrasts between the M.P. and the civil servant in their institutional life-styles. The contrast was dramatically stated by one M.P.:

The greatest difference (between an M.P. and a civil servant) is naturally that the civil service apparatus really functions as a sort of supermarket, and an M.P. is no more than a small independent shopkeeper on the corner—sometimes he (the M.P.) gets half an assistant . . .

Another M.P. stated this in another way:

> Parliament doesn't have its own research apparatus. They are,
> thus, in the power of the ministers who do have a useful *apparaat*.
> On the other hand, ministers who cannot supervise their own de-
> partments results in the civil servants having more power.

Another M.P. stated the difference this way:

> A politician by definition works in a "party way" . . . (M.P.'s) do
> not act exclusively rationally but also emotionally and from their
> instincts. If you as a politician forget that, then you will be quickly
> gone. I think that you as a civil servant . . . can put a greater
> accent on rationality than a politician in direct contact with the
> voters can.

At times, as these leaders discussed each other's tasks and roles, they
revealed a latent tension between them, as some of the above observations suggest. Civil servants often speak of the "decline" of Parliament, that "our representatives are not ideal," or that "Parliament
does not function well." M.P.'s, on the other hand, are inclined by
innuendo or overtly to compare themselves favorably with civil servants. "M.P.'s must be very sensitive," one of them said, "they must
make quick decisions, but that is not natural for a civil servant."

Keeping in mind these images, we can summarize the attitudes of
these leaders toward Parliament. The civil servant's view of Parliament
is a useful point of departure (table 66). Senior bureaucrats emphasize
primarily three Parliamentary tasks: Controlling the government,
lawgiving, and influencing policy. About half also think contacts with
voters and weighing interest group demands are important. Junior bureaucrats are inclined, however, to rank them as less important (on the
average there is a 15 point difference between the two in their proportions). Civil servants do not think that it is very important for Parliament to maintain liaison with the ministries, to respond to citizen
complaints, to take the initiative in policy areas, or to implement party
programs. Thus for 50 to 80 percent of the civil servants lower priority
is placed on these political communication, mobilization, and program
development tasks. In the rank order of tasks it is Parliament's traditional roles that rank the highest.

Comparable data for M.P.'s reveal a rank order of importance of
these tasks that is basically the same, with lawgiving, influencing policy, contacts with voters, and controlling the government being considered by M.P.'s, as by top civil servants, as most important. But
more M.P.'s are inclined to emphasize the importance of other tasks

also. Thus, for implementing party programs, 51 percent of the M.P.'s consider this a very important task (scale positions 8–9) while only 29 percent of the civil servants do. For dealing with citizens' complaints the proportions are 48 percent and 17 percent. For maintaining contacts with the departments, M.P.'s are, interestingly, much more likely to emphasize this task (33 percent of the M.P.'s while only 16 percent of the civil servants).

Evaluations of Parliament's Work

When asked how well they think Parliament is performing its tasks, the top civil servants are consistently more supportive than the high flyers (the latter are on the average 25 points more negative in their evaluations). But even the higher civil servants do not give Parliament high marks. On only three tasks do more than 50 percent of them feel Parliament is doing quite well—controlling the government, lawgiving, and (interestingly) in responding to new problems. On this latter task 67 percent of the top civil servants praise Parliament's work. On many of the other tasks, some seen as quite important by a fairly large percent (such as influencing policy, maintaining contacts with the others), only a minority of civil servants evaluate Parliament at the high-support end of the scale.

One must be careful, however, in using these data to reach the conclusion that top civil servants are very negative. As a matter of fact, most of them are moderately affirmative, or ambivalent, or supportive with reservations. If one looked at the total distribution of responses

TABLE 66. Civil Servant's View of Parliament's Task Performance (in percentages)

Task	Importance of Parliamentary Task[a]	Evaluation of Task Performance[b]
Controlling the government	78	52
Lawgiving	73	54
Influencing policy	64	42
Contacts with voters	53	23
Weighing interest group demands	49	17
Implementing party programs	29	26
Responding to new problems	25	67
Dealing with citizen complaints	17	37
Keeping good contacts with departments	16	29

a. Percentage saying task is very important, rating it 8 or 9 on a scale of 10.
b. Percentage saying task is very important, rating it 7 to 9 on a scale of 10.

on any one item would get the feeling they are in between enthusiasm
and indifference in these evaluations. For example, if we take the task
of maintaining contacts with the voters we see our top civil servants
distributed on our scale as shown in figure 17. Thus, 62 percent of our
civil servants were located in the middle, at scale positions 4–6, and
while only a few ranked Parliament high (23 percent), only a few also
ranked Parliament very low (16 percent).

Generally, one can say that while this is not a particularly strong
evaluation of Parliament by civil servants, it is certainly not an overwhelmingly negative one either. Civil servants do not think certain
tasks are important, and on those they do feel are important 50 percent or slightly fewer rank the job as well done. There is a strong
minority in the top civil service very supportive of Parliament, a small
minority very critical, and the rest seem to be lukewarm, wavering in
between, with moderate support.

One might expect that M.P.'s would evaluate the work of Parliament more positively, but this is not necessarily true for the individual
tasks. On four tasks a majority of the M.P.'s in our sample felt that
Parliament was doing a good job (scale positions 7–9). These were
lawgiving; attacking new problems; maintaining contacts with departments; and handling citizen complaints. On the latter two of these
tasks M.P.'s diverged substantially from the evaluation of top civil
servants; 55 percent of M.P.'s approved of Parliament's performance
on both questions, while only 29 percent of civil servants approved
Parliament's maintenance of contacts and 37 percent approved handling of complaints. On the other two, lawgiving and attacking new
problems, the two elites were very close (M.P.'s 65 and 64 percent,
civil servants 54 and 67 percent). On another task, controlling the
government, more of the civil servants actually approved of Parliament
than did M.P.'s (52 percent to 44 percent at scale positions 7–9).
M.P.'s were most self-critical on the performance of tasks such as
influencing policy, implementing party programs, maintaining voter
contacts, and weighing interest group demands.[2] But again, the picture

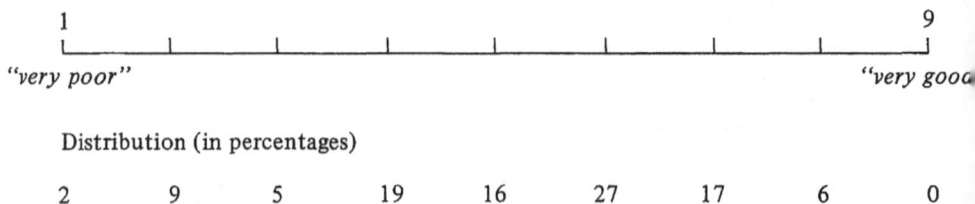

1   9
L____l_____l_____l_____l_____l_____l_____l_____l___J
"very poor"   *"very good*

Distribution (in percentages)

2   9   5   19   16   27   17   6   0

Fig. 17.   Evaluation of Parliament by top civil servants

is one of moderate criticism, with most M.P.'s located toward the middle of the scale (see fig. 18). Almost 50 percent are in the middle scale positions, much as was the case for the top civil servants. M.P.'s are therefore not indiscriminately self-congratulatory. They do tend to feel on the average that they are performing their task better than civil servants feel they are. But the difference is not very great. The average percentages of the three sets of elites evaluating the nine parliamentary tasks as performed poorly (scale numbers 1–4) were: M.P.'s, 20.1 percent; top civil servants, 23.2 percent; high flyers, 37.3 percent. The average percentages estimating performance as good (scale numbers 7–9) were: M.P.'s, 48 percent; top civil servants, 38.6 percent; high flyers, 13.3 percent. Clearly, the high flyers are most negative, while the M.P.'s and top civil servants are most congruent, and inclined to moderation in their evaluations.

Senior civil servants are more inclined to feel that the bureaucracy is more critical for policymaking than Parliament. This emerges from their responses to the following agree-disagree statement that was put to all of these leaders: "Basically, it is not the parties or the Parliament but the civil service which guarantees satisfactory public policy." The results were:

	Agree (pro–civil service)	Agree with Res- ervations	Disagree with Res- ervations	Disagree (pro– Parliament and parties)
M.P.'s	0	9.5%	57%	33%
Top civil servants	6%	40	35	19
High flyers	6	19	56	19

The contrast between M.P.'s and top civil servants (but not the junior bureaucrats particularly) is strong in these distributions. Ninety percent of the M.P.'s are in disagreement with the statement, and thus opposed to giving the civil service such a prominent role, while 46 percent of the senior bureaucrats do think the civil service is more important than Parliament and the parties. Admittedly, the statement

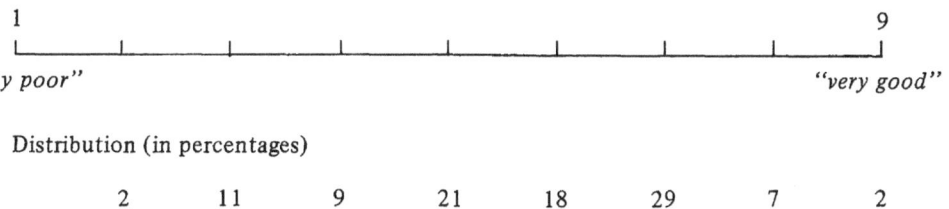

1   9

y poor"   *"very good"*

Distribution (in percentages)

2   11   9   21   18   29   7   2

Fig. 18.   Evaluation of Parliament by M.P.'s

has ambiguities within it and is not ideally phrased to confront elites with a single choice. But it does suggest a tension between the elites, though of moderate proportions, and in the same direction as in the responses about the tasks of Parliament.

Characteristics of Parliament Critics and Supporters

The next question is thus posed: which civil servants and M.P.'s are least supportive of Parliament, and most critical of its work? Of course, high flyers are normally more critical. There are variations, however, in level of support among M.P.'s and senior bureaucrats. Are the critics the older, Weberian types or the younger elites with radical perspectives? Do the critics have distinctive backgrounds and partisan orientations? With whom do they interact, or are they most isolated?

The youngest M.P.'s appear to be the most critical of Parliament (table 67). Although on a certain task like lawgiving the older M.P.'s may also be critical (42 percent saying it was poorly performed), usually the oldest representatives are least critical. Indeed, the average negative proportion for the oldest M.P.'s on these five tasks is 22 percent, while it is 53 percent for the junior M.P.'s. Age does not seem to be a major factor in explaining the views of top civil servants. Actually, the youngest in this group of top bureaucrats are the least critical of Parliament, averaging 21 percent.

Party affiliation is a factor that also discriminates among elites,

TABLE 67.   Age as a Factor in Elite Evaluation of Parliament
(in percentages)[a]

	Top Civil Servants			M.P.'s[b]		
Parliamentary Task	Oldest Cohort	Middle-aged	Youngest Cohort	Oldest Cohort	Middle-aged	Youngest Cohort
Contacting voters	20	50	40	0	23	50
Weighing interest group demands	45	59	28	33	45	44
Handling citizen complaints	37	30	28	18	33	60
Lawgiving	18	14	0	42	29	40
Influencing policy	6	13	8	17	45	70
Average proportion	25	33	21	22	35	53

a. Percentages represent those saying task is poorly done, rating 1 to 4 on a scale of 10.
b. Since M.P.'s were much more inclined to rate Parliament's task performance highly, the scale position used was usually 1 to 5 or 1 to 6 on a scale of 10.

although it works quite differently for top civil servants and M.P.'s (table 68). For the civil servants, those with a rightist partisan commitment are most critical of Parliament, while among M.P.'s it is the Left. The contrasts are striking on some tasks, such as influencing policy or maintaining contacts with the voters. Of course, the interviewing was done before the Den Uyl cabinet (with a socialist prime minister) came into office in 1973. The socialist party members' criticism of the work of Parliament may be partly associated with that time period, although the impression one gets from the lengthy comments of these leaders is that the criticism is more profound and less sporadic than such an interpretation would imply. In any event the distance between the Left deputies and those of the confessional parties is considerable. Within the confessional group of M.P.'s, however, it is Protestant M.P.'s, not the Catholics, who are the locus of most criticism (on the average 33 percent compared to 9 percent).

We see, then, that among M.P.'s it is the younger, socialist representatives, and those with a Protestant background, who consider Parliament as not performing well on these critical tasks. Among civil servants it is inclined to be the middle-aged and those with a right-wing partisan orientation who are unhappy with Parliament's performance.

Are communication contacts of M.P.'s and bureaucrats relevant for their views on Parliament? Our data suggest they may well be. Those civil servants who are in frequent contact with M.P.'s or with interest group representatives or with citizens are much more likely than those civil servants who are more isolated politically to think a task like handling citizen complaints or weighing interest group demands is important. As for elite evaluations, we find those more activist in their contacts to be more critical of Parliament's performance.

TABLE 68. Party Differences as a Factor in Elite Evaluation of Parliament (in percentages)[a]

Parliamentary Task	Civil Servants			M.P.'s		
	Left	Confessional	Right	Left	Confessional	Right
Lawgiving	20	0	7	32	33	36
Contact with voters	22	31	48	39	0	9
Weighing group demands	26	33	57	45	22	45
Handling citizen complaints	13	20	32	52	0	30
Influencing policy	5	13	7	70	11	18
Average Proportions	17	19	30	48	13	28

a. Percentages represent those saying task is poorly done, rating 1 to 4 on a scale of 10.

Thus civil servants with frequent contacts with clientele interest groups feel Parliament's job in representing these groups is rather poorly done (50 percent) compared to the opinions of those civil servants not in contact with such groups (29 percent rating Parliament's performance as poor).

Views Elites Have of Their Relationships with Each Other

Much of our discussion implicity deals with the relationships of Dutch civil servants and M.P.'s, by discussing their contacts and their mutual perspectives and preferences. Such data permit us to determine their congruence or distance in attitudes. Beyond such analysis, however, the question remains: what do these two elite groups think of each other and their mutual relationships, when asked directly? Do they worry about the interference of other elites in their work? Do they feel there is a relationship of trust between elites?

A residuum of discontent in mutual perceptions is found in certain response patterns. When civil servants were asked whether they were worried about the interference of politicians, 17 percent said they were and, while the remainder said no, another 34 percent had some reservation. Similarly, when M.P.'s were asked whether they were worried about the interference of civil servants, 21 percent said they were and another 47 percent indicated some, possibly minimal, concern about such interference. There is no extreme hostility pattern here, but there is definitely a minority of dissidents, possibly one-fifth.[3] Another question in our interview provided some corroboration. We asked these bureaucrats to characterize their relationships with M.P.'s by indicating on a nine point trust-distrust scale what the relationship in general was. The result for higher civil servants is presented in figure 19. There is no evidence here of great mistrust but, on the other hand, there is also considerable ambivalence. Barely half are at the highest scale points (7–9). The same scale, when used with the high flyers, found only 18 percent at these high scale points.

Breakdown   *Mutual t)*
in mutual   *and effec*
trust   *cooperat*

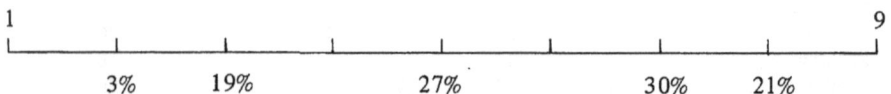

1   9
└──────┴──────┴──────┴──────┴──────┴──────┴──────┴──────┘

     3%   19%   27%   30%   21%

Fig. 19. Bureaucrats' estimations of their relationships with M.P.'s

In probing for the characteristics of those civil servants most worried about their relationships with politicians, we analyzed a variety of possible variables. Two of these are presented in table 69. The right- and left-wing bureaucrats are most likely to feel that their relationships with M.P.'s are conflictual, while confessional party supporters in the bureaucracy are less of that mind. Those relatively low on our trust scale constituted a third or a fourth of Right and Left partisans while being virtually nonexistent for confessionals. Age by itself did not seem important, but we did find that those most recently entering the service were more worried than the civil servants entering many years ago.

Since we are talking here of civil servant perceptions of the harmoniousness of their actual relationships with M.P.'s it was natural to ask whether the patterns of their contacts were relevant. And they clearly were, as the following distributions reveal: 70 percent of the civil servants who had regular contact with M.P.'s rated them high on the trust-distrust scale; of those who had contacts with M.P.'s occasionally, 56 percent rated them high on the scale; only 38 percent of those civil servants who never came in contact with M.P.'s rated them high. There is striking evidence here that contacts between elites are functional to the development of trustworthy relationships. As a final check, we compared those ministries in which we found bureaucrats least in contact with M.P.'s with those ministries most in contact, and there was verification for this basic finding. In those ministries low in contact with M.P.'s only 39 percent reported that relationships with politicians were harmonious and cooperative, compared to 57 percent of those ministries highest in contact with M.P.'s.

TABLE 69. Factors Related to Civil Servant Views of Their Relationships with Politicians (in percentages)

	Relatively Low on Trust Scale[a]	High on Trust Scale[b]
Party Orientation		
Left-wing	35	45
Confessional	6	69
Right-wing	25	43
Year Joined Civil Service		
Up to 1940	14	58
1940–1950	8	61
After 1950	32	42

a. Scale positions 1 to 5 on a scale of 10.
b. Scale positions 7 to 9 on a scale of 10.

All of this suggests that those civil servants entering the bureaucracy later rather than earlier, out of touch with parties and M.P.'s, and tending to favor both Left and Right parties are the locus of concern or unhappiness about interelite relationships. As stated earlier, there is a 25 to 30 percent minority who seem disenchanted. While they seem to be of different backgrounds, they tend to share one major characteristic—they, by their own reporting to us, are somewhat isolated from M.P.'s and party politics.

Conclusion: A Comparison of Public and Elite Evaluations of Parliament

The major direction of our findings for elites is clear. On the average, from 20 percent (senior bureaucrats) to 37 percent (high flyers) think Parliament does its work poorly. About a fifth of the senior civil servants resent the interference of M.P.'s, and 17 percent of M.P.'s resent bureaucratic interference. Most of our respondents talked at length, and many had strong opinions about the Parliament and its relation to the bureaucracy. Neither of these elite sets demeaned each other's role in the system, nor was there violent hostility, but there was a sizable reservoir of discontent with Parliament's work.

It is useful to compare public evaluations of Parliament with those of elites. The 1972 national election survey fortunately included some questions that, although not the same as in our elite project, provide some basis for elite-mass comparison. The public seems to be fairly familiar with the names of members of Parliament, only 18 percent being completely uninformed. When asked to name members, 48 percent can mention five or more, an additional 22 percent three or four members, with 12 percent mentioning one or two.[4] As to the parties represented in Parliament the same level of ability is apparent—78 percent can mention one or more parties, and 60 percent to 70 percent mention the largest parties.[5] They also are generally supportive of Parliament and the need for it in the system. On the question: "Would a government without a Second Chamber appeal to you?" Only 8 percent said yes, 67 percent no.[6] They are cynical, however, in their view of the representative function of M.P.'s, so far as the individual citizen is concerned. On the question, "Do you find that M.P.'s generally do their work well or don't you find that to be true?" 48 percent answered positively and 33 percent negatively.[7] Further, they feel that "politicians in Holland should leave more to other specialists"—54 percent agree, 25 percent do not agree.[8] And in their basic summary evaluation of Parliament's task performance (in response to the question, "Do members of the Second Chamber do their jobs well or don't they?"), 29 percent said they do a good job; 26 percent said they occasionally do a good job; another 26 percent said some members do, some members don't; 5 percent said they don't do a good job; 12 percent don't know; and 1.5 percent did not answer. Two-thirds of the Dutch electorate has a middle-of-the-road position in their evaluations. And actually, 31 percent are rather negative, while 29 percent are quite positive.[9] In this evaluation they fall in between the opinion of high flyers and top civil servants. The average proportions seeing Parliament's performance as good, based on these data and our earlier analysis in this chapter, are as follows: M.P.'s, 48 percent; top civil servants, 39 percent; members of the public, 29 percent; and high flyers, 13 percent. Thus the senior elites are more supportive of Parliament, while the public has more reservations.

Various factors stand out as helping to identify those who are the critics. Age, religious background, and partisan orientation all seem useful in explaining certain types of negative evaluations or feelings that M.P.-bureaucrat relationships are not harmonious. Above all, a variable that seems particularly potent is the frequency of contacts that elites have with each other, as well as with other actors in the system. In some respects the differences in evaluations linked to contacts are striking. And yet many elites who are not interacting are very supportive and sanguine about the counterelite, suggesting again that much political socialization has taken place that is not a function of elite association.

Finally, what one derives from these data is the realization that elites differ considerably in their views about each other and the institution in which they work. They are not of one mind, despite common backgrounds and experiences and positions. However, while not all of one mind, we find for senior bureaucrats and M.P.'s no fundamental disagreement, no extreme dissent, no strong hostility in their mutual evaluations. There is elite noncongruence on some perspectives. There are M.P.'s and civil servants who are critical of Parliament, as well as a minority of both elites who do not reveal mutual trust and acceptance. But severe and deeply felt oppositionism is not manifest in these data. There is much more harmony here than dissonance.

NOTES

1. H. H. Gerth and C. Wright Mills, eds., *From Max Weber: Essays in Sociology* (London: Kegan Paul, 1948), pp. 232–33.

2. One should note that we have found considerable stability in the views of M.P.'s over time. The 1972 survey of Parliament which asked the same basic set of questions with a larger sample (N = 141) found a basically similar pattern of evaluations. For example, on the evaluation of "lawgiving" and "maintaining voter contacts" here were the distributions for the two years:

Sample		Position on Scale				
	Year	*1–3*	*4–5*	*6–7*	*8–9*	N
Lawgiving	1972	2%	6%	57%	34%	141
	1973	2	4	68	26	44
Voter contacts	1972	12	20	50	18	141
	1973	13	29	47	9	44

3. See our earlier article for comparative data on this point: "Elite Perceptions of the Political Process in the Netherlands, Looked At in Comparative Perspective," in *The Mandarins of Western Europe,* ed. Mattei Dogan (New York: John Wiley & Sons, Halstead Press, Sage Publications, 1975), p. 159. In Italy, 79 percent of the bureaucrats resented the interference of politicians; in Germany, 47 percent; in Sweden, 37 percent; in Britain 11 percent.

4. L. P. J. de Bruyn and J. W. Foppen, eds., *Nationaal Kiezersonderzoek 1972–73* (Nijmegen: Instituut voor Politicologie, 1974), p. 214.

5. Ibid., p. 178.

6. Ibid., p. 236.

7. Ibid.

8. Ibid., p. 237.

9. Ibid., p. 236.

CHAPTER 9

Elite Views on Parties and Interest Groups

The highly fragmented Dutch party system has been a dominant characteristic of Dutch politics for a long time. The presence in the lower house of Parliament of many parties (fourteen in 1973 and eleven in 1977) is a basic element in the political culture, for bureaucrats as well as M.P.'s. As we noted earlier, nine political parties are represented in the preferences of our civil servants. We have, then, two sets of elites, each of which reflects the pluralism of party orientations and interests.

In addition, the Netherlands has an interest group infrastructure that is well organized, extensive, and articulate. In the past the labor unions, employer associations, farmer groups, middle-class shopkeepers associations, and many other interest groups were divided along cultural-religious lines, the *zuilen*, which segmented the society. These lines of demarcation are not as rigid today, but the interest groups are as active. Many elites have links to these groups because of their own backgrounds. The attitudes of elites towards the role of these groups in the system particularly during the period of change in consociationalism is very pertinent.

As for the party system, most of our respondents saw important differences in what the parties stood for. Only a minority (17 percent of the civil servants and 11 percent of the M.P.'s) belittled party differences. Further, these differences are seen by bureaucrats less as a mirror of the social and political conflict of the society and more as a sharpening of such conflicts that already exist. For civil servants 74 percent see parties as exacerbating public differences, and 51 percent of the M.P.'s agree. There is more ambivalence on this matter among M.P.'s, however.

Conflict concerns bureaucrats more. Conflict is more often seen by them as unnecessary, and parties are seen as sharpeners of conflict. And top bureaucrats notice party differences affecting the work of their ministries. When pressed with a specific question on this matter 21 percent said they found no evidence of party differences affecting work of the ministry, 25 percent saw little or marginal differences, while 54 percent indicated they felt the effects of differences were evident. This last group comprises the 32 percent who saw the effects primarily in day-to-day work, 11 percent who saw differences primarily in goals, 4 percent who perceived differences in personalities, and 7 percent who did not specify.

The way in which Dutch elites think about party differences is interesting. A comparison of Dutch with British elites highlights the findings (table 70). The Dutch elites are more ideological and more inclined to refer to religious differences. Class and group interests are prominent in the thinking of Dutch elites. Economic questions are salient to them, as in Britain. The scope of government preoccupies British elites much more than the Dutch. Social welfare problems and military and foreign policy preoccupy the thinking of a smaller proportion, about 25 percent. Questions of geography, linguistic, regional, or racial differences, leadership style, crime—these are matters not seen as dividing the parties. Rather the debate or dialogue between the parties is seen as ideological, economic, social, and, to some extent, regarding international policies.

Factors Related to Elite Views about Parties

Background factors play a role, and in surprising ways, in identifying elites that emphasize *ideology* in talking about parties (table 71). Confessional M.P.'s are most likely to talk about ideology, much more than Left partisans in either the Parliament or the bureaucracy. It is interest-

TABLE 70. Topics Most Prominent in Elite Discussions of Party Differences: The Netherlands Compared to Britain (in percentages)

	Netherlands		Britain	
	Civil Servants	M.P.'s	Civil Servants	M.P.'s
Ideology	30	51	12	31
Economic affairs	50	41	31	38
Class or group benefits	46	46	19	28
Religious alignments	10	21	1	0
Proper scope of government	16	28	60	67
Social problems and welfare	22	21	18	21
Military and foreign policy	30	26	4	4

ing also that the oldest M.P.'s and those from middle and lower social class origins are more conscious about ideological differences. Who in these elite groups are the most troubled about party conflicts? We find in every subgroup that the civil servants are more convinced that party diversities distort or exaggerate differences. The majorities who believe this rise to 70 percent for right-wing partisans, Protestants, and the middle-aged civil servants. Here is the location of the greatest concern about party conflict in the system. And the distance between M.P.'s and civil servants on this evaluation is indeed considerable, rising from a small percentage differential of 10 points between the elites of the Left parties to over 50 percentage points for the elites on the Right. The same extreme distance is noticeable for the middle-aged and the Protestants. There is extreme dissension on this point, therefore.

These differences by partisan orientation are strengthened when we look at the role of ideology in relation to perceptions of party conflict (table 72). The conservatives are much more inclined to be critical of parties and to see them as needlessly sharpening conflict. Among civil servants, those opposing state intervention in the society and economy react adversely—50 percent are strongly critical of parties, compared to only 17 percent of those who are liberal on this

TABLE 71. Factors Related to Perception of Ideological Differences among Parties (in percentages)

	Respondents Who See Ideological Differences as Prominent	
	Civil Servants	M.P.'s
Party type		
Left-wing	16	45
Confessional	41	70
Right-wing	33	38
Father's social class		
Highest prestige level	42	27
Somewhat lower levels	24	61
Age		
Oldest cohort	22	60
Middle-aged cohort	29	47
Youngest cohort	40	50
Religion		
Catholic	47	67
Protestant	20	56
No religion	32	36

ideological dimension. It is an even more striking difference between liberal and conservative M.P.'s—56 percentage points.

Further, there is a link between general normative orientations about conflict and elite views of parties. Among civil servants, those who feel political conflict is good for a system are much less likely to criticize parties. There is a tendency in this direction also among M.P.'s but it is less impressive. Clearly, here we have critical orientations toward politics that seem closely related to elite feelings about the party system. It is the ideological conservatives who are worried about party conflict and who feel parties engage in conflictual behavior that goes beyond the pale of propriety.

One must conclude this analysis of elite cognitions of the Dutch party system with an awareness of the salience and considerable concern about party conflict. Both sets of elites see important differences among parties in ideological, economic, and class differences. Civil

TABLE 72. Attitudes toward Conflict and toward State Intervention as Explanations of Elite Views on Party Conflict

	"Parties Exacerbate Conflict Unnecessarily"			
	Definitely Agree	Agree	Disagree	N
	Civil servants			
Ideology				
Opposes state intervention	50	32	18	22
Favors, but has reservations	35	41	24	37
Definitely favors	17	33	50	12
Normative position				
Conflict is good	11	57	32	28
Pro/con	50	23	27	22
Conflict is bad	60	25	15	20
	Members of Parliament			
Ideology				
Opposes state intervention	56	11	33	9
Favors, but has reservations	13	50	38	16
Definitely favors	0	29	71	17
Normative Position				
Conflict is good	16	32	53	19
Pro/con	30	30	40	10
Conflict is bad	12	50	38	8

servants are particularly worried about such conflict per se, with no subgroups exempt from concern. Those from the partisan Right are overwhelmingly critical, and the middle-aged are almost as concerned. But many in the youngest cohort of civil servants and those from the Left partisan persuasion are also ready to deny the necessity of the current character of party conflict, at least the extent of it presently in the country. Young and left-wing M.P.'s are not as ready to express alarm at the exacerbation of party differences, but most other M.P.'s are inclined to be critical.

If there is a basic tendency to "polarity" in these data it is in the relationships of the Left to the Right in Parliament. On the measures used here one sees both considerable agreement and a considerable gap between the two groups. While only a minority of M.P.'s in both parties feel that the parties actually reflect the differences in the country (12 percent of the Right, 15 percent of the Left), only the Right takes the position that parties unnecessarily sharpen political conflicts (100 percent of the Right, 30 percent of the Left). To a certain extent the same pattern exists for the comparison between the youngest and oldest M.P.'s. But within the bureaucracy, while there is disagreement about the extent to which party differences reflect the public's viewpoints, there is very little disagreement on the evaluative issue. Bureaucrats appear to be alienated by party conflict and see it as unnecessarily aggravated.

Elite Attitudes to Interest Groups

One cannot ignore the role of pressure groups in the Netherlands. They still reflect to some extent the major sectors and the vertical pillarization of the society. The provision of a Social Economic Council of forty-five members, in which certain policy matters affecting these groups must be discussed and with which the government must consult, adds a legitimacy to the status and demands of such groups. Changes, however, are taking place. Some evidence of the breakdown of the segmentation of the political society in these terms is manifest in the joint trade union association of Catholics and socialists, which took effect in January, 1976. The rise of new television associations, the decline of the *verzuiling* press, and the dilution of membership in these groups suggests the change away from the rigid interest group pluralism of the past. It is within this reorganized, still somewhat fragmented, but transitional infrastructure of relatively expressive interest groups that Dutch elites must function.

We asked M.P.'s and civil servants at various points of the interview to discuss their evaluations and perceptions of these groups and their roles in the political process. The prominence of interest groups in elite cognitions about politics is evident. As noted earlier in the discussion of party differences, almost half of the elites (46 percent) see the interests and benefits of groups as very prominently distinguishing political parties. In the work of Parliament, the task of weighing interest group demands is considered important; in fact, it ranks as one of the most important tasks, after such obvious tasks as lawgiving, controlling the government, and influencing policy. It ranks close with maintaining contacts with the voters. Only 5 percent of the top civil servants would say that interest group representation is not important, and 49 percent say it is very important.

Parliament is not perceived by most elites as doing an excellent job in dealing with interest group demands. Civil servants are particularly critical. So there is a split in evaluation of how well Parliament is functioning in this respect—the split among M.P.'s is 58 percent to 42 percent in favor of the view that the job is reasonably well done, and for civil servants a 42 to 58 percent split in the other direction.

In the discussion of problems facing the country, we pressed our respondents to discuss approaches to the solution of the problems they mentioned and the obstacles in the way of such discussions. Here one of our emphases in analyzing their responses was on the centrality of groups in elite descriptions of the problem and its resolution. We found that 40 percent of the elites discussed the problem in group terms, that is, with a heavy emphasis on the role of groups in generating the issue, or providing input for its resolution, or creating difficulties for its solution. Another 15 percent referred to groups but not so centrally. Sometimes there was a very explicit recognition of the importance of groups, as in the case of the liberal M.P. who said the most important problem facing the country itself was "class conflict and the relationship between the different functional groups in society." For others, in the context of discussing a particular policy or problem, there was often explicit discussion of the role of groups, or specific vested interests, in opposing change. When asked which groups had been benefiting from governmental policy and which groups had not, the majority of civil servants were able to mention specific groups that had not done well, and 72 percent mentioned groups that had profited or improved their condition. And they were split in their perceptions as to how groups had been treated, that is, lower-class groups and deprived groups were mentioned most often as benefiting most and benefiting least. Dutch elites clearly are group oriented in their thinking about the policy process.

On balance, civil servants were more inclined to express discontent about the role of interest group conflict. When asked to agree or disagree with the statement, "The welfare of the country is endangered by the clash of interest groups," 21 percent of the civil servants agreed strongly, compared to 14 percent of the M.P.'s; 36 percent agreed with reservations, compared to 24 percent of M.P.'s. Twenty-nine percent disagreed, as did 38 percent of M.P.'s; 14 percent disagreed strongly, compared to 24 percent of the M.P.'s. Thus, only 43 percent of the bureaucrats accept a broad role for these groups. But when asked about the role of such groups in the work of the ministries, 86 percent approved (as did 93 percent of the M.P.'s).

Factors Related to Elite Views about Interest Groups

Which leaders, with what types of backgrounds, are most and least concerned about interest group conflict (table 73)? Among M.P.'s there is a clear relationship for most of these variables. Those M.P.'s

TABLE 73. Background Factors Related to Normative Concern over Interest Group Conflict and Pressure (in percentages)

	Agree that Group Conflict Endangers National Welfare	
	Civil Servants	M.P.'s
Age		
Oldest group	58	50
Middle group	64	38
Youngest group	52	30
Party		
Left-wing	40	26
Confessional	71	58
Right-wing	61	50
Religion		
Catholic	67	60
Protestant	56	31
None	54	31
Residence while growing up		
Big city	41	25
Medium-sized city	78	41
Suburban, rural	50	64
Year entered civil service		
Up to 1940	46	
1940–1950	69	
After 1950	69	

most critical of interest groups are the oldest cohort (50 percent feeling interest group conflicts endanger the country's welfare), the Catholics (60 percent), those brought up in rural and suburban areas (64 percent), and the M.P.'s of confessional and right-wing parties (50 to 58 percent). The young socialist deputies from cosmopolitan environments seem much more tolerant of such conflict.

For civil servants, although these same empirical generalizations tend to be true also, the findings are not as clear-cut. Those with a preference for left-wing parties and those most recently admitted to the civil service are most tolerant of such group conflict. Thus, a sizable proportion of elites feel the system should move away from such clashes of interest groups, but this is not an evaluation shared by most of the younger, socialist, or metropolitan parliamentary leaders.

The ideological positions of elites about the role of government and about conflict, again, as with their views about party conflict, are linked to views about interest group conflict (table 74). The conservative leaders, both in the bureaucracy and Parliament, are very clearly those most inclined to see interest group conflict as dysfunctional to the general welfare. The liberals are much more sanguine about such conflict—only 10 percent or less being unreservedly critical of the clash of interest groups, while 43 percent to 67 percent of the conservatives are. Further, the general normative view of conflict is related to the specific evaluations of interest groups. Elites who approve of conflict are less critical of interest groups—the difference is 65 percent to 35 percent for senior bureaucrats and 80 percent to 20 percent for M.P.'s. This suggests a high level of constraint, or structural consistency, in elite views, since we found this to be true in elite views of party conflict also.

If we combine these findings with those about elite views toward party conflict, we can see a pattern or syndrome emerging: ideological liberals, those normatively favoring conflict, and the leftist partisans are more tolerant of conflict in both the Dutch party system and the interest group infrastructure, while the ideological conservatives, those normatively opposed to conflict, and the Center-Right partisans are much more worried about and intolerant of such conflict. This is the basic observation consistently resulting from this analysis.

Finally, we should note that frequency of elite contacts is linked to positive feelings towards parties and interest groups. First, we find that M.P.'s regularly in contact with party leaders rarely feel parties unnecessarily increase conflict (11 percent) compared to those infrequently in contact (62 percent), a striking difference. The same percentages for senior bureaucrats are 25 percent and 40 percent. Contact seems to

| | "The Welfare of the Country is Endangered by the Clash of Interest Groups" | | | | | | | | | |
| | Definitely Agree | | Agree with Reservations | | Disagree | | Disagree Strongly | | N | |
	Civil Servants	M.P.'s	Civil Servants	M.P.'s	Civil Servants	M.P.'s	Civil Servants	M.P.'s	Civil Servants	M.P.'s
Ideology										
Opposes governmental intervention in society	43	67	39	11	9	11	9	11	23	9
Favors, but has reservations	11	6	38	44	35	50	16	0	37	16
Definitely favors	8	0	25	12	50	41	17	47	12	17
Normative position on conflict										
Sees conflict as good	7	11	29	11	50	32	14	46	28	19
Pro/con	23	20	50	30	18	50	9	0	22	10
Sees conflict as bad	40	25	35	38	10	38	15	0	10	8

lead to reduction of critical feelings about conflict. One can, of course, turn this analysis around and demonstrate that it may be *the orientation that determines the contact;* thus, only 5 percent of M.P.'s who believe parties increase conflict unnecessarily have frequent contact with other party leaders, while 42 percent of those M.P.'s who do not believe parties increase conflict unnecessarily have frequent contact with other party leaders. Whatever the direction of the relationship, clearly there is a link of some importance here. We note particularly that M.P.'s frequently in touch with other parties' leaders see considerable differences between the parties, are less likely to see these differences as harmful for the system, and indeed are much more inclined to see these differences as mirroring the partisan differences in the public, rather than exacerbating them.

Second, we find that frequency of contact with party leaders is associated with general orientations supportive of conflict in the system. That is, those in touch with party leaders are more likely to see conflict as functional to social progress. The differences are not great, but there is a modest association. Thus, for civil servants in touch with M.P.'s, 42 percent support conflict generally, compared to 29 percent not in contact with M.P.'s. But more important is the finding that, of those M.P.'s regularly in contact with other parties, only 25 percent feel conflict in the society is irreconcilable (compared to 41 percent of those not in touch).

Third, elite contacts with interest groups also appear relevant for understanding their views about interest group roles in the system. M.P.'s who tell us they are in weekly contact with the representatives of national interest groups are more aware of conflict in the system, but they also are more likely to feel that conflict is healthy (by a margin of 90 percent to 45 percent). However, senior bureaucrats who tell us they are in weekly contact with national interest group representatives remain no less worried about such conflict. Contact does not necessarily lead to the alleviation of bureaucratic concern about the consequences of group conflict.

Concluding Observations

Dutch M.P.'s do not want to be viewed by others primarily as interest group representatives.[1] They are strong partisans. Dutch senior bureaucrats don't want to be seen as partisans. On the other hand, many have frequent clientele relations with interest groups, and 40 percent talk of their mediational role. Both sets of elites see important differences between the parties and are concerned about the meaning of party conflict—two-thirds of the senior civil servants and 50 percent of the M.P.'s feel it is unnecessarily exacerbating. As for interest groups, again a majority of senior civil servants are anxious about its harmful effects, true for over one-third of M.P.'s.

These concerns about the role of interest groups and parties bear a resemblance to public views. In the national survey conducted at the time of the 1972 election the public's attitudes were explored on these questions. Identical questions were not employed, but one can deduce the level of public support from the following data that come from the responses to questions put to an adult sample in that survey.[2] When asked, "Do you think that political parties in the Netherlands do their work well in general or not well?" 23 percent of the national sample responded that parties did well; 13 percent said they did badly; 33 percent felt they worked well sometimes and badly sometimes; 24 percent felt some parties worked well while others did not; and 7 percent did not know or did not respond. There is considerable am- bivalence in this pattern of response. One can interpret it either as more supportive than elite opinion, or as representing the same degree of concern.

When citizens were asked more specifically to respond to particu- lar statements, there was more negativism. Fifty-five percent agreed with the statement, "The political parties are only interested in my vote and not my opinion," while 70 percent concurred that "Political parties promise a lot, but little comes of it." When the voter thinks of his personal relationship to the party system, he is as critical as senior bureaucrats. As to the role of interest groups, the responses to one statement put to this national sample are interesting: 53 percent agreed that "Members of Parliament pay too much attention to the interests of powerful groups instead of the general good." The public does not want its representatives to act primarily on behalf of interest groups and feels M.P.'s are too subservient to such groups.[3]

In short, there is much public opinion critical of parties and of interest groups. There is also considerable elite opinion critical of such groups, and, as we have shown, there are certain pockets of elite opinion in both Parliament and the bureaucracy where these patterns of opinions reveal considerable cleavage and distance. While contacts of elites with these groups seems to add to clarity of perceptions and an acceptance of the phenomenon of group conflict, they do necessar- ily produce more tolerance of others, nor do these contacts resolve the anxiety elites retain about the possible dysfunctional impact of group conflict for the system.

Both parties and interest groups have been undergoing considerable change in the Netherlands. The battle of these groups for a place in the political arena is probably more intense than ever before. Elite and public attitudes and evaluations, therefore, may be a reflection of the transitional period the system is undergoing. Rigid segmentation is declining, and at the same time interest groups are accentuating their roles in the political process, cutting across subcultural lines in their attempts to influence the system. But the conflicts engendered are not seen as healthy by a large proportion of today's citizen public. It seems to be a type of politics to which many, though more politicized than before, have not yet adjusted.

NOTES

1. In the earlier studies of Parliament only one-fourth saw themselves as group representatives. See Hans Daalder and Galen Irwin, "Interests and Institutions in the Netherlands: An Assessment by the People and by Parliament," *Annals of the American Academy of Political and Social Science* 413 (May 1974): 58–71. See also Jan Kooiman, *Over de Kamer gesproken* (The Hague: Staatsuitgeverij, 1976), pp. 104–6. Kooiman distinguishes the "classical" representative function (a delegate concept) from representation as a "link function." For Dutch M.P.'s he classifies 24 percent of them as seeing their most important function as "classical" representation, and 30 percent the "link function."
2. L. P. J. de Bruyn and J. W. Foppen, eds., *National Kiezersonderzoek 1972–73* (Nijmegen: Instituut voor Politicologie, 1974), p. 236.
3. Ibid., pp. 195–97.

CHAPTER 10

Elite Views on
Citizen Participation

The involvement of the public in the political process of modern democracies—the possibility of it, the necessity of it, and the consequences of it for the system, particularly for the performance of elites—is a continuing focus of theoretical argument. Many elite theorists have supported the position of Robert Michels, who claimed in the elaboration of his "iron law of oligarchy" that "every system of leadership is incompatible with the most essential postulates of democracy".[1] With reference to the bureaucracy, Max Weber pointed out the irony that "democracy inevitably comes into conflict with the bureaucratic tendencies which, by its fight against notable rule, democracy has produced".[2]

Joseph Schumpeter's revision of classical democratic theory in which he identified the selection of leadership in competitive elections as the essence of democracy really left no room for other types of citizen participation. "The electoral mass is incapable of action other than a stampede," he argues.[3]

As Heinz Eulau and Kenneth Prewitt have pointed out, more recent theorists are less willing to accept this incompatibility and inevitability, citing Lasswell and Kaplan as rejecting "the common supposition that to put the concept of elite to the fore in political science is to deny from the outset the possibility of democratic institutions".[4] As Eulau and Prewitt say, "elite theorists have (not been successful) in establishing the logical impossibility of democracy." The issue of "whether a social structure is democratic depends not on whether or not there is an elite, but on the relation of the elite to the mass—how it is recruited and how it exercises its power."[5]

Students of bureaucracies have over the years noticed the tension that exists between the civil servant and the citizen. In the United States Leonard White and Pendleton Herring in the 1930s wrote of the conflicts between the administration and the public, and the difficulty of gaining acceptance for citizen participation in the political process. To some there is a fundamental conflict between the rationality of the bureaucracy and the idea of citizen participation. In 1957 a Dutch scholar, Van Braam, published *Civil Servants and Bureaucracy in the Netherlands,* in which he traced the growth and changing character of the civil service. In his epilogue he raises the basic question of the poor relationship of civil servants to the public, the unpopularity of the civil servant, as he put it. In theorizing about this relationship he said:

> In the contact between the civil servant and the public there is often a collision of different social spheres, different ways of thinking and attitudes. . . . The civil servant as representative of the government stands, with respect to the public, as powerholder, as "authority." . . . The citizen approaches the government for welfare, for justice. He feels in a position of subordination, of "littleness" in relation to the "highness" of government. He looks up longingly and expectantly. This makes him exceedingly vulnerable: a friendly word, an encouragement gives him a feeling of support; an unfriendly word, a refusal or a formalistic treatment intensifies his feeling of inferiority. The reaction discharges itself outside the bureau in passionate and negativistic criticism of government and civil servants. It is clear that . . . much of the responsibility and the tact of the civil servants will be questioned. . . .[6]

Although Van Braam had no data on either bureaucratic or citizen attitudes, his study posed the problem of citizen-elite relationships in psychological, sociological, and political terms.

For elite-mass relationships generally, and for bureaucracy-public relationships particularly, the role of the citizen in the political system has thus been a central subject of inquiry, whether from normative or empirical perspectives. Systems vary in the role citizens have in them, in the relationships between elites and masses, and both of these presumably are linked to the images that elites have about the necessity and propriety of such citizen involvement. It is this latter question that we explore here.

Our questions go to the heart of elite-mass relationships. Do elites desire to have more citizen involvement, do they want to open up the system, to expand the polity, so that a variety of groups and individuals with diverse backgrounds and interests have the opportunity to press their interests and make demands? Or, do they prefer a closed system and a passive public? Above all, do elites feel that governance is possible in modern societies, that complex problems can be solved, if there is considerable citizen participation? This is the basic dilemma elites face—maintaining effective decision making while being responsive to citizen demands and pressure, whether by organized groups or by the unorganized.

Elites can respond to this dilemma in three basic ways: (1) by rejecting the idea of citizen participation, on a variety of grounds; (2) by limiting citizen participation to elections, as Schumpeter did, or to other specific channels, or by imposing other qualifications on the expression or implementation of citizen opinion; and (3) by embracing citizen participation as valuable and necessary in a democratic system, as not interfering with effective decision making, and as including much more than electoral participation. In the first type of system the public's role as seen by elites is nonexistent or passive. Historically in many Western systems this was essentially the elite view of the masses. In developing societies today this view still is often prevalent. Frank Bonilla's study of Venezuelan elites is a case in point.[7] The second type of system is presumably much more common; indeed, according to Schumpeter and other later revisionists of classical democracy, it is the system that must prevail in modern societies where elites compete for votes but their political perspectives see very limited utility or propriety for citizen participation beyond elections. Presumably elites in Anglo-Saxon and Western societies, and in new industrial societies as well, should pay homage to the *idea* of citizen participation, submit to it at election time, but clearly see the need to put limits on its expression and canalization. The Dutch system in the past was perhaps an example of this type. It was seen as one where elites made critical decisions at the apex of the system and, as Hans Daalder put it, "elite politics presupposes therefore a rather passive role of the larger electorate."[8]

The third type of system—where elites are enthusiastic about and clearly support citizen involvement and pressure—theoretically should not exist except in the minds of those writers who have argued strongly against the revision of classical democratic theory (such as Peter Bachrach) or those who have studied participation in local government or worker democracy in industry and who argue for more participatory democracy.[9]

Our basic query, then, is, Which of these patterns of elite perspectives towards citizen participation exists in the Netherlands, or do all three exist? How much consensus or dissensus in elite perspectives on the role of the public is there in the content of their beliefs? What factors seem to explain their beliefs: is it their backgrounds, their elite positions, or their ideologies and basic attitudes about the political process? Above all, is there any evidence that Dutch elite political culture emphasizes a particular norm concerning citizen participation in the system?[10]

Major Findings and Illustrations from the Interviews

We used a variety of questions in our interviews in order to solicit elite views on citizen involvement. We asked our respondents in the discussion of Parliament to rate the importance of the task of dealing with citizen complaints and maintaining contacts with the voters, and then to evaluate how well Parliament was dealing with these tasks. We also asked a general question: "In different countries there has been much discussion about increasing participation of citizens in the work of the government and greater influence over the course of governmental affairs. What is your position on this?" We followed this with probes asking them to state both the negative and positive aspects of participation. Finally, we put four agree-disagree statements to them:

1. "In a world as complicated as ours it is a fiction to talk about increased control by citizens over governmental affairs."
2. "Citizens have a perfect right to exert pressure for legislation which would benefit them personally."
3. "The right to vote must exist even if citizens don't make an intelligent use of it."
4. "All citizens must have equal chances to influence governmental policy."

The responses to these questions provide us with a great deal of information about elite beliefs on this subject. Some basic findings are found in table 75. It is clear at once that there is some inconsistency in opinions expressed. When using the agree-disagree items, our respondents seem very supportive of the *norm* of citizen participation. We found only a third opposing the idea of increased participation "in a world as complicated as ours," and virtually no one objecting to giving citizens the right to vote even though they might use it ignorantly. Further, on the right of citizens to exert pressure, 79 percent and 88 percent of the civil servants and M.P.'s, respectively, approved, and almost 100 percent of each group also approved the idea of giving all citizens equal chances to influence policy. Although there is somewhat less willingness to increase participation, there is strong support in both Parliament and the civil service for citizen involvement. Yet, when we used the open-ended question and conversed at length with our respondents, we find far less support among civil servants (but not among M.P.'s) and a great many more reservations about participation. Our coders placed the responses into a five-category scale, revealing a wide range of attitudes. Only a third of senior civil servants were enthusiastic about participation, while over 60 percent of the M.P.'s showed enthusiasm.

It is interesting to compare Dutch elites on this matter with those in other countries. Since we used the same basic questions and codes, such a comparison is possible. Two countries stand out as distinctive— the United States and Germany. A majority of the senior civil servants in both countries (61 percent in Germany and 56 percent in the United States) take a very liberal view of increased citizen involvement. From one-fourth to one-third of the bureaucrats in the other five countries are supportive of the idea, and the Dutch, thus, are very similar to the British (31 percent), Swedish (25 percent), Italian (36 percent), and French (28 percent). The views of M.P.'s in other countries are also similar to those of the Dutch. The most extreme are the Italians, 80 percent of whose M.P.'s are populist on this issue, while the French M.P.'s are not, 49 percent favoring increased public participation. The Dutch, with 63 percent in favor, are thus close to the British (55 percent) and the Germans (57 percent). It is interesting to note that, in all five countries for which we had complete data for both civil servants and M.P.'s, there was considerable distance between M.P.'s and senior

TABLE 75. Elite Attitudes toward Citizen Involvement (in percentages)

	Civil Servants	M.P.'s
General opinion on		
increasing participation		
Very enthusiastic; definitely favors	8	23
Enthusiastic; some reservations	27	40
Pro/con	45	28
Reluctant; tends to oppose participation	15	10
Very reluctant; definitely opposes	5	0
Importance of Parliament tasks		
Dealing with citizen complaints;		
very important (scale positions 7–9)	36	72[a]
Maintaining contacts with voters;		
very important (scale positions 7–9)	76	94[a]
Short answer items		
Agree that "It is a fiction to talk about		
increasing citizen participation."	34	41[a]
Agree that "Citizens should have the right to vote		
even if they do not intelligently use it."	97	100[a]

a. Figures are from 1972 survey.

bureaucrats on this question.[11] The five-country means favoring increased participation are 38 percent for senior civil servants and 61 percent for M.P.'s. The Dutch elites, with comparable figures of 35 to 63 percent, are thus very close to the mean.

Among those who were inclined to support the idea of citizen participation, the discussion often deals with the nature of democracy, of representative government, and the role of Parliament. One civil servant said:

> With the deterioration of the significance of Parliament you must find special substitutes, and perhaps this (citizen participation) is one of the substitutes. It may mean sometimes a hindrance to the realization of pressing matters before M.P.'s. But it has also a very healthy role.

An M.P., very conscious of elitism, philosophized, "I would consider it a very good thing if the work of the government would not be the work of a small elite, rather that on all levels the question would be what concerns the community. . . ."

Those who see negative aspects to participation (and often they are individuals with mixed feelings) emphasized a variety of themes: the difficulty of accountability, the lack of information, the inexpertness of citizens, the tendency for certain minorities to dominate, the difficulty of channeling participation to the proper authorities, the possibility of the input having a stifling effect, and even the concern about demagoguery and the utilization of such opportunities to destroy the system. Examples of such attitudes follow.

> Administration is a function in which you must make decisions and then be responsible also if anything goes wrong. Participation—yes—the people who do not have to measure up, they come with their demands. I feel that participation is good and necessary because you give people the necessary information—so a better understanding results. But it is an illusion to think that administration can function with a great deal of popular (*volksmassa*) involvement.

Emphasizing the problems of citizens in the process, another civil servant said:

> Yes, we must naturally stand positively on that (citizen participation). But I fear actually that for citizens it costs more than for the M.P.'s. It is ordinarily too difficult. You have to know too much . . . I believe sincerely that the ordinary citizen will not be happy at all with this—because he doesn't have a satisfactory interest in it and it is too difficult for him.

The unrepresentativeness of the process bothered some, such as this bureaucrat.

> The man and the group that scream very hard give the suggestion that that is public opinion. That does not have to be the case at all.

Dutch respondents frequently were concerned with the proper channeling of citizen complaints, often seeing other decisional arenas than theirs the proper focus for citizen action.

And then there was the occasional respondent who really saw citizen participation as destructive, as this M.P. did.

> If it were only true . . . if you could do something . . . if the grumblers stayed home, if people who can do something came forward, then I am very much in favor. I have become skeptical. I cheer for it within the system, within the party, naturally. But so often people will destroy the system that I am not for it—on the contrary I am very much against it."

Obviously, many of the respondents were weighing the pros and cons, struggling through a reasoning process in which they saw advantages and then weighing these against their basic concerns as to the consequences of this for the political process. They were confronted with two norms—efficient and responsible elite decision making and the democratic participation of nonelites. They often came down on both sides of the issue, as this respondent illustrates.

> We have attempted in our work to carefully promote a type of participation, and we have realized it. Yet what is the meaning of "participation"? Is it a matter of consulting, opinion giving, or does it go so far that joint responsibility in behavior must occur? Naturally, this last cannot be. Participation without responsibility does not go together.

He has, as a result of his discourse, argued for and against participation! One gets the impression that we have a set of leaders here who do not want to oppose the participation norm, but have a basic skepticism about its implementation.

If we classify the arguments used for and against, the advantages and the dangers, the relative incidence of them is interesting (table 76). Those favoring place great emphasis on a philosophy of democracy and the need for more and different types of input before government acts. A few refer to specific values of an active, involved citizenry. Those opposed are very preoccupied with the effects on the decisional process and the ignorance as well as apathy of the public.

One notes that there are more comments made against participation than for it, but obviously our respondents were inclined to mention arguments on both sides. Actually, 54 percent of the M.P.'s saw negative aspects or dangers and 71 percent of the top civil servants did. In the last analysis, only one-tenth said there were no disadvantages of increased citizen participation.

One must add here that there is considerable feeling that Parliament is only doing a moderately good job in dealing with citizen complaints and in maintaining contacts with the voters; 55 percent of the M.P.'s think they are performing well, but only 38 percent of top civil servants and 18 percent of high flyers agree. It is not only the civil servants who are critical of Parliament in this regard. M.P.'s, too, are self-critical. Indeed, one-fourth think they do a rather poor job on dealing with citizen complaints (scale positions 1–4). We find thus that Dutch elites are inclined to accept the norm of participation in the abstract (two-thirds or more respond properly on our short-answer statements), but most of them have serious, nagging reservations about it, and further, they feel the system (Parliament particularly) is not coping adequately with citizen needs and pressure. The picture is indeed one of a concerned and conflict-fraught elite.

TABLE 76. Themes Appearing in Elite Discussions of Citizen Participation (in percentages)

	Civil Servants	M.P.'s
Arguments in favor[a]		
Foundation of democracy	40	36
Need informed public; opposes demagoguery	2	1
Active public is more realistic	6	11
Quality of representatives will improve	4	1
Government should hear public's		
ideas before taking action	15	19
Other	26	25
Arguments against[b]		
Slow down the decision process	37	31
Frustration in process; demagogic	9	7
Violent struggle for power	2	0
Confusion in demands	2	1
Public ignorant	12	16
Apathy of public	15	9
Violates representative government	2	8
Blurred lines of accountability	2	7
Other	20	22

a. Total number of mentions: civil servants, 47; M.P.'s, 80.
b. Total number of mentions: civil servants, 59; M.P.'s, 101.

Background Factors Associated with Elite Attitudes about Citizen Involvement

One might well expect younger elites to be more supportive of the idea of citizen participation, because they came into office in the 1960s when the Dutch system was changing as a result of student strikes, the appearance of action groups, the breakdown of the rigidity of the segmented society, and the liberalization of Dutch institutions and policy. One would also expect the supporters of the parties on the Left to reveal such supportive attitudes since they were often the groups representing such citizen causes and arguing for reform of the system. It is less clear where the confessional and right-of-center party supporters should stand on citizen participation, since these parties were undergoing internal transformation as well.

We do indeed find these two variables of *age* and *party* to reveal some relationship to elite attitudes (table 77). Our data reveal a relationship between age and citizen involvement attitudes for civil servants, but not for M.P.'s. Only 23 percent of the oldest civil servants (fifty-eight to sixty-five years of age) are enthusiastic about participation, compared to 48 percent of the young cohort (thirty-eight to fifty years of age). For M.P.'s the norm seems to have penetrated all age groups, but we do find that the newcomers (those entering Parliament after 1970) are somewhat more enthusiastic.

As for differences by party, our expectations are certainly confirmed, since the Left partisans are clearly more inclined to favor citizen involvement (50 percent of the civil servants with leftist inclina-

TABLE 77.   Relevance of Age and Party
for Elite Attitudes toward
Citizen Participation
(in percentages)

	Favors More Participation	
	Civil Servants	M.P.'s
Age		
Oldest cohort	23	50
Middle age	33	75
Youngest cohort	48	50
Party		
Left-wing	50	68
Confessional	47	60
Right-wing	20	38

tions and almost 70 percent of similar M.P.'s) Adherents to the Catholic and Protestant parties are also high in support, compared to those on the Right who, both in the bureaucracy and the Parliament, are least enthusiastic (only 20 percent of the civil servants and 38 percent of the M.P.'s). It is the M.P.'s on the Left, therefore, and the civil servants in the youngest age cohort who are most populist.

Role Conceptions and Views of the Political Process as Linked to Views of Citizen Involvement

Expanding the role of the citizen in the political process of modern societies is controversial, and we would assume that leaders' views on the matter would vary with their other views about politics and about the roles they see that leaders have. It is not enough to note that age and party preference are relevant to preferences about citizen roles. The question is whether preferences about citizens' roles are part of a "perspective structure" about politics.

One could expect that civil servants who see their roles as political (or less narrowly bureaucratic) might be more inclined to favor citizen involvement. In order to test this relationship we can use the codes for our respondents for a variety of role definitions, the most pertinent of which we present in table 78. The first concerns the role of the civil

TABLE 78. Role Conceptions as Related to Views of Bureaucrats about Citizen Participation (in percentages)

	Enthusiastic About Citizen Participation (overall code)	Desires Much Influence For Voters (code 7–9)	Approves More Citizen Say Despite Complexity of Governmental Problems	N
Policy role of civil servants seen as				
very important	41	60	68	46
of lesser importance	21	46	61	29
Broker role seen as				
important	45	69	76	29
not important	28	44	58	46
Active or passive role of civil servants in policy process?				
active	38	58	64	53
unsure or passive	21	23	64	14

servant in formulating policy (seen as important by over 60 percent of Dutch higher bureaucrats). The second concerns activity in mediating and resolving conflicts of interest (emphasized by 40 percent), a role which presumably will bring them into associations with citizens or representatives of citizen groups. We also used here conceptions of themselves as having an active or passive role in the policy process (over 70 percent of the Dutch emphasized activism). The data suggest a consistent relationship between these role conceptualizations and their views about citizen involvement. They suggest the appearance of a top bureaucrat who is both political and procitizen, who conceives of his role in political terms and holds affirmative views toward citizen participation. Those civil servants who define their jobs as political, and the majority do so define their jobs, are somewhat more inclined to favor expanding the citizen's role, while those who see themselves less actively political in these senses (possibly the Weberian types) are not.

There is additional evidence supportive of this finding. We asked civil servants to tell us whether they felt technical considerations were more important than political factors in solving today's problems. Two-thirds took the latter position and were consistently more affirmative on citizen involvement (56 percent compared to 22 percent).

There remains the question of ideology and its relevance to this matter. Do the liberals (who are for a more socialistic order and for more change in the system in that direction) feel more inclined to support citizen participation than the conservatives? Table 79 presents findings indicating that ideological orientations may be very influential. The differences are considerable between those who support state intervention and those who do not. Among civil servants the ideological liberals are from 40 to 60 percentage points more inclined to support citizen involvement. Among M.P.'s the spread can be even greater— over 60 percentage points. Those elites who are consistently for radical change in the system, and who favor more of an interventionist role by government, particularly on behalf of egalitarian objectives, are the defenders of citizen involvement in both the civil service and the Parliament. This, of course, fits well with our earlier findings that age and partisan leanings are linked to these views.

Conclusions: Elite and Mass Views Compared

What stands out in these data is, first, the distance between M.P.'s and bureaucrats in their actual enthusiasm for citizen participation. Bureaucrats accept the *norm,* but not the *practice.* Two-thirds of the M.P.'s are enthusiastic, but only one-third of the civil servants are.

TABLE 79. Ideology as Related to Elite Views on Citizen Participation (in percentages)

	Civil Servants		Members of Parliament		N	
	Enthusiastic about Citizen Participation	Desires Much Influence for Voters	Enthusiastic about Citizen Participation	Desires Much Influence for Voters	Civil Servants	M.P.'s
Overall code on state involvement						
Desires more involvement	55	55	77	77	33	31
Prefers present balance or more free enterprise	16	47	14	43	38	7
The doubts and fears about government intervention in society and economy are						
justified	13	43	33	56	23	9
somewhat justified	39	51	60	81	37	16
not justified	73	58	79	67	11	17

Second, one notices the not-so-latent concern throughout these interviews with the problems, complications, and dangers of encouraging citizen action. Many civil servants particularly see this norm as conflicting with the norm of efficient policymaking. Third, there are distances and gaps between leadership subgroups in their support for the idea of citizen involvement, between old and young, between the Left and the Right. Fourth, we note the highly political role conceptualization of Dutch civil servants and the close relationship of this to views about citizen involvement. Similarly, ideological orientations seem to distinguish elites. Dutch elites are deeply concerned about conflict in their system and they also differ on the extent to which government should be interventionist in the society and economy. These views that divide them seem also to divide them on their enthusiasm for more citizen involvement. Fifth, it is nevertheless essential to remember that many of that large group of civil servants and M.P.'s who oppose radical change and also are not liberal ideologues on policy are supportive of citizen involvement. This suggests that the norm of participation is not merely the symbol of the radical innovators, but is also coming to be the accepted belief of many of the more moderate, even conservative, status-quo oriented bureaucrats and politicians.

These elite views should be evaluated in the light of the views of Dutch citizens about the influence of voters. In the 1973 study 1,036 voters were asked two questions that bear on this matter: (1) "When important decisions are made in Holland . . . how much say do you think the voters have?" and (2) "Do you consider that voters have too much, too little, or enough influence on important decisions in Holland?"[12] To question (1), 31 percent responded that voters had no say whatsoever; 54 percent thought they had little say; 12 percent thought they had great say; and 4 percent did not know or gave no answer. To question (2), 78 percent responded that voters had too little influence; 16 percent found enough influence; and only 6 percent felt there was too much voter influence. There is obviously considerable cynicism here about citizen involvement. And the contrast with elite views is great. While 78 percent of the citizens want a greater role, only 35 percent of the senior civil servants support this. M.P.'s are more enthusiastic (particularly the Left M.P.'s), 68 percent favoring more participation. On the other hand, both M.P.'s and administrators feel Parliament is not doing a good job in maintaining contacts with the voters. There is some tension, therefore, between elites and the public, as well as within and between elite sectors over the adequacy and the necessity of citizen involvement in the political process.

Elite contacts with citizens seem to produce a "boomerang effect" in the Netherlands—contacts lead to less enthusiasm for citizen involvement (table 80)! If we dichotomize our M.P.'s into those who are in weekly contact with citizens and those who are in contact less frequently, we note that 40 percent of the latter are very enthusiastic about citizen participation, while only 17 percent of those M.P.'s in weekly contact are. Similarly, senior bureaucrats in frequent contact are less enthusiastic than those more remote from citizens. Not only is there disagreement, then, between elites and citizens, on whether citizens should have a greater role, but contact with citizens, something more and more emphasized as requisite for elite behavior, leads to greater caution about the value, necessity, or practicality of greater public involvement.

We started this chapter by posing the basic dilemma that elites face in modern society—performing effective decision making while being responsive to citizen input. Some theorists have argued that elite decision making precludes meaningful citizen involvement; others claim the two are compatible. While Dutch leaders are obviously worried about effectuating a compatible relationship between the two, many of them are obviously also engaged in attempting to implement democratic dogma. They believe in citizen participation as a basic norm. They tend to be more than Schumpeterian in their views. Many do not reject the citizen role, nor do they confine it to elections. They are not all yet ready to accept the third approach, of optimism and enthusiasm about the feasibility of increased citizen involvement. But, with the exception of some of the older, more right-wing, elites and those who are conservatives ideologically, many Dutch leaders adhere to the democratic norm and appear to be working at its implementation.

In 1933 Leonard White asked the critical question, "Faced with the steady growth of technological operations in government, to what extent and in what way can citizen participation in administration be preserved?" He maintained that "the reconciliation of democratic institutions and a professionalized bureaucracy. . . . is one of the major perplexities of the future."[13] Today, forty years later, Dutch elites, M.P.'s as well as top-level bureaucrats, are still wrestling with that problem. Clearly, however, many are very inclined today to support the *idea* of more citizen involvement in the political process. It is the practical implementation of this belief and the consequences for the system which continues to trouble a large segment of the elite stratum.

TABLE 80. The Boomerang Effect: Elite Contacts and Their Views on Citizen Participation

	Attitudes toward Citizen Participation							
	M.P.'s				Civil Servants			
	Very Enthusiastic	Somewhat Enthusiastic	Total Enthusiastic	N	Very Enthusiastic	Somewhat Enthusiastic	Total Enthusiastic	N
Weekly (for M.P.'s) or regular (for civil servants) contacts with citizens	17%	41%	58%	30	5%	29%	25%	20
Less regular, but contact does occur	40	30	70	12	9	35	44	23
No contact or seldom in contact					12	24	36	25

NOTES

1. Robert Michels, *Political Parties* (New York: Collier Books, 1962), p. 364.
2. H. H. Gerth and C. Wright Mills, eds., *From Max Weber: Essays in Sociology* (London: Kegan Paul, 1948), p. 226.
3. Joseph Schumpeter, *Capitalism, Socialism and Democracy* (London: Allen and Unwin, 1943), p. 283.
4. Harold Lasswell and Abraham Kaplan, *Power and Society* (New Haven: Yale University Press, 1950), p. 202.
5. Heinz Eulau and Kenneth Prewitt, *Labyrinths of Democracy* (New York: Bobbs Merrill Co., 1973), p. 11.
6. Arie Van Braam, *Ambtenaren en bureaukratie in Nederland* (Zeist: de Haan, 1957), pp. 355–59.
7. Frank Bonilla, *The Failure of Elites* (Cambridge, Mass.: MIT Press, 1970), pp. 279–80.
8. Hans Daalder, "The Consociational Democracy Theme," *World Politics* 26, no. 4 (July 1974), pp. 604–21.
9. For a brief review of some of these studies see, for example, Carole Pateman, *Participation and Democratic Theory* (Cambridge: Cambridge University Press, 1970).
10. We have sought in this analysis to parallel fairly closely that of the American scholars Joel Aberbach and Bert Rockman, who used the same type of data as part of our comparative project. Their paper, "Administrators' Beliefs about the Role of the Public: The Case of American Federal Executives," was presented to the Annual Meeting of the American Political Association in September, 1975, in San Francisco. We have borrowed a great deal here from their analytical schemes.
11. The Swedish and American legislators' data were incomplete at the time of this writing.
12. L. P. J. de Bruyn and J. W. Foppen, eds., *Nationaal Kiezersonderzoek 1972–73* (Nijmegen: Instituut voor Politicologie, 1974), pp. 391, 399.
13. Leonard White, *Trends in Public Administration* (New York: McGraw-Hill, 1933), p. 340.

CHAPTER 11

Elite Images of the Influence Structure of Their Political World

Having discussed in detail elite views of the roles of certain particular actors and institutions—Parliament, parties, interest groups, citizens— we now turn to an examination of their views of the total influence structure of the polity, in terms of the relative power of particular political and social sectors. Our interest is both in the views of the elites concerning what the role of a particular actor is, and in what it should be. We wish to determine the extent to which there is congruence or diversity in elite views of who has power and who they think should have power. This description should then lead us to some appraisal of the extent to which there is perceptual and evaluative distance within or between Dutch elite sectors. The issue is basically whether in this transition period there is suggestive evidence that the views of elites are changing concerning the influence structure, whether they seem to be developing new images not in accord with the consociational model.

Perceptions of Actual Influence— Reality Consensus among Elites

The general, comparative picture of elite views of who has influence in the Dutch system is presented in figure 20. This is based on questions concerning the influence of various actors in Parliament's decisions, in which we asked each respondent to rate each actor on a nine point scale. Although both the M.P.'s and top civil servants agree on the overwhelming importance of two actors (M.P. specialists and ministers) there is some disagreement on most other actors and extreme disagreement on the roles of certain ones. Perhaps the outstanding example of dissonance here concerns trade unions, which the civil servants put at the top of the list, 77 percent of them according unions considerable actual influence (compared to 44 percent of M.P.'s). Similarly, top civil servants think national party organization leaders outside of Parliament have considerable power (62 percent) but M.P.'s tend to downplay their role (only 26 percent say they are very influential). Other differences are also apparent. Top civil servants are generally inclined to ascribe more power to these actors, except for themselves. Most do not feel that they as civil servants have an influential role (only 37 percent do), while 58 percent of the M.P.'s feel civil servants are influential. On the other hand, many civil servants perceive action groups, newspapers, radio, and television as influential, while M.P.'s tend to think otherwise.

On certain groups there is considerable agreement, notably churches, employer organizations, and farm organizations. No elite group thinks churches are influential, but all elite groups are inclined

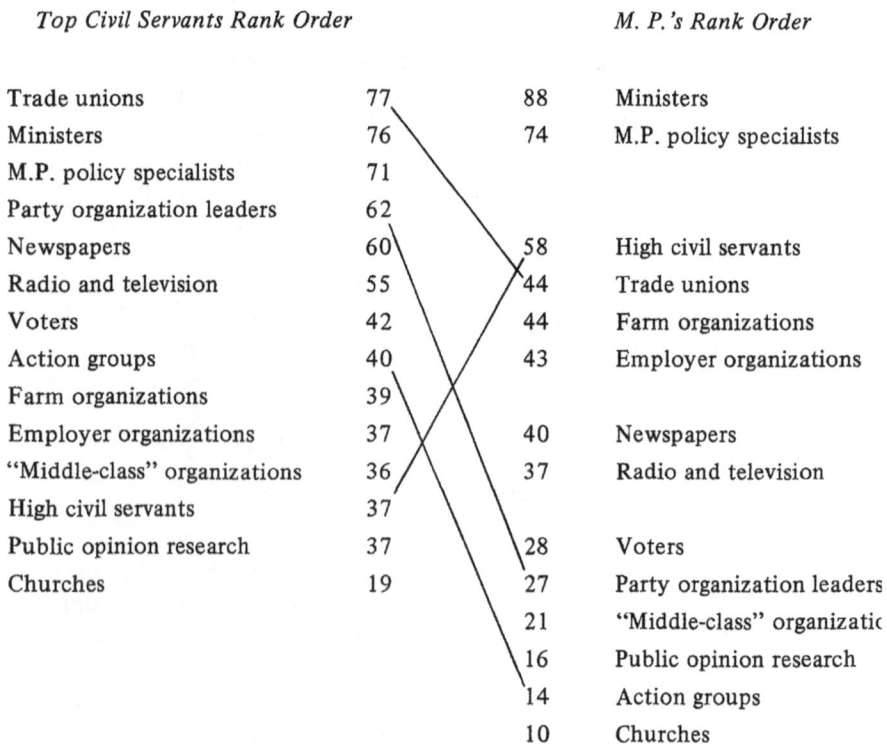

Top Civil Servants Rank Order			*M. P.'s Rank Order*
Trade unions	77	88	Ministers
Ministers	76	74	M.P. policy specialists
M.P. policy specialists	71		
Party organization leaders	62		
Newspapers	60	58	High civil servants
Radio and television	55	44	Trade unions
Voters	42	44	Farm organizations
Action groups	40	43	Employer organizations
Farm organizations	39		
Employer organizations	37	40	Newspapers
"Middle-class" organizations	36	37	Radio and television
High civil servants	37		
Public opinion research	37	28	Voters
Churches	19	27	Party organization leaders
		21	"Middle-class" organizatic
		16	Public opinion research
		14	Action groups
		10	Churches

Fig. 20. Influence perceptions of Dutch M.P.'s and civil servants (percentage who feel each actor *has* considerable influence)

to place farm and employer organizations at an intermediate position. That is, about 40 percent of M.P.'s and civil servants feel that these groups are relatively important in the system. One should note also the generally low ranking of voters, particularly by M.P.'s, only 28 percent of whom rank them at the upper level of the influence scale.

A close scrutiny of these rankings of political influence reveals three different patterns:

1. *High congruence, low conflict in perceptions.* For example, both M.P.'s and senior civil servants see ministers as influential, *and* both elite groups use extreme scale positions in ranking ministers. On the other hand, both groups see voters relatively low in influence, and they do not vary much in the extremeness of their views.

2. *Some evidence of basic disagreement, but no real extremeness in their positions.* Their mutual perceptions of the role of civil servants illustrates this pattern. M.P.'s see civil servants as more influential, and both elite sectors take both moderate and extreme positions, but they do not conflict basically in extremeness of scale positions.

3. *Clear evidence of polarization in perceptions.* In the cases of trade unions, party leaders, and action groups one notes the conflict in perception. In the case of action groups, M.P.'s say they do not have much influence (and many take the extreme low positions), while civil servants say they have considerable influence (and a sizable minority take the extreme high positions).

Many interesting queries could be posed, of course, on the basis of these findings. The major conflicts of view over the actuality of power are clear. How much influence in reality do labor unions have in the Dutch system, and how much more than other groups? Who is right on this question, M.P.'s or civil servants? Are national party executive leaders as unimportant as M.P.'s claim? Is it merely a sense of insecurity or actuality that prompts civil servants to discount their own role in the system, and is the judgment of M.P.'s more accurate? Who is correct on the role of the mass media, top civil servants, who say they are influential on Parliament's decisions, or the M.P.'s who say no? Are action groups accurately perceived by civil servants, both top and lower officials, as having influence superior or equal to other interest groups, or is the M.P. tendency to demean their role a more reliable perception? These are the key questions we cannot answer here. What these data show is not necessarily a picture of objective reality, but the images of elites. And the divergence in elite images is striking at times.

Before leaving the discussion of actual influence perceptions we shall note that our top civil servants have a somewhat different picture of who is influencing *departmental* decisions. Civil servants tend to see their political system's decisions as being made in somewhat different pressure and power contexts. Parliament's decisions are primarily and immediately the product of M.P. experts, ministers, party organization leaders, labor unions, and to some extent the mass media. But bureaucratic decisions are seen as a product of civil servant and interest group input with some recognition of M.P. influence. These images of the decisional and power process suggest that there indeed may be two different images of the world in power terms for these elite participants.

Cross-National Comparison of Elite Perceptions

Since our international project used the same questions in most countries, a comparative description of elite power perceptions is possible. As table 81 reveals, the way elites view their systems can vary greatly by country. In the four countries we selected there is high agreement on the considerable influence of governmental ministers, but one finds striking differences for the other actors. In Italy the role of M.P.'s (as viewed by M.P.'s) is very low, while the church's role is relatively high. In Britain the influence of civil servants is believed by M.P.'s to be very high, while in Germany and the Netherlands fewer M.P.'s rate bureaucrats as influential. The Dutch M.P.'s are the only ones to deemphasize the role of party leaders, the press, and, together with Britain (perhaps surprisingly), of the trade unions. The role of the

TABLE 81. Comparison of M.P. Images of the Power Structure in Four Nations (in percentages)

Actors Seen as "Very" or "Rather" Influential	Netherlands	Britain	Germany	Italy	Range
Ministers	88	100	96	70	30
M.P.'s	74	56	68	25	49
Senior civil servants	59	92	55	78	37
Leaders of party organizations	26	83	93	85	67
Trade unions	44	48	74	89	45
The press	39	58	85	60	46
Churches	10	6	22	59	49

press is considered high particularly in Germany, as is that of trade unions in Italy. On the basis of these comparative elite judgments the distinctive character of the British images is their heavy emphasis on national party organizations and senior civil servants; in Germany it is the role of national party leaders, the press, trade unions, and M.P.'s; in Italy it is the church, the trade unions, senior civil servants, and national party leaders; in the Netherlands it is the dominant role of M.P.'s and to a lesser extent of senior civil servants.

These comparative data also point out certain cross-national uniformities in the disagreements of senior civil servants and M.P.'s in their judgment about who has influence. Civil servants seem consistently to play down their own role and that of M.P.'s (table 82). Only in Italy did we find the latter not to be the case (47 percent of the civil servants rated M.P.'s rather or very influential, while only 25 percent of the M.P.'s did). Otherwise, M.P.'s insist that they have more influence than civil servants accord them. In Britain the discrepancy is particularly high (30 percent of the bureaucrats rate M.P.'s as influential, compared to 56 percent of M.P.'s). Further, civil servants seem to exaggerate the influence of party organization leaders and of trade unions in comparison to M.P. perceptions. This suggests that the bureaucrat's contacts and socialization experience leads him to interpret the reality of power distribution differently than does the M.P. Some of the basic differences we find, thus, between the power images of Dutch M.P.'s and senior bureaucrats are not distinctive to the Netherlands.

Desired Influence of Political Actors—
Normative Consensus Among Elites

Turning now from reality perceptions, we can look at the basic power *preferences* of Dutch elites. The rank orders as presented in figure 21 show both the extent of consensus and for which groups there is impor-

TABLE 82. Cross-National Tendencies for Senior Bureaucrats to Disagree with M.P. Judgments of Influence (in percentages)

Actors Seen as "Very" or "Rather" Influential	Netherlands		Mean for Four Countries	
	Civil Servants	M.P.'s	Civil Servants	M.P.'s
Senior civil servants	37	59	52	71
M.P.'s	71	74	51	56
Party organization leaders	62	26	83	72
Trade unions	77	44	79	64

tant disagreement.[1] The sharpest difference is in the role of ministers, a 42 percentage point differential. The M.P.'s show some reluctance in saying ministers should have a great deal of influence over Parliamentary decision making. They do not say, however, that ministers should have minimal or no influence (less than 5 percent do), but they are more likely to place them at scale positions 4, 5, and 6. Voters, party organization leaders, and trade unions are emphasized more in M.P. preferences, but one should note that 55 percent of the civil servants say voters should have considerable influence, and virtually none of them discount voters completely (no more than 4 percent). Similarly, the civil servants play down the role they would like party organization leaders to have, but only 17 percent say they should have minimal influence. It is inter-

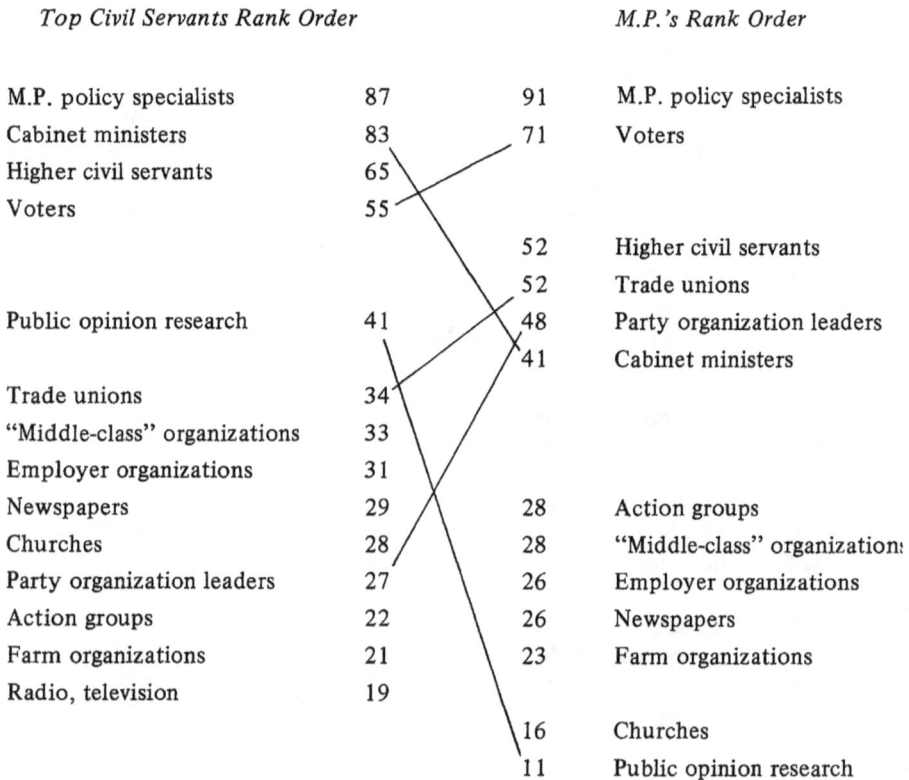

Top Civil Servants Rank Order			M.P.'s Rank Order
M.P. policy specialists	87	91	M.P. policy specialists
Cabinet ministers	83	71	Voters
Higher civil servants	65		
Voters	55		
		52	Higher civil servants
		52	Trade unions
Public opinion research	41	48	Party organization leaders
		41	Cabinet ministers
Trade unions	34		
"Middle-class" organizations	33		
Employer organizations	31		
Newspapers	29	28	Action groups
Churches	28	28	"Middle-class" organization:
Party organization leaders	27	26	Employer organizations
Action groups	22	26	Newspapers
Farm organizations	21	23	Farm organizations
Radio, television	19		
		16	Churches
		11	Public opinion research

Fig. 21. Elite power preferences for fourteen actors in the Dutch system (percentage of elite which desires much influence in Parliamentary decisions for each actor, i.e., places them at position 7–9 on a nine-point scale)

esting that civil servants place much more importance on public opinion
research than do M.P.'s, perhaps reflecting an interest in providing a
more scientific basis for representing citizen opinion.

There seems to be no serious conflict in influence preferences
between M.P.'s and top civil servants for key groups (except trade
unions), for higher civil servants, and for the mass media. Civil servants are placed at a relatively high ranking, and interest groups and
the media are ranked rather low in preferences by most elites. More
civil servants feel the churches should have considerable influence (28
percent) than do M.P.'s (16 percent), but it is clear there is no sizable
body of support in any elite sector (except, as we shall see later, for
the older civil servants) for a significant role for the church in Dutch
national decision making. The Dutch leaders see the church and other
interest groups as properly having some influence but not a great or
dominant role. This is clear when we note the proportions who advocate little influence for these groups (i.e., who rank them at scale
positions 1–3):

	M.P.'s	Civil Servants
Employer organizations	14%	6%
"Middle-class" organizations	14	6
Farm organizations	10	11
Action groups	4	21
Churches	25	23
Trade unions	4	8

At the low end of the preference scale there is remarkable congruence.

The critical dissensus is not concerning interest group involvement, but the relative weight to be given to ministers, party organization leaders, and trade unions in Parliamentary decision making. If
there is serious normative dissensus among Dutch elites, it lies in opinions about those key groups.

A final observation should be made here concerning the comparative preferences of civil servants on who should have influence over
departmental decisions, as distinct from Parliamentary decisions.

Senior civil servants accept the role of M.P.'s on departmental decisions, and, above all, they accept the relevance of interest groups for the
bureaucracy. While 78 percent scale interest groups as very important
for departmental decisions, no more than 34 percent rate interest groups
that important for the decision making of Parliament. It is interesting to
note also that more civil servants think interest groups *should* have great
influence than think they *now* have influence on departmental decisions; 65 percent say their influence *is* great, and 78 percent say it *should*

be great. Yet, they also take the same position for M.P.'s—52 percent say their influence *is* high on departmental decisions, and 61 percent say it *should* be high (87 percent say M.P.'s should have a strong influence on Parliament's decisions). They envision a bureaucracy which has to be more responsive to both M.P.'s and clientele groups. Civil servants do not seem to think that the mass media should have a strong effect on either Parliament's or departmental decisions—no more than 29 percent feel mass media influence on Parliament should be high, and only 14 percent feel the same about the departments.

Age as an Explanatory Variable

Among both M.P.'s and civil servants, there is strong consensus across age cohorts on the influence roles for M.P.'s (table 83). For other actors there is less agreement. The youngest M.P.'s and civil servants are less enthusiastic about the roles of ministers and civil servants. In the case of voters, M.P.'s are more inclined to prefer more influence than do civil servants, but except for the youngest elites the difference is not great. There is considerable consensus for the place of farm groups and action groups—only a minority wish them to be influential. There is much more distance, however, in power preferences when we consider the roles of unions, for example, or churches. The older civil servants agree with all M.P.'s in their preferences concerning unions, but the distance between the oldest and younger bureaucratic cohorts is rather large. As for the role of churches the pattern differs, with considerable distance existing between older civil servants and all other age groups of both elites. The older M.P.'s are more inclined to support the idea of influence for interest groups, while the youngest M.P.'s have limited enthusiasm for all such groups except trade unions and action groups.

At the upper age levels of the bureaucracy, one finds the greatest support for the influence of key interest groups; then, below this older cohort, there is a sharp drop in the proportions who support the influence of these groups. Consider the cases of churches, unions, and employer organizations. The percentages of bureaucratic age cohorts desiring high influence for those groups are as follows:

	Churches	Unions	Employer Groups
Older civil servants	52%	48%	48%
Middle-aged civil servants	13	22	22
Young civil servants	18	35	26
High flyers	6	30	30

TABLE 83. Variations in Elite Power Preferences by Age Cohorts (in percentages)

Percentage Who Desire the Following Actors to Have Much Influence (Scale Positions 7–9)	Oldest Cohort (58–65 years)	Middle-Aged Cohort (51–57 years)		Young Cohort (38–50 years)		Youngest Cohort	
	Civil Servants	Civil Servants	M.P.'s	Civil Servants	M.P.'s	High Flyers	M.P.'s
M.P. specialists	82	83	83	100	100	59	80
Ministers	86	78	60	87	46	30	20
Civil servants	68	64	58	59	55	47	40
Party leaders	29	23	42	30	54	24	44
Voters	50	48	67	61	64	30	90
Action groups	27	30	17	9	32	18	33
Unions	48	22	50	35	50	30	56
Churches	52	13	25	18	18	6	0
Farm organizations	32	9	33	23	23	24	11
Employer organizations	48	22	33	26	27	30	11
"Middle-class" organizations	48	22	42	30	23	30	0
Average for six interest groups	43	20	33	24	29	23	19

In each case, there is a break between the older civil servants and the other age groups, not a gradual decline in support as one moves from the oldest to the youngest age cohorts. This disagreement is much less apparent for action groups and farm organizations. It suggests that the traditional preferred association between the civil servants and clientele groups of the ministries is not as valued among the younger civil servants.

The distance between age groups in Parliament again reveals striking examples of disagreement. The younger M.P.'s agree with older M.P.'s on the influence role of unions, they want more influence for action groups, but they are less supportive of other interest groups, particularly middle-class organizations. In this respect they resemble the young civil servants. Both rebel against giving churches, employer groups, and small-business organizations much influence. But the key difference is that the young bureaucrat is also less inclined to support the idea of union influence than the oldest civil servants, while the young M.P., to the contrary, prefers considerable influence for unions. Here, then, is a basic conflict between M.P.'s and bureaucrats in the lowest age cohorts. Furthermore, there is also strong disagreement among certain of these young elites on the role of the ministers. The older M.P.'s are much more inclined to desire a major influence role for the minister than are the younger M.P.'s. The younger civil servant, however, is strongly supportive of ministerial influence. The following summary data for M.P.'s document their support for these elements of society:

	Unions	Small Business Organizations	Ministers	Action Groups
Older M.P.'s	50%	42%	60%	17%
Middle-aged M.P.'s	50	23	46	32
Young M.P.'s	56	0	20	33

Again there is a hierarchical pattern here.

The picture that emerges from this analysis is one of significant differences in preferences about the roles of certain actors in the system—*within* the bureaucracy and *within* the Parliament, and *between* the Parliament and bureaucracy, particularly for the youngest age cohorts. The data strongly suggest that the younger elites are not accepting completely the images of their seniors. In developing their own orientations they quite probably are responding to the new political pressures and emphases of their generation.

Differences on Power Perceptions Among Elites by Religion

Views about who shall have influence in the Dutch system differ considerably by the religion of the elite respondent. The variations are noticeable in both the Parliament and the bureaucracy. One notes first that Catholic elites have the most consistently negative power preferences. In *every case* the Catholic civil servants desire less influence for a group or actor, including churches, than do the Protestant civil servants or those with no religion. For Catholic M.P.'s this is not as true—they make exceptions for ministers, civil servants, M.P.'s, and small-business groups. However, for all other actors Catholic M.P.'s also are less positive. The following data show percentages of civil servants, by religious affiliation, who desire much influence for voters, unions, and action groups:

	Voters	Unions	Action Groups
Catholic civil servants/M.P.'s	40%/60%	27%/30%	7%/ 0
Nonreligious civil servants/M.P.'s	50 /65	33 /44	25 /38%
Protestant civil servants/M.P.'s	67 /81	38 /75	26 /38

Differences in Elite Influence Preferences for Political Party Groups

Party supporters among elites reveal as great differences in influence preferences as one finds for religious categories. Indeed, for some actors the distance between elites by party is greater (table 84). M.P.'s are perceived as ranking high across the board for all elites irrespective of party, and ministers rank high except among Left M.P.'s. Only 18 percent of Left M.P.'s think ministers should have considerable influence, in contrast to 55 percent and 75 percent for the Right and confessional parties, respectively. This is a striking difference and helps to locate again the antiministerial prejudices among elites. Another major difference is in the preferred role of action groups. Both the left-wing civil servants and M.P.'s are much more inclined to accord them influence in the system; the other elites do not. The differences are dramatic—56 percent compared to 6 percent for civil servants, 48 percent compared to 0 percent for M.P.'s. In fact, one of the striking reverses in the findings concerns the preferences of Left M.P.'s *and* civil servants for action groups and unions compared to employer groups.

The distance among elites of the same political outlook (between

TABLE 84. Power Preferences of Elites by Party Orientation (in percentages desiring much influence for actor)

Actors	Civil Servants			M.P.'s		
	Left-wing Parties	Confessional Parties	Right-wing Parties	Left-wing Parties	Confessional Parties	Right-wing Parties
Ministers	94	81	83	18	75	55
M.P.'s	78	94	93	87	100	89
Civil servants	78	53	59	52	67	33
Voters	56	44	59	74	67	66
Action groups	56	6	14	48	0	13
Unions	47	38	31	56	50	38
Newspapers	41	25	24	14	33	44
Party leaders	38	25	21	48	45	50
Churches	38	19	28	17	25	0
Employer organizations	24	31	34	9	50	38

Left civil servants and M.P.'s, for example) can also be striking. The distance is extreme (76 percentage points) in the views of Left M.P.'s and civil servants concerning the role of ministers. This is the greatest gap between elites of the same party persuasion and suggests the importance of elite position as influencing perceptions. The differences between confessional elites are most apparent for preferences for party leaders and employer organizations. For right-wing supporters in both elites the differences are great as to the role of civil servants, churches, and party leaders. On the left of the political spectrum there is less congruence among elites in power preferences.

Elite Contacts in Relation to Power Perceptions

One would assume that the pattern of elite contacts would influence their views of who has and should have power in the system. Our data suggest, in some rather interesting ways, that this is so. First, we find that contact often is related to perceptions of low influence in the system. For civil servants, particularly, we find that those in contact with citizens, party leaders, and M.P.'s are inclined to feel that these actors have less influence than do those civil servants not frequently interacting with those actors or groups. Thus we find that 75 percent of those civil servants with less frequent contact with M.P.'s feel the latter have a great deal of influence, while only 54 percent of those who have much contact with M.P.'s feel the same way. Forty-four percent of civil servants who have only infrequent contact with citizens think they have a powerful influence; 33 percent of those civil servants with frequent contact agree.

There is a "boomerang effect" as reported earlier, in certain types of elite contacts as related to *desired* influence. This is not true for contacts with ministers—both M.P.'s and senior civil servants in weekly contact with ministers desire a great deal of influence for those officials. But civil servants in contact with citizens are less inclined to desire a larger role for them. Of those elites in weekly contact with citizens, only 25 percent of the bureaucrats desire more influence for voters, compared to 77 percent of M.P.'s; of those with less frequent contact, 55 percent of bureaucrats and 58 percent of M.P.'s would increase citizens' influence. Familiarity with citizens seems to lead to more concern among civil servants and less of a desire to give them influence.

In summary, it appears that elite contact relationships may be associated with their power structure perceptions and preferences. Some contacts lead to negative reactions to an actor. Other contacts lead to a belief that it *is* low and *should* be increased; the latter tendency is particularly relevant for M.P.'s. Thus, 65 percent of M.P.'s in weekly contact with citizens see their influence as relatively low and 77 percent wish to see it high. The same tendency exists in their perception of union influence, as well as that of party leaders.

Differences in Elite and Mass Perceptions of Influence

How do elite perceptions of the nature of the influence structure compare with the public's views? A unique opportunity was provided for such an analysis as a result of the national postelection adult survey of 1972–73, in which very similar questions were put to a sample of adults. The findings, placed alongside our elite data, reveal certain similarities in perceptions (table 85). Elites and masses, as aggregates, agree that ministers and M.P.'s are very influential and that churches are not. But as for the other actors there is a varying degree of distance in perceptions. The greatest disagreement is on the influence of farm and small-business associations, action groups, the press, unions, and voters. The distance between the public's perception and those of

TABLE 85. Comparison of Elite and Public's Power Perceptions, 1973 (in percentages feeling that a given actor has "much" influence)

Actors	Public	M.P.'s	Civil Servants	Difference between Public and M.P.'s	Difference between Public and Civil Servants
Ministers	77	88	76	11	1
M.P.'s	75	74	71	1	4
Voters	12	28	42	16	30
Unions	60	44	77	16	17
Farm associations	10	44	39	34	29
Small business associations	10	21	36	11	26
Employer associations	49	43	37	6	12
Senior civil servants	43	58	37	15	6
Press	38	40	60	2	22
Action groups	12	14	40	2	28
Churches	6	10	19	4	13
Average differences				11	17

Note: The categories in the two studies are not exactly identical. In the elite study "M.P. policy specialists" was used, while in the citizen survey "the Second Chamber" was used. The "press" was divided in the elite study into "newspapers" and "radio and TV" (we used the former).

Source: De Nederlandse Kiezer '73 (Alphen aan den Rijn: Samson Uitgeverij, 1973), p. 49, for data on public.

the M.P.'s is usually smaller than between the public and the senior civil servants. For example, a much larger proportion of senior civil servants feel voters (42 percent) and action groups (40 percent) have much influence, than do members of the public (only 12 percent in both cases feel they have much influence). There is some tendency for greater elite than public optimism about the influence role of others.

As to the attitudes of the public and elites concerning how much influence actors should have, our data are not as comparable. Nevertheless, some rough comparisons are possible by using the data available.[2] The public was asked whether the influence of each actor was too little, too much, or satisfactory. If we combine these data with their responses to the influence these actors actually have, we can conclude that for the public there are six actors which they wish to have considerable influence: ministers, M.P.'s, voters, actions groups, farm organizations, and small-business associations. The first two groups they see as having much influence and do not feel it is too much. For the last four they see the influence as slight, and a large proportion wish to give them more influence. Elite views generally accord with public preferences for ministers, M.P.'s, and voters (although civil servants are less enthusiastic about citizen influence than M.P.'s). Elites are much less interested in having action groups, and farm and small-business associations have much influence. Further, a majority of elites think senior civil servants should have much influence, but the public is more ambivalent on this matter. Thus 43 percent of the public feel senior bureaucrats are very influential and of the total public sample 30 percent feel this is too much influence, 10 percent too little, and 60 percent say their influence is about right. M.P.'s and civil servants are more interested in increasing their own influence—53 percent of M.P.'s and 43 percent of senior civil servants—than are the public.

There seem to be differences in the views of elites and the public on the role of labor unions and employer organizations also. The public is inclined to support the M.P. position on labor unions—52 percent of M.P.'s want much influence for unions (only 34 percent of senior civil servants take that position). Of the public, 60 percent see the unions as already having much influence, and the public is divided as to whether this should be increased (22 percent), reduced (23 percent), or is satisfactory (50 percent).

An analysis of party differences reveals that consistent partisan variation in power perceptions and preferences exist at the citizen level, just as we found them at the elite level. On the critical question of the role desired for voters, unions, and action groups, the findings are strikingly similar by party orientation. For example, the percentages of the public, M.P.'s, and civil servants desiring much influence for action groups compare as follows:

	Left partisans	Confessional partisans	Right partisans
Public	56%	41%	24%
M.P.'s	48	0	13
Civil servants	56	6	14

Clearly, strong congruence between party elites and the public is suggested by these findings.

Concluding Observations

One major observation which emerges is that it is a gross oversimplification to speak of the consensus or congruence, and dissensus or distance, between the Parliament and the bureaucracy. Immersion in this analysis of the age, religious, and party differentials among elites and the way in which these variables are linked to power perceptions underline the heterogeneity of Parliament and the top bureaucracy. If one wishes to locate the antipower sentiments within the elite groups, it is as often that we find the conflicts *within* the structure as *between* them. An example of that is in the character of the antiministerial feeling in the Parliament. Those M.P.'s who really are opposed to the high influence role of ministers are essentially a combination of partisan leftists, plus some Protestants and usually a few M.P.'s who are relatively young.

A second conflict pattern seems to exist within the bureaucracy, in which the Right (and sometimes the confessional) party supporters, and the oldest cadre are opposed to the other top civil servants. This is notable particularly on the question of power for action groups, with only 6 percent of the left-wing civil servants opposed to their influence, compared to almost half of the older, right-wing and confessional party supporters.

A third pattern emerges in which only the very youngest elites, particularly the high flyers in the bureaucracy, are opposed to the power of a certain group. It is only they who are really antiministerial in the bureaucracy (24 percent) and who feel voters should have minimal influence (36 percent). Other elements within the civil service may have some doubts about the roles of these actors, but the high flyers often are distinctive.

A fourth pattern finally must be mentioned, lest the wrong impression is conveyed that there is great conflict in perceptions for all actors. On the role of M.P.'s, civil servants, farm organizations, and the media, we do not find great conflicts within the bureaucracy or within Parliament. There is strong consensus in the civil service on the roles of M.P.'s and party leaders, the one rated high, the other rated low. Age, religious, and party groups within the civil service are in remarkable agreement. The same pattern of essential consensus exists among M.P.'s for the desired role for civil servants, voters, and unions.

As further evidence of the similarity in influence perceptions of M.P.'s and top civil servants we combined perceptions of actual influence and desired influence for each other (table 86). We find a remarkable congruence in their levels of satisfaction about M.P. influence—53 percent of both the M.P.'s and senior civil servants feel M.P.'s have too little influence. There is not as much congruence concerning the levels of satisfaction about civil servant influence. While 43 percent of the top civil servants want more influence, this view is shared by a smaller percentage of M.P.'s—21 percent. Nonetheless, a large minority of M.P.'s *do* share this view and, overall, M.P.'s and civil servants' views are relatively close concerning each other's proper status in the system.

We do find discontent in the bureaucracy and the Parliament as to their power roles, but it is not a basic conflict in perceptions *between* M.P.'s and civil servants over each other's roles. It has to be precisely specified for certain types of M.P.'s and civil servants. One of the most interesting conflicts is between the *oldest* civil servants and the *youngest* M.P.'s; this may be the pattern of conflict between these structures which is most extreme. We can illustrate this by listing percentages of those groups who desire high influence for five of our aforementioned social elements:

TABLE 86. Index of Elite Satisfaction with the Power Status of M.P.'s and Top Civil Servants (in percentages)

	M.P.'s Influence			Top Civil Servants' Influence			
	Too Much	Too Little	Adequate	Too Much	Too Little	Adequate	N
M.P.'s	7	53	40	23	21	56	43
Top civil servants	8	53	39	15	43	42	67

Note: This classification was based on the questions dealing with how much influence the actor actually had and how much the actor should have. The nine point scale used for each question was divided into three segments (low, medium, and high influence) for the determination of the respondent's location in this typology.

	Oldest Civil Servants	Youngest M.P.'s
Churches	52%	0
Small-business groups	48	0
Employer groups	48	11%
Voters	50	90
Ministers	86	20

This pattern did not, interestingly enough, obtain for the perceptions of unions. But obviously there is conflict between senior civil servants and junior M.P.'s on the preferred roles of certain key groups in the polity. This is not a conflict pattern that exists to the same extent in the opposite comparison (between the older M.P.'s and the junior civil servants), although these two groups do differ on the roles of voters and ministers. The basic, recurring disagreement is between older civil servants and junior M.P.'s. It is a conflict which in fact may be disappearing with the aging and retirement of the older bureaucrats. We find our middle-aged bureaucrats in much less conflict with the younger M.P.'s. The only exceptions to that, again, would be in the roles of voters and ministers.

A complex mosaic of conflict patterns of elite and public power perceptions thus emerges. Older civil servants versus young M.P.'s, Catholic civil servants versus Protestant M.P.'s, supporters of the left parties in either structure and their partisan opposition in the structure. On the role of certain actors in the system an oppositional mentality certainly does exist. Not on the roles of M.P.'s themselves—this is a conflict which does not in reality exist. And the disagreement over certain other groups, such as farm organizations, is minimal. But as to other actors in the political arena conflict between certain types of parliamentarians exists, and is often extreme.

The relevance of these data for the performance of the Dutch system, whether seen as still a consociational system or a postconsociational system, is not easy to assess. One gets the impression that the system is indeed in transformation. Lijphart in a sense may be right in his feeling that elite images are ambivalent, in aggregate terms. They certainly are varied and not homogeneous. The difference is the views of the older civil servants, middle-aged civil servants, and younger elites, both in the bureaucracy and in Parliament, strongly suggests a system which is in a state of change, and one with different power emphases than previously. The earlier model of the Dutch system posited that elites should view the role of the citizens and voters as passive, as Daalder and others have said. Our data do not confirm this theoretical expectation for all our elite groups. M.P.'s are particularly deferential to voters, although only 28 percent feel that in fact voters are very influential. But most civil servants accord voters a relatively influential role in their rank order of power preferences, close to civil servants themselves, in fact. The only subgroups that rank them relatively low are Catholic civil servants and the high flyers, who take a surprisingly negative view. For the others the role of the elector is ranked high, implying a democratization of perspectives.

As for the influence status of interest groups, the response is varied. With the exception of trade unions, whom civil servants see as very influential (and whom they would prefer not to be influential), interest groups are not seen as ranking high in the actual decision-making system. And there is great difference of opinion as to whether they should be. The older civil servants are surprisingly supportive of an influence role for unions, churches, employer organizations, much more so than junior civil servants. They are more similar to M.P.'s in this respect. No elite group, including the Protestant and Catholic civil servants, is particularly supportive of the role of churches. The major conflict in the role of interest groups really occurs in the partisan comparisons. The supporters of the socialists and other parties of the Left are strong supporters of the influence of unions and action groups. Those of the Right and those who support confessional parties are not extremely opposed to the role of unions, but toward action groups they are very negative. On the other hand, they are supporters of employer organizations, while the left-wing partisans are not. It is this dichotomy that is particularly manifest in the data, suggesting again that the classic earlier consociational interest group picture of reality may be changing, at least in the minds of these elites.

One should keep in mind in all this that we do not see much serious conflict in mutual perceptions of the roles of M.P.'s and civil servants themselves. This runs quite counter to the theoretical perceptive picturing the classical bureaucrat confronting and disagreeing with the member of Parliament in perceptions about each other's power in the system. True, civil servants are inclined to deprecate their roles in the system (only 37 percent saying they have real influence, while almost 60 percent of M.P.'s attest to their influence). There is some tendency for right-wing and younger deputies, plus some Catholic civil servants, to play down the civil servant's role. But on balance there is moderate to high support for the civil servant's preferred status in the system. And of course the M.P.'s role is not disputed, actually or preferentially. The disagreement is really not over the roles of M.P.'s and civil servants, but over the roles of ministers, party leaders, and particular interest groups. The relevance of these conflicts in power preference for consociationalism may be more than symbolic.

NOTES

1. For an earlier discussion of these data see our chapter, "Elite Perceptions of the Political Process in the Netherlands, Looked At in Comparative Perspective," in *The Mandarins of Western Europe,* ed. Mattei Dogan (New York: John Wiley & Sons, Halstead Press, Sage Publications, 1975), pp. 143–45.
2. These conclusions are derived from the data presented in *De Nederlandse Kiezer '73* (Alphen aan den Rijn: Samson Uitgeverij, 1973), pp. 49–52.

CHAPTER 12

The Emergent Elite Culture: Less Accommodation and More Conflict?

We began this study with certain basic theoretical positions. The first was that the relations between M.P.'s and civil servants were central in modern democracies, and that it was essential to study their roles, interaction patterns, and political orientations if one wished to understand the character of the political elite structure of these societies, whether cohesive, conflicting, or convergent. A second position was that a knowledge of the attitudes and beliefs of political elites, the sources of such perspectives, and the patterns of elite consensus or conflict would help us describe and understand the bases and conditions of elite performance—their styles of thinking about social and political problems, their theories for the resolution of such problems, and the value and ideological preferences which they bring to bear in dealing with such problems. We were primarily interested in assessing elite political culture in the context of system needs. Finally, we hoped that such analysis of elite political culture would suggest the directions which the system was taking, how it might be changing in the seventies from what the system presumably was like in the earlier post–World War II period.

All three of these theoretical stances are particularly relevant for the Netherlands. The politics of accommodation long ago prescribed the elite structural conditions, roles, and requisites for the roles of politicians and bureaucrats which, together with the prescribed roles of other actors, were functional to the achievement of a stable democratic society. And elite congruence on basic political orientations and rules of the game has always been extremely important in theories of the proper functioning of the Dutch system. Finally, even though we were studying Dutch elites at one point in time (1973) our findings can be very suggestive in a longitudinal sense. If we accept the argument that

223

1967 was the dividing point, and posit certain conditions as existing during the pre-1967 period of consociationalism we can view our findings in a temporal perspective. Indeed, in our introductory chapter we spelled out in detail what the expectations were for elite attitudes in the postconsociational period after 1967. We can also, of course, analyze elite orientations by age cohort and, hopefully, from this infer the extent of change (or potential change) in the system.

We have, therefore, three major theoretical concerns in terms of which to attempt a summing up of our data: elite integration (and polarization), elite accommodation, and elite transformation.

Elite Integration

A major theoretical concern in this study has been the character of the relationship between M.P.'s and top civil servants. How unified are these two sets of elites and, if not unified, in what respects are they in conflict? That has been a central inquiry throughout this book. Too much elite cohesion may not be healthy for a system, leading to limited perspectives, inadequate representation of alternative viewpoints, and nonadaptiveness to societal needs and demands. Too little cohesion could mean such disparate values, goals, and styles in the policy process that governmental effectiveness is seriously threatened. How much cohesion or conflict do we find for Dutch elites?

Common Social Backgrounds?

The first dimension of elite integration is common social backgrounds. For some scholars this is the real test of integration, as Quandt and Porter argue.[1] There are many others who question this, but one can argue that homogeneity of social background *plus* other factors may lead to cohesiveness. Together with adult socialization and elite contacts, intra- or extrainstitutionally, social background variables may be relevant.

For senior bureaucrats and M.P.'s in the Netherlands educational backgrounds are indeed common—93 percent and 80 percent, respectively, have attended universities. But in addition, these elites reveal great diversity of backgrounds in religion, type of community in which they were raised, father's socioeconomic status, family socialization, and university training. Important historical changes have taken place in educational level: Kooiman shows that since 1930 the percentage of university educated members of Parliament has risen from 44 to 62 percent. The percentage of members with only a primary education has dropped from 18 percent in 1930 to 2 percent in 1972.[2] Another important trend is the change in curriculum. Among M.P.'s the study of law still is the most popular: lawyers constitute half of the politicians with university education (the same number as in 1930). Of the other majors economics has become most important.[3] Our own analysis shows that most of the older civil servants also have a law background. The younger ones are more likely to be economists.

What our data on paths to elite status suggest, then, are the following observations concerning the "integration" of elites:

1. University education is the key credential for getting into a senior bureaucratic or parliamentary position. This is the underlying common, and, presumably, integrating, social background characteristic.

2. High family economic status was also evident for a large proportion of these leaders, but socioeconomic origins were more diverse, for M.P.'s especially. M.P.'s from lower-class families did get to the university and then to Parliament, partly recruited through the parties, both socialist and confessional. In this sense there was less integration of elites.

3. On other background variables both sets of elites were very diverse, not coming from similar milieus at all.

4. There is no strong evidence that these elites were integrated in their views on politics and government *because* of their social backgrounds. Many background variables are not closely linked at all to their views. Other variables, such as education, may be indeed linked to their views, but by no means produce an identity of view. Thus we noted that the university curriculum of bureaucrats (natural science, social science, and law) seemed to produce individuals who later differed in their perceptions of the role of the bureaucrat, as well as on such matters as the role of citizens in the political process. The educational system may have produced persons committed generally to the system, but by no means having the same political views or preferences about the governmental system.

5. Adult socialization experiences *after* university probably were more influential—the type of ministry of the bureaucrat, the type of party for the M.P., and the associations and interactions which their position and roles in these contexts led to. These resulted in great differences in views about politics, as well as considerable consensus on certain beliefs.

Mutual Role Perceptions?

A second test of integration concerning role perceptions is clearly passed successfully by Dutch elites. There is high congruence in the way they describe each other's roles, or the traits associated with being an M.P. or bureaucrat. Both agree overwhelmingly (over 70 percent) that the senior civil servant has a policy role and is an advisor-counselor. Both elites agree that civil servants do not have representative, ideological, or charismatic roles. Similarly, there is a strong agreement on the task of the M.P. He is involved in policymaking, has an intellectual responsibility, and is a political representative. Virtually no one in either set mentions organization or mediating tasks. There is some difference in the two groups, with a minority of M.P.'s seeing charismatic and sociability traits as important, which finds little agreement among civil servants. The latter also see M.P.'s as ideologues or advocates (38 percent) but, interestingly, only 10 percent of the M.P.'s talk about this aspect of their role. The M.P. is seen as the mobilizer or the facilitator, while the senior bureaucrat is viewed much more as the legalist, the technician, and the interest group representative in the policy process. The major point is that in own role definitions and in role prescriptions among both groups there is strong consensus.

There are indeed pockets of dissent within both the bureaucracy and Parliament over role perceptions. We found a subgroup of 17 percent among senior bureaucrats that we call Weberians because of their consistent emphasis on technical expertise, hierarchical loyalty, and a deemphasis on political approaches to the solution of problems. We also found in Parliament a tendency for Left partisans to emphasize more the representative role of M.P.'s as well as their technical expertise. But the internal dissensus in either Parliament or the bureaucracy is minimal on role perception. On balance our analysis clearly documents that in mutual role acceptance this is an integrated set of elites.

Close Networks of Elite Contacts?

A third test of the integration of elites is their sociometric ties to each other and to other actors in the political system. In terms of *lateral* communication between M.P.'s and senior bureaucrats, this is not a very integrated elite. Few (16 percent) of the bureaucrats see M.P.'s regularly, while 29 percent of the M.P.'s claim to see higher civil servants weekly (and another 31 percent regularly). There is an imbalance here. Senior bureaucrats, whether because of limited opportunities or limited feelings of dependency, do not seek such political contacts. They are frequent interactors within the bureaucracy; indeed, for many this is their major, if not exclusive arena for interaction. Variations in contact patterns were found, however, by ministry.

In terms of political linkages *upward* (to ministers), *outward* (to interest group leaders and party leaders) and *downward* (to citizens) these elites are differentially active and specialized. But they are by no means isolated from the other major actors in the system. The major focus of senior bureaucracy is with interest group leaders (64 percent see them regularly, compared to 29 percent who have regular contact with citizens and 4 percent with party organization leaders). Our analysis of M.P.'s revealed a complex mosaic of multisectored and multilevel contacts. We found also that a majority of M.P.'s saw leaders of other parties, one-fifth regularly or weekly. Weekly contact with citizens was reported by 72 percent of the M.P.'s. The M.P.'s are continually active in communication relationships. But *together* the bureaucrats and M.P.'s do not constitute a close-knit sociometric elite. There is enough variation in contact pattern, however, to suggest that this is a very open elite system. M.P.'s vary considerably, for example, in contacts with other parties, with interest groups, and with ministers. These differences in contact patterns are often linked to different views about the political process.

While the Dutch elite is not an integrated elite in personal interactions, there are clear integrative tendencies in these relationships which are probably functional for the Dutch system. First, there are certain points in the system where contacts of M.P.'s and bureaucrats converge: the ministers and interest group leaders are the two best illustrations. Second, the contacts of each elite set seem particularly relevant to their roles in the system. Third, there is a considerable amount of cross-level and elite-mass communication. Fourth, the contacts across party lines are considerable and engaged in particularly by young M.P.'s. And finally, when contacts occur between civil servants and M.P.'s, for example, or with citizens, or between parties, these contacts seem to move in the direction of producing more consensus than conflict. Thus civil servants in contact with M.P.'s are inclined to be less Weberian in their orientation and to be more willing to recognize the importance of political considerations in policymaking. Contact patterns indicate, therefore, significant integrative elements in elite relationships, even though elite sociometrics are immensely varied and open.

Value Consensus?

Dutch elites have certain value emphases which distinguish them from other western European leaders. They are less interested in material welfare and security, and indicate a greater commitment to a value called belongingness (or reference to community). Dutch M.P.'s are more likely to emphasize social justice and equality. While distinctive, Dutch M.P.'s and senior civil servants do not share values completely. Bureaucrats intend to be more explicitly bourgeois (25 percent, compared to 11 percent of the M.P.'s). The latter are inclined to be more explicitly postbourgeois in their value priorities (46 percent, compared to 15 percent of the senior bureaucrats). The major value cleavage is within Parliament, between the partisans of the Left and the confessional and right-wing parties. There is a striking contrast between the 6 percent of the confessionals and rightists who espouse values of social justice and equality, and the Left, 62 percent of whom place such postbourgeois values at the top of their hierarchy of values. There is no such value cleavage in the bureaucracy. The bureaucracy, therefore, seems an integrated institution in value terms; the Parliament appears to have significant value cleavages within it.

Ideological Agreement?

A fifth test of elite integration concerns the classic question of the role of the government in the economy and society, and the extent of acceptance or rejection of the social order. On both of these beliefs Dutch M.P.'s and civil servants differ considerably. Thus 80 percent of the M.P.'s favor some more or much more state involvement, while 47 percent of the senior bureaucrats do. M.P.'s are enthusiastically in favor of planning (74 percent) while less than half (35 percent) of the bureaucrats are. On the other question 57 percent of the civil servants will accept the present social order with no changes or reforms, but only 22 percent of the M.P.'s will. The contrasts in these ideological positions are striking.

Again, it is the partisan Left which is least satisfied with the existing social order and which prefers more governmental intervention in both the bureaucracy and the Parliament. On balance, one must say that this is no monolithic ideological elite. Contrasts are also evident by age, the findings on which we will summarize later.

Congruence in Perceptions of the Political Process?

There is a great variety of interpretations one can arrive at if we apply this sixth test of the integration of elites. In probing for their views about the performance of Parliament we find considerable agreement in evaluations of M.P.'s and senior civil servants. They both feel Parliament performs certain tasks reasonably well, and other tasks (such as responding to the voters) poorly.

Elite views on the nature and utility of party and interest group conflict diverge considerably, however, The bureaucrats are very concerned about such conflict—three-fourths feel parties unnecessarily sharpen conflicts, and close to 60 percent say interest group conflict is harmful. While M.P.'s also express concern about group conflict, it is not as great nor as widespread among them. Within the Parliament the Left deputies and those in the youngest age group are most sanguine about conflict, while the older and Center-Right deputies are most alarmed.

The attitudes of elites toward citizen participation in the political process demonstrate further the dissonance in their views. While 63 percent of the M.P.'s are enthusiastic about increasing citizen participation, only 35 percent of the senior bureaucrats feel the same way. The latter believe that they can support the principle of participation but react negatively to the idea of increasing participation. Again, it is partisans of the Left in both the bureaucracy and Parliament who are the strongest supporters of citizen involvement. And the youngest civil servants (but not M.P.'s) are clearly most procitizen.

When we turn to elite images of the power structure, we note again the lack of harmony in their views. To some extent M.P.'s and senior bureaucrats see their political world differently. The bureaucrats place trade unions at the top of their list of actors with great influence, even above ministers. They also feel party organization leaders and action groups have considerable power. The M.P.'s tend to downplay the role of unions, and very few think party organization leaders and action groups have power. The distance and extremeness in differences in actual power perceptions is considerable. As for the amount of influence seen as desirable, again in some respects they differ. Thus 83 percent of the civil servants wish ministers to have a great deal of influence, but only 41 percent of the M.P.'s do. And a majority of the latter wish unions to have much influence, but only one-third of the civil servants do. As for the preferred influence status of M.P.'s and civil servants, there is little disagreement, nor is there for other groups, such as churches and employer organizations. There is disagreement within each institution, however, by party subgroup concerning influence preferences. The Left is much less interested in giving power to employer organizations or ministers, for example. M.P.'s and civil servants do not disagree on their own or each other's power roles, but for other actors and groups they often disagree. This is not an elite, therefore, which is cohesive in power preference terms.

Do Elites Trust Each Other?

The oppositionism of elites in terms of feelings of trust or distrust is a seventh type of test of elite integration which to some scholars is of overriding importance. Is there mutual respect or mutual hostility? Our data partially shed some light on this question. Some M.P.'s and civil servants do have reservations about each other. But in the final analysis, based on all available evidence, one must conclude that although there is a 30 percent minority of discontented, possibly distrusting, leaders in each elite set, one finds strong evidence of trust and limited evidence of strong, hostile distrust and antagonism. In this sense this is a rather impressively integrated elite.

These seven different tests of elite integration applied to the Netherlands reveal clearly that this is a convergent elite system, if we return to the basic elite interaction theories which we discussed in the introduction. It is not a self-conscious, close-knit, cohesive power elite, nor is it a set of elites in fundamental conflict. There is much diversity in viewpoints within each set and between them. But there are also strong commonalities, as in mutual role perceptions, certain power preferences for other actors in the system, and certain evaluations of institutional performance, such as that of Parliament. There is also evidence of mutual trust rather than hostility. The impression one gets from these data is that the bureaucracy has indeed been politicized. As it has assumed in its own mind a more important role in the political process, it has also developed (or maintained) good relations and many shared attitudes about politics with the M.P.'s.

Polarization Between M.P.'s and Bureaucrats?

There is evidence of conflict within and between these elite cadres over ideology, over values, and in the styles with which these leaders approach their administrative and political tasks. Whether this lack of integration will produce (or is producing) serious friction within or between these elite sets, friction which is polarizing, is the key question to which we can now address ourselves. It may very well be that these elites are convergent in many respects, but if they hold to polar positions in ideological and philosophical terms, effective relationships between them and effective government may be difficult. There are scholars who fear that polarization has arrived among Dutch elites. As noted earlier, Daalder wrote in 1974 of a conscious polarization "which can lead to increasing conflicts between politicians and higher civil servants."[4] The question here is whether in 1973 when this study was completed we did in fact find such polarization, whether conscious or not.

The first point to be made is one previously emphasized: there are indeed considerable differences between M.P.'s and senior bureaucrats on ideological and perspective dimensions. Thus, while 80 percent of the M.P.'s favor more state intervention in the society and economy, only 47 percent of the bureaucrats do. While 51 percent of the M.P.'s favor important or radical changes in the social and political order, only 25 percent of the bureaucrats do. While 63 percent of the M.P.'s are enthusiastic about more citizen participation in the political arena, only 35 percent of the bureaucrats are. While only 37 percent of the M.P.'s are inclined to compromise in politics, 73 percent of the senior bureaucrats are. While 52 percent of the M.P.'s see conflict as functional to social progress, only 32 percent of the senior bureaucrats do. These types of findings clearly indicate basic differences in views of politics and society. And on value priorities 46 percent of the M.P.'s are concerned primarily with social justice, equality, and institutional reform, but only 15 percent of the civil servants espouse these values. There are certainly differences, then, in M.P. and civil servant beliefs; the question is whether they are polarizing. Do these differences represent basic antagonisms, and are they based on beliefs which are strongly held?

A second point which should be made here is that the differences between Dutch M.P.'s and senior bureaucrats are the largest differences on almost all of these ideological and belief measures of all the European countries in our international survey, with the exception of Italy. We can demonstrate this by comparing the Dutch data (the gross differences in percentages between the two elite sectors) with the *mean* differences between elite sectors for the other countries, for a few of these perspectives:

	Netherlands	Means for All Countries
Favoring state intervention in society and economy	33%	25%
Believing conflict is healthy	13	8
Enthusiasm for citizen participation	28	28
Tolerance of others' ideas	12	9
Inclination to compromise	36	17
Approval of party conflict	22	13
Holding social justice, equality, and reform values	31	24

We do not mean to imply by this that Dutch elites, M.P.'s or bureaucrats, are necessarily more liberal or conservative, more democratic or antidemocratic, than in other countries. Rather, the important point here is that the *distance* between the Dutch M.P.'s and civil servants is greater than in other countries, suggesting more extremeness in attitudes and beliefs.

The third point related to the concern over polarization is that often these contrasted attitudes cohere, so that those holding a particularly distinctive position on one perspective also hold a distinctive position on another perspective. An illustration is in the connection between ideological views about state intervention and about democratization of the political process. From 70 to 80 percent of M.P.'s and bureaucrats who strongly favor state intervention also favor increased citizen participation, but only 13 percent of civil servants and 33 percent of M.P.'s who are conservatives on state intervention approve of increased citizen participation. And we must note again that the degree of distance or the coherence of attitudes is greater in the Netherlands than in other countries. The data can be summarized as follows; the percentages listed represent those in each state intervention category who are also enthusiastic about citizen participation in government.

	Very Strongly Interventionist	*Strongly Interventionist*	*Noninterventionist*	*Differences between Very Strong and Noninterventionist Types*
Dutch civil servants	73%	38%	13%	60%
Dutch M.P.'s	79	60	33	46
Civil servants from other countries (mean)	56	50	47	9
M.P.'s from other countries (mean)	76	67	58	18

There is striking evidence of the tendency in Dutch elite positions to cohere and to be extreme, in comparison to other European political elites.

The fourth point to note in the discussion of elite polarization is that the distinctive, and sometimes extreme, positions which elites take are apparently tied to partisanship. An illustration of this is in their acceptance, rejection, or desire to reform the political social order. We find the striking contrast by party shown in table 87. The polarization by party within these elites is considerable based on these data. For

TABLE 87. Evidence of Partisan Polarization in Elite Attitudes (in percentages)

	Left Partisans	Confessionals	Right Partisans	Differences between Left and Right
Percentage of elites rejecting present order and seeking reforms				
Dutch M.P.'s	59	18	0	59
Dutch civil servants	15	6	0	15
Percentage of elites approving present order without change				
Dutch M.P.'s	5	37	50	45
Dutch civil servants	30	65	70	40
Percentage of elites enthusiastic about increased citizen participation				
Dutch M.P.'s	71	60	38	33
Dutch civil servants	50	43	9	41
Other European M.P.'s (mean)	66	52	56	10
Other European civil servants (mean)	61	36	41	20

M.P.'s, another illustration concerns views of conflict—9 percent of the Left partisans take considerably negative views toward political conflict, while 50 percent of the confessionals and 55 percent of the Right (VVD and DS'70) are consistently opposed to conflict. And as noted earlier, elite views about citizen participation show fairly large differences by party. Note from table 87 how extreme the Dutch differences by party are in comparison to other countries.

As we survey the great variety of data in our study, we cannot escape the reality of many of these findings. Although there is little evidence of the overt hostility, suspicion, and distrust (such as our Italian data reveal), there *is* evidence of a latent attitudinal and normative oppositionism within the parliamentary and upper bureaucratic elite structure which could pose problems for the resolution of conflicts and for making progress on key social, economic, and political problems. Dutch elites come from high social status backgrounds and similar educational environments. They seem to accept each other's roles in the system. They give strong evidence of mutual trust. But they are divided, sometimes deeply, on the crucial questions of the role of the state and society, the value priorities for the system, the need for important and radical reforms, the democratization of the political process. Their divisions are more partisan than dependent on elite position. And since we find that the younger elites are inclined to be more dogmatic in cognitive orientations than the older leaders (50 percent of the M.P.'s under the age of thirty-eight are dogmatists, compared to none of those fifty-one years old and older) there is the strong possibility that the oppositionism and polarization that we find in the system from our data is being reinforced and increased today and for the future.

While all of these findings may induce concern for the stability of the system, the overarching question is whether these polarizing tendencies really interfere with elite commitments to the system, their willingness to work together, and their capabilities in achieving problem resolution. These are perhaps the dimensions of elite performance which, for the Dutch system at least, are most critical. That leads us, then, to a careful evaluation of our evidence in the context of accommodation.

Incidence of Accommodationism

Throughout this study we have linked our findings to the consociational model of Dutch democracy. According to this model, elites at the apex of the system are required to be, and realize that they must be, accommodative if the historically segmented Dutch system is to maintain its viability. Accommodationism, of course, means many dif-

ferent things and can be operationalized variously, emphasizing different types of elite attitudes and behavior. Without reviewing all these
approaches, it seems to us that accommodative behavior and orientations rest essentially on an awareness by elites of the existence of social
and political conflict, a belief in the resolution of such conflict, and a
willingness to work actively to resolve conflict. If the system is accommodative then it has elites who, despite social and political group
differences, believe in the need for conflict resolution while remaining
genuinely aware of the sharpness of conflicts in society and the difficulty of their resolution. Presumably, this is what the Dutch system has
had at the elite level for a long time in order to be a viable democracy,
and theoretically this is what it still needs today.

The data from our study permit us to explore the extent of accommodationism at the elite level, even though we do not have information on the attitudes and behavior of cabinet ministers, where historically the bargaining on the crucial issues of Dutch politics takes place,
finally and authoritatively. While the cabinet is the first authority, the
accommodationist perspectives of elites in Parliament and in the senior
bureaucracy are not irrelevant. Indeed, despite their limited roles in
the process of reaching accommodation, their attitudes toward the
system and the resolution of conflict in that system are important. The
attitudes of M.P.'s and senior bureaucrats constitute both the expectation environment within which the cabinet works and the support infrastructure which the cabinet, collectively and as an individual ministers, must appeal to. While their roles in arriving at the final bargains
are secondary at best, they are elites who indeed have to be taken into
consideration in the functioning of the system. Therefore, the extent to
which accommodative perspectives are found in the Parliament and
bureaucracy constitutes both an underpinning for the cabinet in its
work and a reflection of the direction which they, as M.P.'s and bureaucrats, see the system taking.

To probe the extent of accommodationism, we combined our data
on elite awareness of the extent of conflict with their belief in, and
willingness to work toward, conflict resolution. Two basic codes we
used for that purpose are

1. *conflict perception:* prominence of conflict of interest in (M.P.,
   civil servant) perception of politics and society and
2. *reconcilability of conflict:* response to: "Are these conflicts irreconcilable or not?"

In addition, other aspects of the respondent's attitudes towards the
resolution of conflict interested us. One in particular concerned elite

proposals for dealing with the most important problem facing society (which we had discussed with him at length). Another was the attitude toward compromise and the extent of tolerance of the ideas of others. The accommodation concept assumes leaders who seek solutions to political conflict and who have some willingness to work out compromises. Starting, therefore, with the leader's basic view of conflict, we can assess the extent to which both policy initiative and compromise willingness exist among these elites.

If we combine the two variables—conflict perception and reconcilability of conflict—we discover the distributions in table 88. There are three major observations: (1) the majority of both elites see conflicts of interests as typical or dominant; (2) a minority of both elites see conflict as irreconcilable (although there is considerable ambivalence and uncertainty in both groups); (3) a smaller minority see conflict as dominant *and* irreconcilable—12 percent of the senior bureaucrats and 17 percent of the M.P.'s. At most the pessimists concerning the reconcilability of conflict (who are also very conflict conscious) consist of 21 percent of the bureaucrats and 31 percent of the M.P.'s.

One could conclude from this that there is a strong tendency toward accommodative perspectives in both elites—at least only a minority reveal extremely negative orientations towards the settlement of conflict. This would be premature, however, and before arriving at such a conclusion one should look at other related attitudes. On attitudes towards political compromise, for example, we find only a minority who are negative about the solution to conflict *and* who say compromise is dangerous (31 percent of M.P.'s and 16 percent of civil servants). Even the most pessimistic M.P.'s do not ordinarily oppose the idea of compromise in politics. The great majority seem committed to accommodationism.

Another test of this basic observation concerns the readiness of elites to propose policy alternatives to deal with the important problems facing society. In our discussion with them of the most important problem(s) facing the Netherlands we probed for their proposals for solving these problems. Some were very skeptical and presented no specific proposals, others discussed the matter in terms of general principles, while one-third presented clear policy proposals. The interesting question is, who are these elites who do propose specific policy initiatives? Particularly, are those who see conflict as irreconcilable those who are incapable of, or unwilling to, suggest policy solutions? The interesting finding in this connection is that often the most pessimistic elites (so far as the resolution of conflict is concerned) are the policy idea men in Parliament and the bureaucracy. Over 50 percent of

TABLE 88. Distribution of M.P.'s and Senior Bureaucrats by Conflict Perception and Conflict Reconcilability (in percentages)

Reconcilability of Conflict	Senior Bureaucrats' Conflict Perceptions				M.P.'s Conflict Perceptions				Total	
	Little Conflict; Mostly Cooperative	Pro/con	Conflict Typical	Conflict Dominant	Little Conflict; Mostly Cooperative	Pro/con	Conflict Typical	Conflict Dominant	Civil Servants	M.P.'s
Definitely reconcilable	8	3	3	1	5	3	0	0	15	8
Usually reconcilable	1	15	10	10	14	11	8	0	36	33
Pro/con	1	6	7	8	3	5	3	14	22	25
Usually *not* reconcilable	1	1	8	8	0	5	11	3	18	19
Definitely *not* reconcilable	0	1	1	4	0	0	3	14	6	17
Total	11	26	29	31	22	24	25	31		

Note: The pro/con category here includes a few cases (six M.P.'s and five civil servants) whose position was unclear on these variables. The percentages do not add exactly to 100 percent because of rounding.

the M.P.'s who are pessimistic about conflict resolution nevertheless do have policy proposals to present. One senses that when they say conflict is irreconcilable they are stating an abstract philosophical position about society, but pragmatically many of them believe conflicts can be resolved. Close to 50 percent of the senior bureaucrats do also. Those more sanguine about conflict are much less specific when they discuss solving the most important problem. Even the elites most concerned about conflict are inclined to work towards its resolution. They are the policy activists and probably the most creative in thinking about the solution to problems. This reduces the hard core of negativists to a very small minority of less than one-fifth of both M.P.'s and civil servants in our sample. Although there is certainly much ambivalence among elites about conflict and its reconcilability, and although many elites do not discuss the solutions to problems as explicitly as one might wish, on balance the great majority of them (by these tests at least) demonstrate a commitment to accommodative behavior.

It is interesting to compare the Netherlands with other systems in elite accommodationism. Table 89 presents these data, revealing the relatively high incidence of theoretical nonaccommodationism among Dutch elites. In Sweden, for example, less than 30 percent see conflict and feel it is not reconcilable, but in the Netherlands it is 44 percent for bureaucrats and 58 percent for M.P.'s. French and Swedish elites in this study were particularly inclined to ignore conflict and to be san-

TABLE 89. Conflict Accommodation Index (in percentages)

	Predisposed to Accommodation: Conflict Reconcilable		Predisposed to Non-accommodation: Conflict Irreconcilable or Unsure about Reconcilability[a]		The Sanguine: Feel There Is Little Conflict	
	Civil Servants	M.P.'s	Civil Servants	M.P.'s	Civil Servants	M.P.'s
Britain	37	32	25(12)[a]	36(18)	38	32
France	21	32	18(6)	15(9)	61	53
Germany	30	40	45(34)	49(22)	25	11
Italy	45	29	22(19)	54(33)	33	17
Netherlands	42	22	44(23)	58(36)	11	22
Sweden	16	21	29(13)	24(15)	55	55
United States		52		16(9)		32
Six country means (not U.S.)	32	29	31(18)	39(22)	37	32

a. Figures in parentheses refer to those who feel conflict is *definitely* irreconcilable.

guine. German and British elites saw conflicts but were more optimistic about resolving them.

Among these leaders who are concerned about conflict and feel they may be (or are) irreconcilable, there are also cross-national differences in the percentages submitting specific policy proposals. With 47 percent of their bureaucrats and 55 percent of their M.P.'s having specific policy ideas, the Dutch rank high in the capacity of their elites to initiate policy proposals despite their worry and pessimism about conflicts. They are close to the British in this respect (53 percent of bureaucrats, 73 percent of M.P.'s), outrank the Germans (39 and 52 percent), while the Italian elites seem to be relatively immobilized (29 and 42 percent).

Finally, we should note that parties are important in the development of accommodative perspectives. A comparison of the Dutch M.P.'s with those in other countries demonstrates the strong relationships (table 90).

M.P.'s are sharply divided by partisan membership in accommodation propensities. In all countries except Germany the party representatives of the Left are those who think conflict irreconcilable. The mean differences are considerable, among the largest we have found— 53 percent of the Left are nonaccommodative, compared to 35 percent of the Center and Right. The distance is extreme for Italy and the Netherlands, but considerable also for Britain and Sweden. The Left in European Parliaments (but not in the United States) is clearly the location of great conflict awareness and pessimism.

We must conclude these observations with considerable reservation. It appears that there is a hard core of philosophical pessimists among these elites, conflict theorists who see no end to conflict and, at the abstract level of reasoning, no clear solution to it. The extent of this phenomenon varies by country, but on the average, in terms of basic predispositions, as many as one-third of the bureaucratic and parliamentary elites can thus be characterized. On inspection of other basic attitudes of these elites toward problem resolution and political compromise, however, one finds that even the most negative often reveal orientations which suggest that probably a majority are pragmatic leaders committed to seeking answers to problems, proposing policy initiatives to that end, and in practical terms manifesting accommodative behavioral preferences. Perhaps the major concern is the linkage of nonaccommodative propensities to ideology and, above all, to party or to partisan direction. Given their basic feelings about the conflictual character of the society and the political system, the Left in European politics, particularly in Parliament, must in most of these

TABLE 90. Party Differences among M.P.'s and the Index of Accommodation (in percentages)

	Party Membership													
	Britain		Germany		Italy		Netherlands		Sweden		USA		Means	
	Left	Right	Left	Right	Left	Center	Left	Center/Right	Left	Others	Demo-crat	Repub-lican	Left	Center/Right
1. Sees little conflict	18	47	8	14	0	33	5	44	20	84	35	33	14	43
2. Sees conflict as														
a. reconcilable	34	30	48	34	18	42	15	31	40	5	57	52	35	32
b. nonreconcilable	24	10	16	28	55	8	50	19	27	5	11	6	31	13
c. uncertain	24	13	28	24	27	17	30	6	13	5	11	6	20	12
Nonaccommodative (2b and 2c)	48	23	44	52	82	25	80	25	40	10	22	12	53	25

countries overcome a much greater philosophical negativism by working affirmatively for conflict solutions than is the case for the political
Center or Right, who in most countries are no less aware of conflict
but are much more confident about its management. The Dutch elites
manifest these tendencies in parallel to the elites of other European
nations.

Elite Transformation

Are Dutch administrative and parliamentary elites changing in their
views about politics? We can attempt an answer to this question although our data are not designed for, nor entirely adequate to, that
task. We do not have data about these leaders at different times on the
crucial dimensions which concern us. We cannot report on the attitudinal reorientations of incumbents in these positions from one time period to the next. We can, however, approach this analytical question in
two other ways: (1) we can contrast our 1973 findings with what theoretically was the situation under the consociational model in the pre-
1967 period, as specified in chapter 1; and (2) we can compare the
characteristics of the younger elites in our study with the middle-aged
and older elites. This should provide us with some time perspective on
elite attitudes.

To most elite theorists, changes in the social composition, skills,
and orientations of elites are inevitable, linked to changes in socioeconomic relationships in the system, to the rise of new social forces,
and to the changes in the roles and character of particular political
institutions, as well as to other factors. The question is whether in
our data, interpreted in the two ways indicated above, there is evidence that Dutch administrative and parliamentary elites have been
changing in their political attitudes and orientations, particularly
through the recruitment by the parties (for Parliament) and by the
civil service (for the bureaucracy) of young elites whose views about
politics are distinctive.

There can be no question that the education, skill backgrounds,
and economic status of Dutch elites have changed in the last forty to
fifty years. Previous research has demonstrated, for example, that the
proportion of M.P.'s with college educations increased since 1930 from
44 percent to 62 percent. In our own study, 93 percent of the senior
civil servants attended college and 84 percent completed undergradu-
ate studies. We note also that these elites reveal more specialization
recently in economics in their university curricula, challenging the earlier emphasis on law. Thus, 36 percent of the youngest cohort among

our senior bureaucrats took economics (32 percent took law), compared to the 17 percent who studied economics among the oldest cohort (50 percent studied law). While it is important to note these
trends, the more significant question is whether there has been a new
orientation in political views, whether or not linked to the skill and
social composition characteristics of elites.

One of the most consistent patterns in our data is the acceptance
of the importance of politics, particularly parties and parliamentary
politicians, by the younger members of the top bureaucracy. We noted
earlier that the senior bureaucrats as a group are inclined to emphasize
their active roles in the policy process. The young civil servants go
beyond this and reveal more trust in politicians as a group, less concern about the interference of politicians, and less criticism of parties
as conflict-exaggerating structures than do the older civil servants. An
interesting bit of evidence of this is their responses to a short answer
item we put to them asking them to evaluate the contributions of the
civil service in relation to that of the parties and Parliament in the
making of public policy ("It is not the Parliament and the parties but
the civil service which guarantees reasonably satisfactory public policy"). We find a significant, although gradual, decline in support for
this statement from the 50 percent of the bureaucrats fifty-one years
and older, to 36 percent support from those in the thirty-eight to fifty
year old bracket, to the 25 percent support among our young cadre of
high flyers. We note also that those entering the civil service most
recently are less likely to emphasize the importance of technical expertise for their jobs than those entering the service over thirty years ago.
Although the age differences on these attitudinal variables are not in
all respects a matter of dramatic contrasts, there is considerable indication of an incremental socialization of younger bureaucrats to more
acceptance of politics, political roles, and partisan approaches to public
administration and its policymaking function.

The younger elites in our samples are much less committed to the
historic group pluralism of Dutch politics. They hold rather distinctive
power images and preferences. The older bureaucrats are much more
likely to favor an important political influence role for such groups as
churches, employer organizations, farmers, and even unions. For six
key types of interest groups, 43 percent of the oldest cohort of bureaucrats, on the average, favor much influence, compared to an average
of 20 percent to 24 percent for the middle-aged and younger bureaucrats. For the young M.P.'s there is the same basic tendency—only 19
percent, on the average, favor much influence for these six types of
groups, compared to 33 percent for the older M.P.'s. The two excep-

tions to this basic finding for M.P.'s are unions and action groups, whose influence is supported somewhat more by the youngest M.P.'s. Nevertheless, the old clientelism in power perspectives of Dutch elites seems to be less acceptable to both sets of young elites.

Another theme apparent in our data, although the differences are often marginal and not unanimously in the same direction, is that the younger elites are more populist; that is, they are more inclined to support the idea of increased citizen participation. Their power preferences reveal this as well as their views about the role of citizens in the political process. In both elites the youngest cohort is more inclined to desire much influence for voters (a 29 percentage point difference among M.P.'s and an 11 percentage point difference for senior bureaucrats). We coded 48 percent of our young bureaucrats as enthusiastic about increased citizen participation (and only 4 percent as opposing the idea), which is twice as large a proportion of support as for the older bureaucrats. Further, in examining the contact patterns of these elites we note that for both M.P.'s and civil servants the younger cohorts report that they are more in regular contact with citizens than are the older elites. While it is true that this increased role of citizens in politics is acknowledged by both M.P.'s and civil servants, the older bureaucrats are much more skeptical of it.

The contact patterns of the youngest elites are distinctive also in their emphasis on contacts with party leaders and other nonbureaucratic actors. It is the youngest civil servants who reveal the most contact with M.P.'s, and the youngest M.P.'s who reveal the most contact with national party leaders of their own and other parties, by their report to us. The youngest elite cadres, then, are the most activist and interactive with a variety of other actors in the system.

What does all this mean for consociationalism and for political accommodation? The question in the basic sense is whether the rules of the Dutch political game are being altered as a result of new attitudes towards politics, and whether this is occurring with the acquiescence, if not active support, of younger elites in comparison to older elites. If the accommodation system is changing, it means that new attitudes and views are held about key elements of the consociational system concerning elite compromise, anonymity, tolerance of conflict, citizen involvement, activist policy roles for administrative elites, and the place of ideology. Are the younger elites revealing a tendency to deviate from consociational expectations; are they interested in more publicity, less compromise, more support for social and political conflict, and the like? That in a sense is the key empirical question of Dutch elite transformation analysis.

We have already noted the tendency of younger elites to espouse an increased role for citizens. We note further that the rule of anonymity in bureaucratic operations, presumably an important condition for accommodation, is one which younger bureaucrats are more willing to see relaxed than are the older bureaucrats. Most higher civil servants are against a change in the rule, but the youngest cohort is more open-minded on this matter.

Compromise has been the hallmark of the politics of accommodation. M.P.'s are now much less committed to compromise than are civil servants. But, more important, our analysis of cognitive styles reveals that the dogmatists in Parliament are much more likely to be in the youngest age group—a proportion of 50 percent for the youngest cohort, compared to none in the oldest cohort. In the bureaucracy all age groups are more open-minded in style, by our index.

What is especially noticeable for the bureaucracy is that the youngest age group is also less committed to compromise than is the oldest age group. This suggests that there is some movement for the younger levels of the bureaucracy, while remaining yet basically open-minded (much more so than M.P.'s), to demonstrate less willingness to compromise, an attitudinal orientation found also in Parliament. For our index of accommodation, the bureaucracy appears split in its attitudes about conflict, for all age groups. But in Parliament it seems clear that there is more evidence of nonaccommodative propensities in the youngest age cohort. The young M.P.'s are much more articulate about conflict, more aware that it is typical or dominant in the system, and much more inclined to be dubious about its reconcilability. Thus 70 percent of the young M.P.'s see conflict as irreconcilable, compared to 40 percent of the oldest M.P. group. (For the bureaucrats, pessimism is at the 40 percent level for both old and young cadres). The young M.P.'s also defend conflict in normative terms more than do the older M.P.'s.

Finally, there may be an incremental change taking place in value orientations. We find in both the bureaucracy and in Parliament that the younger leaders, those under forty-five, are more preoccupied with social justice, equality, and institutional reform. Such values are at the top of the value hierarchy for 50 percent of the junior M.P.'s (in age terms) compared to 40 percent of the older M.P.'s; similarly, such values are highest priority for 28 percent of the youngest cohort (under forty-five) of our senior bureaucrats, compared to 5 percent of the older bureaucrats (fifty-six years and older). This, combined with the greater concern of younger elites for citizen participation, less acceptance of the social order as is, and approval of conflict, may be part of a syndrome of perspectives distinguishing the newer, younger elites. In addition, our data reveal that younger elites in the bureaucracy talk more about conflict, such as party differences, in ideological terms, than do older bureaucrats (an 80 percent to 45 percent difference). Those who entered the bureaucracy before 1945 are much less likely to discuss party conflict from an ideological standpoint than those who entered after 1960 (35 percent of the former, contrasted to 83 percent of the latter). In terms of basic value orientations and ideological stylistic emphases in thinking about politics, then, there is evidence that change may be occurring.

If elites' orientations in the pre-1967 consociational model (see chap. 1, fig. 3) manifested disapproval of conflict, a sanguine attitude toward its resolution, as well as a limited role for the public in politics, a politically neutral, nonideological and nonpartisan bureaucracy, an emphasis on compromise and tolerance of others' ideas, anonymity in the administrative operation, and pluralistic respect for the influence of interest groups, then there is some evidence in our data that change is taking place, indeed has taken place, in both the bureaucracy and Parliament. And change is manifest particularly, though not extremely, in the youngest elite cohorts. It is not dramatic, but modest, change, and perhaps less pronounced in the top bureaucracy than in Parliament. But despite this lag, it does seem to be occurring. Both elites today are better educated than previously and have high socioeconomic status. One might expect such trends in social status to lead to more commitment to the status quo, or to tradition, or to the maintenance of conservative values. But this does not appear to be the case. Along with the developments in socioeconomic status, and despite them perhaps, there has been a gradual, marginal reorientation of elite perspectives towards the political game and elite roles in it. In a sense this is a politicization and a democratization of perspectives, as well as a retreat from the old pluralism and automatic accommodationism. If the older elites are replaced systematically by new, younger elites revealing more and more the types of attitudes beginning to appear in our data, a considerable modification of the Dutch political process could be the product. In the long run this could indeed mean elite, and system, transformation.

We have discussed integration, polarization, and accommodation in this analysis without reference to the level of the system. As David Easton has suggested, it might be helpful to distinguish three levels of the system: the community, the regime, and the specific authority levels.[5] At the *community* level we speak of elite accommodation and polarization. At the *regime* level we speak of rules of the game. At the

authority level we think of the specific actors in politics and administration in their day-to-day interrelationships. At what level of the Dutch
system do we find change occurring? Probably at all levels, but in
varying degrees. The Dutch society (community) has certainly been
changing in the postwar period, in its economic structure and in its
cultural-traditional form. Political behavior is responding to that. As
Lijphart noted, the rules of the game have been changing, among
elites and in the relationships of elites to the masses. And there can be
little doubt that at the authority level the day-to-day style of politics in
the Netherlands is changing greatly. Our data suggest differences between top bureaucrats and M.P.'s in orientations linked to all three
levels.

There can be no question that the Dutch political system is in a
state of change. The developments at all levels have produced problems which could lead to long-term polarization and cleavage. How
elites cope with these problems and how they settle their differences at
all levels is critical. Some observers see a hardening of positions.[6]
Rather than that, what is needed perhaps is a new pacification model.
Both M.P.'s and bureaucrats seem sensitive to new aspects of politics
(such as citizen participation, openness and publicity, a political process role for the bureaucracy), and are adapting to these new elements
in the political system. If this is true, then this transition period need
not necessarily lead to more polarization and extreme conflict but,
despite legitimate conflict, to the politics of a new pacification, including both elites and masses, based on new elite perspectives towards the
political system, a new elite political culture responsive to a new, developing mass political culture.

NOTES

1. William Quandt: "The integration of a political system may be viewed in
   terms of the degree to which members of the political elites share common
   socialization experiences." *The Comparative Study of Political Elites* (Beverly Hills, Calif.: Sage Professional Papers in Comparative Politics, 1970),
   p. 198; John A. Porter: "Even if they have never met before . . . their
   identity of interests stemming from their common social characteristics and
   experience facilitates communication." *The Vertical Mosaic: An Analysis
   of Social Class and Power in Canada* (Toronto: University of Toronto
   Press, 1965), p. 528.
2. Jan Kooiman, *Over de Kamer gesproken* (The Hague: Staatsuitgeverij,
   1976), p. 86.

3. A. Van Braam, "Enkele aspecten van recrutering van hogere ambtenaren in de Nederlandse rijksdient," *Civis Mundi,* 1974, pp. 23–213, 206.
4. Hans Daalder, *Politisering en lijdelijkheid in de Nederlandse politiek* (Assen: Van Gorcum, 1974), p. 69.
5. David Easton, *A Systems Analysis of Political Life* (New York: John Wiley & Sons, 1965).
6. M.P. C. M. van Schendelen, "Verzuiling en restauratie in de Nederlandse politiek," *Beleid en Maatschappij,* February 1978, pp. 42–54.

Methodological Notes
for the Study

Elite research has a short tradition in the Netherlands. Professor Hans Daalder called for such research in his inaugural address in 1964. It is worthwhile to quote Daalder here at length

> First, there is a need for more systematic elite research; it should be directed to the past as well as to the present in order to show important shiftings in political selection. The elite concept will have to be defined rather broad by including not only ministers, members of Parliament, higher civil servants and mayors but also leaders of pressure groups, party officials and party members. . . . Besides objective data about milieu, education, religion, and the like, data on more subjective political attitudes are desired; for the present these data are partly to be obtained by survey techniques; for the past one is forced to go back to an analysis of dominant opinions appearing explicitly from ideological pamphlets and implicitly from parliamentary records and bureaucratic files. [H. Daalder, *Politisering en lijdelijkheid in de Nederlandse politiek* (Assen: Van Gorcum, 1974), p. 34, our translation].

In 1968 and 1972 Daalder and his associates organized extensive interviews among members of Parliament. In 1968 attention was concentrated on social background data of members of the upper and lower houses of Dutch parliament. In 1972 attitudinal questions about role perceptions, recruitment patterns, and influence patterns in society as well as within parliamentary parties and committees were the focus. The second time the study concentrated only on members of the lower house.

The Dutch elite study in 1973, reported here, was part of an international elite research project which included the United States and six European countries. We followed the basic design for the international project in all major respects. Consequently, the methodology employed was constrained by the demands of that design. On the other hand, the special aspects of the international project opened up opportunities for comparative elite analysis. The methodological approaches and problems of this project have been discussed previously in three special papers: Joel D. Aberbach, James D. Chesney, and Bert A. Rockman, "Exploring Elite Political Attitudes: Some Methodological Lessons," *Political Methodology* 2 (Winter 1975), pp. 2–27; Bert A. Rockman, "Studying Elite Political Culture: Problems in Design and Interpretation" (unpublished); Theo van der Tak, "Problems and Complications in Comparative Elite Research: The Dutch Case," Paper presented to the International Conference on Cross-National Research in the Social Sciences, Ann Arbor, October 3–8, 1977. These papers discuss a variety of problems in this project in detail. We will draw on them in the discussion of the Dutch project which follows.

One of the purposes of our study was to explore elite attitudes and their mutual relationships. As this kind of research was never done before in the Netherlands for higher civil servants, the study had an exploratory character. This meant that the interviews could not be too structured, and our aim was to conduct them like normal conversations. To emphasize this special character frequent use was made of open-ended questions. All interviews were tape-recorded. These two characteristics caused several other problems in data management, data analysis, and reporting. We will also comment upon these complications.

Interviews were conducted with 44 members of Parliament and 76 higher civil servants. Fieldwork started in March 1973. By the end of June all 120 respondents were interviewed. Most interviews with members of Parliament were held in March; most civil servants were interviewed in April and May. This timing of the interviewing may have influenced the findings, although there is no clear evidence that this was so. At the time of interviewing, the formation of the Den Uyl cabinet was still going on or was just finished. Politicians, for instance, were mostly talked to in March, when the formation was in full swing. Likewise, the civil servants were interviewed in a period when there was no cabinet, but when the composition of the new cabinet was becoming clear. (The new cabinet presented itself on May 11, 1973.)

Despite timing difficulties, we are inclined to conclude that we profited by the special circumstances under which we interviewed. The atmosphere of the interviews was described as good, and many discussions took more than one hour. The average duration of the interviews with bureaucrats was two and a quarter hours. The range was, however, considerable: the shortest interview lasted one hour, the longest four

hours and forty-five minutes. This at least suggests a very willing attitude of the Dutch civil servants for this kind of interviewing. Meetings
with the members of Parliament took less time, because the questionnaire was shorter (134 questions, compared to 178 for the bureaucrats).
The average duration of the interview with a member of Parliament was
about an hour and a half. The shortest discussion here took three
quarters of an hour, the longest three and a quarter hours. These numbers also indicate a very easy accessibility of Dutch political and bureaucratic elites for political research. Future researchers should be aware of
this relative openness of Dutch elites, but warned that there is some
skepticism among them about the purposes of these studies. Also, the
easy access to Dutch politicians and higher civil servants may have had
something to do with the formation of the Den Uyl cabinet, which was
taking place at the time. Formations always give higher civil servants
more time, for the pressure on them is not high. Our suggestions may be
supported by the finding that the interviewing in the United States took
less time. The average interview time of civil servants was sixty-six
minutes, of Congressmen forty-three minutes. The interviews with the
Dutch elite lasted twice as long! Our respondents made a very good
impression on our interviewers. Politicians were thought to be somewhat less interested than the bureaucrats, but this may be accounted for
by the fact that the formation period is a very crucial one for parliamentarians. Also, to some of them it was the second time within two years
that they were interviewed extensively. The fieldwork of the parliamentary survey conducted by Daalder and his associates took place in February and March, 1972. This also may account for some weariness
among politicians.

It is interesting to note that the Second Chamber (the lower house
of Parliament) has developed an official policy towards scholars. Every
member who is being approached for research or an interview is to
inform the chairman of the Chamber. The chairman then looks into the
credibility and research purpose of the scholar(s). When more than one
parliamentary party is to be involved in the research, the chairman gives
an advisory opinion on whether to cooperate or not. If only one party is
approached, the executive committee gives advice to its members.

Our interviewers found the discussions with members of Parliament somewhat more frank than those with the civil servants, a situation we found true in all countries except Sweden. Civil servants are
not accustomed to public interviews nor to political interviews. M.P.'s,
on the other hand, are much more accustomed to publicity; they even
actively seek this publicity for their own party's sake. We had four
senior civil servants who objected to the political character of some of

our questions. Refusals to be tape-recorded (only three) were all found within the bureaucracy. This may also have something to do with the civil servant's fear of internal misuse of data.

The Elite Sample

The hierarchical structure of Dutch departments is depicted in figure 22. The minister is the head of the department, responsible to Parliament. Usually he is supported by one or more *staatssecretarissen*, who are responsible for part of the ministerial task. *Staatssecretarissen* are also responsible to Parliament and to their minister. They come and go with the cabinet. The highest civil servant is the *secretaris-generaal*. He is responsible for nearly all that is going on in the department. Sometimes he is described as the most powerful man in the department, including the minister. He is no specialist, but a general manager, varying in power from department to department.

Below the *secretaris-generaal* is the *directeur-generaal*. He is responsible for some part of the ministry's task. For instance, in the Ministry of Health and Environment, there are two *directeuren-generaal,* one for health, another one for environmental affairs. These general directories are further subdivided into directories: the heads of these directories are called *directeuren.* The actual number of these higher civil servants may vary from department to department. In 1972, for example, the Finance Ministry consisted of five *directeuren-generaal* and twenty-four *directeuren.* The Agriculture Ministry, on the other hand, consisted of two *directeuren-generaal* and nineteen *directeuren.* These two levels form the population of our study of higher civil servants, excluding those of the Defense and External Affairs Ministries.

From the government directory we calculated the actual number of *directeuren-generaal* and *directeuren* in the Dutch civil service: 42

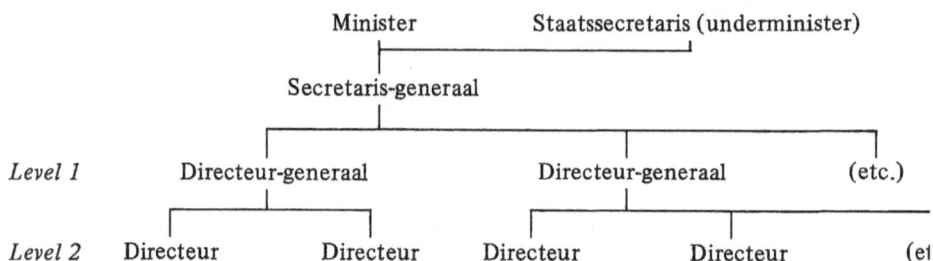

Fig. 22. Hierarchical structure of Dutch departments

directeuren-generaal and 179 *directeuren* (Ministries of External Affairs and Defense not included). Of these bureaucrats 15 *directeuren-generaal* and 85 *directeuren* were randomly selected. This sample had to be diminished because of budget reasons: the final sample consisted of 87 higher civil servants, of whom 87 percent participated in the survey.

Of the 150 members of the Dutch Second Chamber, 53 politicians were randomly selected. Forty-four finally cooperated, so that our sample covers about 30 percent of the original population. Half of these parliamentarians had already participated in the parliamentary survey conducted by Daalder and his associates. Background data and some questions of the same format were taken from the earlier parliamentary study.

Coding

Coding was done by three coders. One of them did all the closed questions, which is relatively easy. This work was finished within one month after the interviewing. The coding of the open-ended questions took a lot more time. The structure of the study required that all conversations be typed out. After that a very long session with the coders was necessary to inform them about the purpose of the codes. The two coders who finally did the open-ended questions also interviewed half of the respondents. These two coders kept in close contact with our fieldwork supervisor. Together they solved problems arising from the code book. This code book was largely derived from the British, German, Swedish, and Italian counterparts of the study. So in the Netherlands we had to work with a given framework for coding open-ended questions. In some cases this led to difficulties. Check coding for the closed questions was done by the coder and the fieldwork supervisor.

The Questionnaire

1. To begin, I would like to ask you what you consider to be the two or three most important problems facing the Netherlands at this time. Which is *the* most important?
2 (for the most important problem) Do you see a solution for this problem? (if yes) How? (if no) Why not?
3. (in case a solution is advanced) What obstacles could stand in the way of such a solution?
4. Are you optimistic or pessimistic over the chances of arriving at a solution?
5. One question asked in this research in all countries concerns economic planning. What is your own position on economic planning here in the Netherlands? How far should the government go, and what role should the government play in this? Should the role of the government be expanded or restricted?
6. Do you think economic planning is primarily a technical matter or more a matter where primarily political considerations should have weight?
7. (civil servants only) Now I would like to ask you about special aspects of the civil service. If you think for the moment of your work as a civil servant, what do you think is the most satisfying aspect?
8. (civil servants only) And what aspect is the least satisfying?
9. What do you see as the most important problems which the bureaucracy must deal with? What are the causes for these problems?
10. I would also like to talk with you about the role of the *senior* civil servants.
    a. What do you think are the most important tasks of senior civil servants?
    b. And what personal qualities must they have?
    c. Have the characteristics of the typical civil servant changed over time? Do you approve of this trend or not?

11. If you now make a comparison between the characteristics of the senior civil servants and the M.P.'s, what conclusions would you come to?

12. Do you think there are still special qualities which M.P.'s have which are specifically necessary for M.P.'s, or don't you think that is so?

13. Do you think that the characteristics of the typical politician have changed much over time? Do you approve of this trend, or not?

14. (civil servants only) There is sometimes talk of a tendency towards a merely advisory and more independent position for senior civil servants in the preparation and implementation of policy. What do you think of that?

15. (civil servants only) It is said sometimes that a senior civil servant often operates in a gray area, between administration in a strict sense and politics—what is your opinion on that? Do you agree with this position? (in case of a positive answer) Do you also see negative sides, or not? (In case of a negative answer) Do you also see positive sides, or not?

16. (civil servants only) In your own work is there much difference noticeable when you have another minister or not?

17. (civil servants only) Do you find it personally difficult to be involved in formulating or carrying out policy which is at variance with previous governmental policy? And if you personally do not agree with this policy?

18. (civil servants only) How do you feel about the suggestions for relaxing the traditional rule of anonymity and public silence for civil servants? (in case of a positive answer) Are there also negative sides to this, or not? (in case of a negative answer) Are there also positive sides to this, or not?

19. One hears these days critical and concerned expressions about the place and functions of the Parliament in the Dutch political system. What is your opinion of this?

20. In different countries much is said these days about the *increased participation* of citizens in the work of the government, and the *greater influence* of citizens in public affairs. How do you feel about that? (in case of a positive answer) Are there negative aspects to that, or not? (in case of a negative answer) Are there positive aspects to that, or not?

21. What in your opinion are today the most important questions on which the political parties differ?

22. Does one notice differences between the parties in the work of this ministry?

23. Do you think that these party differences are a mirror of the differences in the public, or are these differences a distortion (an exaggeration) or a sharpening of the differences in the public?
24. Do you find differences within political parties to be helpful or harmful?
25. If there is an important difference of opinion between yourself and the majority of your party, what would you then do?
26. Concerning social relations in general, some people say that there will always be conflicts and cleavages between interests, while others say that groups and classes in society generally have the same interests. What is your opinion on this? (probe) What groups are you considering here? (in case there is no response) Do you think there are conflicts between employers and employees? geographical interests and groups? religious interests and groups?
27. Do you consider social conflict a sign of social health or social illness?
28. Do you think these conflicts are irreconcilable, or not?
29. In case there is a conflict where one side seems to you in the right and the other side wrong, do you think that the side which is in the right should stick to its guns, or would you personally be inclined to seek a compromise?
30. Which groups are treated less well by the government? Which groups have benefited the most recently from governmental policy?
31. (M.P.'s only) I would like to ask you a few questions now about your work in Parliament. What do you consider to be the most important functions which you as an M.P. must fill?
32. (M.P.'s only) If you consider your work as an M.P., what do you feel is the most satisfying aspect?
33. (M.P.'s only) And now look at the other side of the coin—what do you feel is the least satisfying aspect?
34. I have here on this card a list of more or less important tasks of members of Parliament. Will you tell me for each task whether you think the Parliament fulfills the task well or poorly?

Scale:

```
very   1——+——+——+——+——+——+——+——9   very
poor      2   3   4   5   6   7   8      good
```

Tasks:

a. Lawgiving
b. Controlling the government
c. Handling citizen complaints

    d. Weighing interest group demands
    e. Responding to new problems
    f. Keeping good contacts with the departments
    g. Influencing policy
    h. Implementing party programs
    i. Maintaining contacts with voters

35. Members of Parliament must look at all opinions in dealing with public affairs. Would you tell me how much influence the following groups or actors *should have* in parliamentary decisions?

Scale:

little   1 ——+——+——+——+——+——+——+——9   very great
influence   2 3 4 5 6 7 8   influence

Participants whose influence is ranked:

    a. Civil servants with special expertise
    b. Ministers
    c. Labor union representatives
    d. Party leaders (outside of Parliament)
    e. Representatives of farm organizations
    f. M.P.'s with a special expertise in an area of policy
    g. Action groups
    h. Representatives of employer organizations
    i. Representatives of small businessmen (or shopkeepers)
    j. Churches
    k. Radio and television
    l. Newspapers
    m. What M.P.'s hear from the voters
    n. Public opinion research results

36. (using the same scale and the same fourteen actors as in question 35) How much influence do you think each of these actors in fact does have?

37. If you would characterize the relationship of M.P.'s and senior civil servants generally, where on this line would you put your opinion?

Scale:

breakdown in   1 ——+——+——+——+——+——+——+——9   trust and
trust, and   2 3 4 5 6 7 8   effective
conflicts   cooperation

38. When you were young was there much politics discussed in your home? Some? None at all?

39. For which party did your father vote? And your mother?
40. Was your father a member of a political party? (if yes) Did he also hold a position in the party?
41. Was your mother a member of a political party? (if yes) Did she hold a position in the party?
42. (civil servants only) Could I ask you which political party you have a preference for? Are you a party member? (if yes) Have you ever had a party administrative position? (if not a member) For which party did you vote in the last election?
43. (M.P.'s only) Here is a list of governmental positions. Could you tell me which of these you held before you entered Parliament? (A list of sixteen positions was provided, from local to national positions).
44. (M.P.'s only) Have you ever been a civil servant? (if yes) At what governmental level?
45. How old were you when you developed an interest in politics? How did it happen that you became interested in politics?
46. When did you first become active in politics? Why?
47. What was your first political position?
48. Have you been continuously active since then, or did you break your political activity at some time? (if interrupted) When did you interrupt your activity?
49. We are particularly interested in your contacts with other leaders, groups, and citizens. Using the following list, could you tell me how frequently you have contact with each actor?

	More than once a week	Once a week	Not weekly, but regularly	Less than regularly but often	Occasionally	Never
1. National leaders of your party (outside of Parliament)						
2. State or regional leaders of your party						
3. Local leaders of your party						
4. National leaders of other parties						
5. Regional, state, or local leaders of other parties						
6. Ministers						

	More than once a week	Once a week	Not weekly, but regularly	Less than regularly but often	Occasion-ally	Never
7. Senior (national) civil servants						
8. Senior officials of the state governments						
9. Local government officials						
10. Representatives of national (interest) groups						
11. Representatives of state or local (interest) groups						
12. Ordinary citizens						

50. I have here a list of a number of representative, political, and administrative positions. Can you tell me for each of them which of these positions your father held? And your grandfathers on your father's and mother's side? And other family members?

	Father	Grandfather on father's side	Grandfather on mother's side	Other Relatives
1. Upper house of Parliament				
2. Lower house of Parliament				
3. State assembly				
4. Local government council				
5. Minister or undersecretary				
6. Mayor				
7. Local government civil servant				
8. Senior civil servant in a department				
9. Military				
10. State government civil servant				
11. Other				

51. What was the highest education of your father? (respondent given a list of educational levels)

52. What was your father's major occupation? Was he in business independently?
53. In what community were you brought up as a young person?
54. Do you have a religion (or religious conviction)? (if yes) In what church?
55. What type of lower school did you go to? What was the highest education that you achieved?
56. In what religion were you brought up?
57. How active are you in religion now? How often do you attend church?
58. What was your occupational training (or educational curriculum)?
59. What was the first occupation you held?
60. (M.P.'s only) What occupation did you hold just before you entered Parliament?
61. (Civil servants only) If you were to make an overall evaluation of the nature of your contacts with other senior civil servants— whether over technical and organizational aspects of your work or political aspects—what number on this line would you point to? And in your relationships with the secretaris-generaal? And in your relationships with the minister? And with the Staatssecretaris?

    Scale:

    exclusively   1——+——+——+——+——+——+——+——9 exclusively
    technical   2   3   4   5   6   7   8   political
    organizational

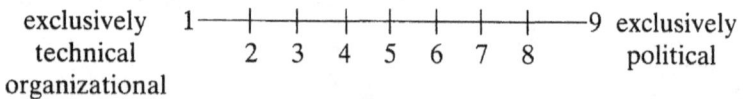

62. (Civil servants only) I would like to ask you where you get most of your information which you need in your work in order to be well informed? What is for you the most important source for the administrative and technical aspects of your work? (rank order)

    a. Trade literature
    b. Bureaucratic materials
    c. Talks with colleagues in the government
    d. Talks with other administrators outside of government

    And now for the political aspects of your work. What is the most important information source? (rank order)

    a. The press
    b. Information from politicians
    c. Discussions with colleagues in the government
    d. Contacts outside the government

63. Finally, we have a list of short statements which we ask you to give your opinion about, indicating whether you agree, agree strongly, disagree, or disagree strongly with each statement.

a. In a world as complicated as the modern one, it doesn't make sense to speak of increased control by ordinary citizens over governmental affairs.
b. The disadvantages of an (administrative) parliamentary career are more than offset by the personal satisfactions.
c. Abstract principles of right or wrong seldom are of help in solving social problems.
d. In contemporary social and economic affairs it is essential that technical considerations have more weight than political factors.
e. Certain people are better qualified to lead this country because of their traditions and family background.
f. The only way to help the poor is to take something from the rich.
g. Citizens have a perfect right to exert pressure for legislation which would benefit them personally.
h. Often those who enter politics think more about their own welfare or that of their own party than about the welfare of the citizens.
i. Many of the doubts and fears expressed about the growing intervention of the state in the economic and social spheres are fully justified.
j. To compromise with our political adversaries is dangerous because it normally leads to the betrayal of one's own side.
k. Generally speaking, in political controversies the extreme positions are to be avoided, since usually the right answer is in the middle.
l. It will always be necessary to have a few strong, able individuals who know how to take charge.
m. Public discussion of policy disagreements between officials is harmful to the work of government.
n. When one group or individual gains something, it usually means that another group or individual loses.
o. The interference of (civil servants) in affairs which are properly the business of (members of Parliament) is a worrisome feature of contemporary public affairs. (This statement is reversed for the other elite group.)
p. Politics is the "art of the possible," and therefore the leaders of

the country must worry more about what can be done in the short run than about ambitious ideals and long-range plans.

q. The general welfare of the country is seriously endangered by the continual clash of special interest groups.

r. Basically there is no conflict of interest between private enterprise and government.

s. Few people really know what is in their own best interest in the long run.

t. Although parties play an important role in a democracy, often they uselessly exacerbate political conflicts.

u. The strength and efficiency of a government are more important than its specific program.

v. Relations of close collaboration between a department and the groups and sectors most affected by its activities are improper and unnecessary.

w. Really, it is not the parties and Parliament, but rather the public administration which guarantees a fairly satisfactory politics in our country.

x. It is only social conflicts which bring about progress in modern society.

y. People should be allowed to vote even if they cannot do so intelligently.

z. All citizens should have the same chance of influencing government policy.

Index

www.ingramcontent.com/pod-product-compliance
Lightning Source LLC
Chambersburg PA
CBHW030644270326
41929CB00007B/203